Consumer Culture and Personal Finance

Consumption and Public Life
Series Editors: Frank Trentmann and Richard Wilk

Consumption and Public Life
Series Standing Order ISBN 978–1–4039–9983–2
Hardback 978–1–4039–9984–9 Paperback
(*outside North America only*)

You can receive future titles in this series as they are published by placing a
standing order. Please contact your bookseller or, in case of difficulty, write to us
at the address below with your name and address, the title of the series and the
ISBN quoted above.

Customer Services Department, Macmillan Distribution Ltd, Houndmills,
Basingstoke, Hampshire RG21 6XS, England

Consumer Culture and Personal Finance

Money Goes to Market

Jacqueline Botterill
Brock University, Canada

palgrave
macmillan

First published 2010 by
PALGRAVE MACMILLAN

Palgrave Macmillan in the UK is an imprint of Macmillan Publishers Limited, registered in England, company number 785998, of Houndmills, Basingstoke, Hampshire RG21 6XS.

Palgrave Macmillan in the US is a division of St Martin's Press LLC, 175 Fifth Avenue, New York, NY 10010.

Palgrave Macmillan is the global academic imprint of the above companies and has companies and representatives throughout the world.

Palgrave® and Macmillan® are registered trademarks in the United States, the United Kingdom, Europe and other countries.

ISBN 978-0-230-00867-0   hardback

This book is printed on paper suitable for recycling and made from fully managed and sustained forest sources. Logging, pulping and manufacturing processes are expected to conform to the environmental regulations of the country of origin.

A catalogue record for this book is available from the British Library.

A catalog record for this book is available from the Library of Congress.

10   9   8   7   6   5   4   3   2   1
19   18   17   16   15   14   13   12   11   10

Printed and bound in Great Britain by
CPI Antony Rowe, Chippenham and Eastbourne

Contents

List of Illustrations and Table

Acknowledgements

I acquired many social debts during the writing of this manuscript that I would like to acknowledge. The University of East London provided a sabbatical that allowed me to undertake much of the initial research, as well as a stimulating intellectual environment in which many of the ideas in this book took shape. Helen Powell and Iain MacRury gave invaluable collegial succor. I owe a special debt to Mica Nava who provided just the right mix of rigorous criticism and friendly support.

I am indebted to Kayla Foster for her bibliographical work and beholden to Soya Felix and Alan McEwen who kept me going in the final phases of completing this book, while they diligently tidied my mistakes and clarified my prose. I own all errors that remain.

Finally, the intellectual and personal support generously given by Stephen Kline, quite simply, bankrupts me. I dedicate this book to my father, Stanley Botterill.

Introduction

In 2005, Richard Cullen of Bath, England was found behind the wheel of his car, asphyxiated by carbon monoxide from the running engine. Although the coroner's report called it suicide, the press coverage implied a kind of foul play, depicting Mr Cullen as the victim of an emerging cultural pathology they dubbed 'debt related suicide' (Ronson, 16 July 2005). They explained that Mr Cullen was an ordinary man in every way; his troubles started with an innocent loan to pay for a private hospital operation for his wife. As the illness progressed, Mr Cullen had to take time off work to care for her. This loss of income quickly drained his savings and made him dependent on his credit cards. He began to miss bill payments, discovering he could only pay for his wife's treatment by juggling a mountain of debt, which grew to £130,000 by the time he sought to escape the only way he knew how.

Looking for motives, journalists found the banks guilty, submitting the smoking gun in Richard Cullen's mail pile as evidence: among the aggressive collection letters from the banks they found seductive flyers inviting Mr Cullen to assume even more easy credit through debt transfer to manage his mounting financial worries (BBC One, 2003; Morgan, 16 April 2004). Mr. Cullen's death, journalists implied, was at the hands of heartless debt-promoting bankers. In 2005, as bankers counted up their large bonuses, their insensitivity towards the plight of the ill-starred debtor became increasingly egregious. When he fell victim to fate, he had no alternative to the financial institutions' easy credit schemes, aggressive marketing, high interest rates, service charges, and heartless collection strategies. Journalists asked: is not the bank's aggressive advertising of easy credit as hypocritical as the church's sale of papal bulls (Dunn, 24 October 2004, p. 31). They labelled the banks 'uncaring fat cats' and modern day loan sharks. The banks responded that they were simply answering to a credit-hungry public while carrying out the consumer-led economic strategy of the Labour government whose popularity rose with escalating house prices and falling unemployment.

Although Mr Cullen's situation foreshadowed the looming credit crisis that was to unfold in Britain during the following few years, few commentators paid much attention to the cultural underpinnings of the consumer-led expansionism of the first decade of the twenty-first century. Yet amid the economic downturn of the 1990s, psychologists Lunt and Livingstone had sounded similar unheeded warning bells. Their survey showed that people thought about and talked about money a lot – especially about debt. But debt-ridden consumers were *less troubled* by feelings of social shame or fear of public humiliation – the plight of nineteenth century debtors – than with a sense of enslavement and the loss of personal liberty that their growing indebtedness imposed. The most deeply indebted consumers especially expended considerable psychological resources to manage their complex and contradictory feelings towards money – which both empowered them as consumers and enslaved them as debtors (Lunt & Livingstone, 1992).

In his growing indebtedness, Mr Cullen was no different from millions of Britons for whom getting and spending defined the pivotal preoccupation of living. Since WWII, impatient for the good life, mortgage lending and bank loans had significantly accelerated many consumers' access to a middle-class lifestyle: homeownership grew from 48% of the population to 70% in 2006. So too cars, TVs, and appliances in every home were the ready signs that consumerism was a democratizing historical trajectory. In Britain's burgeoning economy, domestic consumption now accounted for 70% of GDP. Yet amid growing affluence, per capita savings had declined while personal debt now exceeded the Gross National Product (£1.16 trillion). In 2006, the UK became the world's most credit-card-intensive nation, with 67 million credit cards for a population of 59 million people – even more than American where the cards were invented (Ronson, 16 July 2005).

In this respect it is possible, from the historical perspective, to claim that the dilemma that Mr Cullen faced was symptomatic of the underlying changes taking place in Britain's consumer economy. After WWII, successive governments mandated the banking sector to provide more banking services to consumers. To achieve this goal, they began to loosen financial regulations. The British banks, which for years had specialized in large-scale short-term credit, best suited for the needs of the state, industry, and wealthy families shifted, sometimes painfully, to focus on everyday consumers – and their personal finances. Margaret Thatcher's 1986 'big bang' deregulation of the financial sector allowed foreign ownership of banks. Money – the most abstract and yet material of all commodities – went to market. American banks brought their marketing approach, financial methods, and technologies which had proven popular within their own peculiar financial system, into the square mile of the city challenging those gentlemanly British bankers, who once viewed themselves stewards of the commonwealth, to modernize their attitudes. In the competitive swirl of global finance, they learned to become market-oriented financial institutions selling to the masses. Emphasizing profits and market expansion, the marketing-oriented banking sector sought out the previously excluded members of the public (especially the working poor, immigrants, the young, and women). Overdrafts and credit cards were now sold like soap and beer in the mediated marketplace with television advertising campaigns. A quarter century of economic policy-making seemed to encourage a fundamental shift in the public's values, attitudes, and practices involving money: interest rates, credit ratings, and managing dizzying mortgage debts were normalized aspects of Britain's consumer society.

Most consumers recognized that access to money was essential for their happiness in the consumer society (Bernthal, et al., 2005). To be denied credit was to be, in some way, excluded from the basic necessities of living – of hope, possibility, freedom, and self-esteem. It is now impossible to book a hotel room, tickets to a concert, or shop online without a credit card. Looming debts became normalized in a consumer society in which cash became passé and debit cards the preferred medium of financial exchange. As a result Britons have three times more unsecured debt on their credit cards than other European countries. If economic expansion depends on the ability of consumers to manage their increasing debt loads, then the consumer-led boom years were taking Britain into uncharted territory.

The shadow history of personal finance

Academic firewalls erected between cultural and economic analyzes have done little to aid the appreciation of the psychosocial forces underwriting the consumer-led boom years. While some writers argue generally that the formation of the consumer culture and the expansion of the market economy were intertwined trajectories (Wilk, 1996; Polany, 2001; Slater, 1999), debates about consumerism have remained split between two camps: the economist side focusing on globalized systems of accelerated capitalism, high tech production, and transnational distribution that expands commodity flows; and the culturalist camp emphasizing the spectacular modes of fashionable display, entertainment, and lifestyle aesthetics that dynamize the mediated marketplace and promote indebtedness.

Focusing on high rather than low finance, political economists on the right and the left excluded everyday money experience, motivation, and financial anxieties from their calculations operating at a level of numerical abstraction far removed from the daily flow of money through pockets and piggy banks. Macroeconomics dissects and measures the capitalist marketplace with statistics about sources of economic growth – emphasizing variously, corporate taxes, technological innovation, unemployment, investment strategies, state regulation of markets, the size of government debt, interest rates and subsidies, the division of labour, and recently corporate ethics and entrepreneurial management to understand the pace of market expansion.

From historical accounts, economists know that tinkering with mortgage interest rates and credit terms impacts the market system profoundly: when it comes to consumer demand, they survey consumer confidence and study aggregates of individual household expenditures, accounting for consumer preferences by measuring a normative basket of goods. Having their eyes set on the management of a post-industrial economy has meant that the domestic economy – and consumers' ability to buy houses, cars, and clothes and make ends meet by paying off spiralling debts – has been relegated to the back burner. Armed with gross statistics, it is hardly surprising that economists, until recently, minimized the social implications of financial deregulation and ignored the social communication dynamics which helped agitate growth of GDP: they simply bracketed the social circumstances and discourses – from divorce to religion which shape savings and spending patterns.

While economists neglected everyday culture and low finance, cultural analysts skirted the issue of personal finance too. During the 1980s and 1990s scholars investigated the social, psychological, and political circumstances of growing affluence in Britain finding common ground by shifting their analysis from the modes of production to consumption and the social use of goods in everyday life (Nava et al., 1997). Consumption could no longer be theorized simplistically as the satisfaction of biological needs, they argued, in a social order where goods are employed as totems of resistance, as carriers of memories, as conduits of desire, as markers of gender, and generally as resources for identity. In a market economy, the arts, media, and leisure industries were fully commodified – and ruled by the logics of market exchange so, as a consequence, popular entertainment, leisure, travel, and media were included in the analysis of consumer culture. The contribution that the new cultural intermediaries – designers, marketers, advertisers, even sales clerks – played in the consumer economy was acknowledged. They set out to chart their contribution to the emerging lifestyles of rich and poor, men and women, immigrants and aristocrats. They examined how fashion, novelty, style, cultivated taste, even ethical considerations underscored the expanding vortex of consumption. But, these same researchers who pledged allegiance to interdisciplinary study refused to admit banks and building societies among these new cultural institutions or examine the part that the banks' promotional discourses were playing in popular culture.

This rethinking of commodified culture had a profound impact on how we talk about and study consumerism. Researchers' acknowledgement of the expanding role that retailing, marketing, and advertising sectors play within consumerism was crucial in melting the line that separated high arts from crass economics. Their critical analyzes of cultural industries revealed how patriarchy, sexism, racism, humanism, and even modernism itself constrained individual identity and reframed class conflict. Nevertheless, a line was drawn in the sand around money itself. Yet as Stuart Hall noted, fearing crass reductionism, culturalist scholars turned away from economic explanations. As a consequence, rather than produce alternative ways of thinking about the economic conditions Hall finds 'a massive, gigantic, and eloquent disavowal' (Hall, 1996, p. 96). Most who commented on consumerism ignored the money it took to acquire it or the way it shaped identity and social judgement. The commodity that made the acquisition of all other commodities possible – money – passed under the radar of cultural research even while its importance as a prerequisite for acquiring a lifestyle and managing the pecuniary side of this exploding logic of consumer desire increased.

One way we can account for their refusal to bring money into the analysis of consumerism is that compared to celebrities, fashion shows, and Superbowl games, scholars of culture find money boring. As Lendol Calder has argued, compared with 'the history of goods,' 'the history of how goods were paid for appears tedious in the extreme' (Calder, 2001, p. 16). Money, he argues, must be given a visual form to become 'the object of social, political, or economic discussion': account books, computer databases, and spreadsheets simply have none of the sex appeal of advertising, the popularity of television programs, or the glamour of fashion models. Consumer culture researchers would rather write about the spectacular (pink Cadillacs, punk rockers and goth fashions) and the exotic aspects of consumerism (the collector, the avant garde, rare objects). Moreover, scholars rarely deigned to study banks (until recently) which remained the staid Other of humanism – the apposite of culture. To cultural studies researchers, financial organizations and the people who populate them continue to be associated with the banal and crass, in comparison to the edifying world of arts and music. And so money largely circulates unwitnessed by cultural studies exchanged in private contracts, with handshakes, deposited in bank machines, or discreetly hidden in wallets, fanny packs, and fine leather handbags.

Bridging the economic and cultural divide

I agree with Kopytoff that economic determinism is a blunt instrument to carve out the history of personal finance with (Kopytoff, 1988). To breach the disciplinary walls that separate cultural and economic ways of thinking about personal financial relations, I have tried to build on the insights of Raymond Williams' historical approach which acknowledges the materiality of financial discourses and the discursiveness of institutionalized social relations (Williams, 1983). This book seeks to shed light on these financial relations by weaving together a cultural history of the social context within which saving and borrowing practices were forged in modern Britain. Like Williams, my ambition is to show how information, stories, moral debates, and ideals are complexly interwoven into the consolidation of the social practices of savings and credit – and vice versa. Focusing on communication historically allows us to see how moral media and political discourses responded to institutionalized cultural forms but also informed the changing money practices, institutions, and social relations emerging in the modern period. Cultural historians are faced with the complex task of unravelling the weave of a complex tapestry, and as we shall see, social practices, laws, and daily life are constantly being reworked as new discourses contested prior practices, attitudes changed, commerce expanded, and new rhetorics crystallized around new frameworks of social organization of monetary exchange – from tallymen and pawn shops to hire purchase and debit cards. Although I provide a sweeping overview of the long march from usury to credit-led booms, my intent is to throw into relief the cult of domesticity and the moral issues, gender dynamics, and public debates that have underpinned its formation as the fulcrum of the expanding consumer economy.

Beyond usury

Obviously current economic discourses drew from and built upon the past. In this respect my work is also inspired by Max Weber's complex theorization of the relationship between economy and culture that emerged from contemplating capitalism's moral foundation in Protestantism. Weber's contribution to modern sociology was to expose the connection between religious discourses and productivity (Weber, 1958). Capitalism's expanding wealth, Weber suggests, cannot be explained by greed, an interest in earning more, or social mobility alone. Rather, it was the Protestant ethos which celebrated hard work, saving, and prudence that explains the rise of the merchant classes.

Weber's analysis stressed the work ethic. Protestantism held that a man seeking God's grace 'gets nothing out of his wealth for himself, except the irrational sense of having done a good job' (Weber, 1947, p. 71). But work was both a moral and economic force because of the ways it motivated new forms of enterprise. Weber also noted the important role that the discourses of thrift played in the mercantile classes' practices of wealth accumulation. The thrift ethos commanded that need, usefulness, durability, simple pleasure, and lasting contentment should govern consumption decisions for the danger was that unmindful consumption might lead people to relax 'in the security of possession, the enjoyment of wealth with the consequence of idleness and the temptations of the flesh, above all of distraction from the pursuit of a righteous life'. A prudent man therefore avoided 'ostentation and unnecessary expenditure, as well as conscious enjoyment of his power, and is embarrassed by outward signs of the social recognition he received'. His manner in life is, in other words, 'often ... distinguished by a certain ascetic tendency'. Forgoing immediate gratification, saving and investing in the future, stood as high water marks of graceful living.

As Christians, Quakers warned against 'worldly vanity' and condemned acts of 'ostentation, frivolity, and the use of things having no practical purpose, or which are valuable only for their scarcity'. Yet, whereas the medieval church condemned all money rent, the Protestant faith sanctioned 'prudent investment' that emphasized future yield, addressed real needs, provided for others, and supported self-reliance in their community. In this sense borrowing money was not wrong in itself. Weber argued that the thrift ethos 'allowed, even encouraged, expenditure on objects that yielded future gains' (Weber, 1958, p. 277). Although Weber had little to say about debt, a popular 1692 Quaker pamphlet deemed debts just if they were 'paid on time and without complaint'. The sermon warned the congregation not against the evil moneylender but to avoid 'trading and commerce beyond their capabilities to discharge with a good conscience towards all men'. Nor were Friends advised to 'contract extravagant debts endangering the wronging of others and their families' (Barty-King, 1991, p. 50). Persecuted for their religious beliefs throughout the seventeenth century, Dixon (2007) suggests the London Quakers earned the respect of the community because of their honest conduct in financial affairs (Horrell & Oxley, 1999). Prudent investment guided by strict utilitarian principles which secured future well-being for family and community not only secured the grace of God but also the respect of other merchants.

Usury, meaning the excessive interest charged by the moneylender or banker, was morally sanctioned in medieval Britain because it defied Christian ideals of brotherly love, charity, and self-sacrifice. The moral sanctioning of money rents is the much-commented theme of Merchant of Venice in which the Jewish moneylender is humiliated for demanding his pound of flesh. But the hatred of the banker was well established: 'Canon law in the middle Ages forbade usury, which was generally interpreted as a loan repayment exceeding the principal amount' (Persky, 2007, p. 227). The thrift ethos promoted by Protestantism helped erode the Catholic churches' moral injunction against usury, which was honoured in its breach by kings and paupers alike. What Weber failed to comment on however was how Protestantism also popularized a new language and set of practices that helped reconfigure moneylending as an economically productive practice with the notion of providential investment.

But moral discourses alone do not change social practices and long-established economic arrangements. Debtor's prison awaited those unable to uphold these Christian ideals. But even here the voice of redemption sang. Daniel DeFoe, imprisoned for his debts in 1692 and 1706, found a novel escape route – in both senses of the word. Unable to live up to his own ideals, he confessed his deep regret towards his insolvency and the stain it cast on his good name: 'I freely name myself, with those, that are ready to own, that they have in the Extremities and Embarrassments in Trade, done those things, which their own principles Condemn'd' (in Novak, 2001, p. 96). Yet prison proved the mother of invention, for to pay his debts he also began to publish prolifically including what is considered a prototype of the modern novel. His passionate antiprison screeds sought to mobilize legal reform by winning public sympathy for the plight of the indebted tradesmen.

His writing – one-part prison confessional and one-part manifesto for mercantile classes, proposed a new way that debt could be understood. The threat of imprisonment was so harsh, Defoe warned that it dampened the traders' enthusiasm for taking the risks necessary to expand the commonwealth: 'How could men with heads in the gallows work to pay off their debts?' (Rogers, 1971, p. 451) Defoe reviled the morally tainted term 'usury', speaking instead of investment's magical force: 'the true Spring of the Greatness of our Trade. ... By this strange thing call'd Credit, all the mighty Wonders of an exalted Commerce are perform'd' (Owen & Furbank, 1986, p. 496). Nor was he a friend of the moneylender arguing that the 'customary encroachments of Usurers, Money-Lenders, Scriveners and Bankers' was 'the scandal of the times' (Coleman, 1951). Acknowledging the repayment of debts as the foundation of commerce, he praised only the 'Honest Man' who garnered 'the trust of others, thus was able to secure capital irrespective of his resources' (Bardon, 1690, p. 27).

Defoe honoured the honest man but, like many of the faithful, fell short of being one. His confession of guilt, plea for forgiveness, and commitment to perpetual self-improvement probably appealed to the largely Protestant merchants and traders (Seaver, 1985, p. 37). So as an alternative to prison, Defoe became an advocate of what he called 'savings banks' which could help provide the investment needed by traders. And he put this idea to test founding the Mutual Marine Insurance Society, taking a first step towards the wider acceptance of institutionalization of savings and lending.

But it wasn't until 1787, when Bentham published a tract called the Defence of Usury, that the moral force of the thrift ethos replaced usury. Gilbert K. Chesterton (1933) identified Bentham's essay on usury as the very beginning of the 'modern world' (Persky, 2007, p. 228) because it convinced Parliament to remove governmental restrictions on the charging of interest between merchants. 'On what legal grounds can kings, queens and aristocrats set rates of interest while tradesmen cannot', he demanded and why are money rents acceptable on property, but not in trade (Bentham, 1787). Bentham pointed out that the expansion of trade called upon creditors to extend vast sums of finance over long periods. When someone lent money for one project, capital could not be then used in other projects yielding quicker returns. According to Bentham, it was just for investors to receive interest for the risks they took. But 'what rate of interest is there that can naturally be more proper than another? What natural fixed price can there be for the use of money more than for the use of any other thing?', he argued (Bentham, 1787).

Laying the foundations of modern notions of liberalism, Bentham maintained tradesmen should be entitled to construct their own contracts (Bentham, 1818; Jones, 1989; Kerridge, 2002). The state's prime interest in moneylending, he proposed, was in ensuring the rational character of contracts, plain language, disclosure, and information sharing but not setting the terms of engagement. As Persky notes, Bentham's notion of money contracts was the keystone for legalizing market relations generally: 'The market offered opportunity to individual creativity and a harsh respect for even the poor. And no market did so more explicitly than that for borrowing and lending money (Persky, 2007, p. 235). And unlike Defoe, Bentham lived to see his advocacy of contract law for investments precipitate a vote in Parliament. In 1789, Parliament revoked the Usury laws while establishing chartered banks mandated to regularize credit transactions in an expanding mercantile investment economy. Moneylending was thus recast in the more morally neutral lexicon of the money commodity – credit, principal, and interest – in the benefit of high finance.

Towards a cultural history of personal finance

Chapter 1 explores how the financial institutions forming around prudent investment played an important role not only in Thatcher's 'big bang' but in the Victorian cult of domesticity that she invoked as its cultural end. This chapter looks backward, suggesting that Margaret Thatcher's invocation of enterprise culture, a homeowner democracy, and the thrifty housewife drew rhetorical strength from long-standing nineteenth century British values and discourses. Like Bentham, Thatcher demonized state interference in financial markets of any kind while paying homage to the ordinary values of hard work, thrift, and self reliance that was exhibited by the Victorian housewife to keep the British economy in check. Yet working-class historians following the brush strokes of E. P. Thompson have noted that, ignored by the corporate banks and major financial institutions until the 1970s, most people made their own banking arrangements in difficult circumstances (Thompson, 1963).

As historians have shown, as the yoke of canonical laws faded, lending and saving became well established in village life. Since the eighteenth century butchers, widows, and shopkeepers made surplus cash available for community loans, sometimes for profit, but also out of a sense of social obligation (Finn, 2003). The financial collectives that some craft-workers formed pooling their coins to enable some to purchase tools for work, mark the beginning of important local financial institutions. The Friendly and Building Society movement proved popular by providing a place to earn interest on saving for some and mortgages to others. Mandated as a communal, non-profit lending organization, this uniquely British institution helped to broaden homeownership, becoming a symbol of thrift and self-reliance that was protected by the state until Thatcher's 'big bang'.

Simmel's *The Philosophy of Money* also recognized the extent to which money had become a force for modernization in the nineteenth century. Unlike Marx, he acknowledged the productive capacity of money exchange not only within the industrial economy but within working-class communities (Simmel, 1990). During the early Victorian period, financial innovations such as penny banks, building societies, and hire purchase contracts spread the acceptance of a money commodity. Soon savings banks, hire purchase contracts, and building society loans began to supplement the financial needs once fulfilled by the pawn shops, street lenders, and tally men who had provided credit to working communities.

Unlike many social critics, Simmel did not mourn this transition in traditional social life. Instead, he understood that money could both alienate and liberate the individual. Money, he argued, was ambiguous. It provided a common system of exchange that released the individual from the indentured labour of the past, promoting social mobility and freedom. With money, one could suspend the mutual obligations of custom that bound the farmer to the land, experience a new sense of freedom, and explore places and tastes beyond the local and familiar. Yet money at the same time eroded the lifelong social obligations of the gift circle to a contract that was meaningless upon delivery of the debt – an impersonal form of social relation that was antithetical to those established in rural and working-class communities. Yet in the industrial society, money was essential not only to make ends meet, but for acquiring houses, furniture, and clothes. As a universal manifestation of individual worth, money also provided a universal scale for establishing relative value and worth, not only of goods but also of people. The hot passions of traditional social obligations gave way to the rational assessment indicated by their ability to manage money. Ultimately, as he suggests, money is intimately woven into modern identities through the notion of pecuniary respectability. The formation of savings and lending institutions proved particularly important in the late nineteenth century as ideals of private homeownership began to define the notion of domestic respectability for all classes. The cult of domesticity, I hope to show, formed the core cultural hook upon which the normalization of penny banks, building societies, hire purchase arrangements, and credit cards was hung.

Viviana Zelizer's *The Social Meaning of Money* builds upon Simmel's work by rejecting its modernist thrust (Zelizer, 1997). She showed how money was made meaningful by the context of its use – within families where it is shared, in friendships and gift exchanges, in rituals, rites of passage, and ceremonies of reciprocity where mutuality and sociality were consolidated. People, she argued, did not simply reduce all economic transactions to a quantum or exchange value but moralized it by distinguishing between blood money, pin money, our money, and fun money. Arguing against the view that a rational calculus of equivalence governs all monetary relations, she illustrated the many ways people used the abstract commodity of money to continue impassioned relations of traditional cultures. Money was used as much as a tool for social bonding and mutuality, argued Zelizer, as it was a source for radical individualization and hedonistic self-expression.

Simmel and Zelizer offer persuasive and sophisticated arguments that demonstrate that personal finance is more than just a means of acquiring resources. It is also a medium through which identity and social affiliation are thought through and carried out. Demonstrating this idea further, literary critic Jennifer Wicke finds no legitimate basis for maintaining the theoretical divide between culture and economy. '[T]he market is at least as much an aesthetic phenomenon as it is anything else, and that neither art nor economics can be separated out of it or given an artificial primacy as instigator or reflector' (Wicke, 1994, p. 8) of the growing importance of market transactions. Wicke goes on to suggest that fiction is as legitimate a part of everyday discussion of money as are the proclamations of economists. Indeed, money comes to play as important a role in modern fiction as romance. The great characters of nineteenth century literature – from Scrooge to Madame Bovary – revealed how money had became a plot device that shaped characters' actions, posed moral dilemmas, fuelled conflicting belief systems, and excited various emotions. The gambling cad, the drunkard who failed to provide for his family, or the generous donor who enabled class mobility, spoke to and reinforced the complex relationship between money management and humanistic sentiments.

These authors have made it clear that the economy is culturally bound. Discourses shape the economy, and money provokes public discussion. In this, consumerism is as much shaped by the circulation of meaning as it is by the calculation of price. Since the early 1990s, a growing number of social scientists began highlighting the role that information and communication plays in shaping the contemporary economy (Dodd, 1994; Callon, 1998; Leyshon & Thrift, 1997). This thesis adds three dimensions pointing out the role that journalism plays in the diagnosis and commentary of the consumer economy, the part played by banks as promotional cultural institutions, and the part played by everyday talk and anxiety about money in our daily lives – the moralities.

Chapter 2 explores how Victorian culture, in the context of digesting the profound changes wrought by industrialization and the expansion of the money economy, attempted to fix masculine identities to public breadwinning and feminine identities to bread-buying and the domestic sphere. As recompense for their unacknowledged labour nineteenth century household management books encouraged women to see the value of constructing graceful sanctuaries to edify others and the nation (Sutton-Rampspeck, 2004). Authors Mary Ward, Sarah Grand, and Charlotte Perkins Gilman struggled to win recognition for women's domestic work and thrift.

Social reformers measured women's housekeeping against the idealization of thrift. Samuel Smiles' mid-nineteenth century self-help books instructed men to value a woman's thrift as much as beauty. He stressed that the spendthrift wife could shake the stability of a family as profoundly as any drunken husband who spent the mortgage money on beer. Yet, no one was more capable of stretching a penny further, or putting it to better use, than a woman – a theme Margaret Thatcher resurrected in the 1980s. Working-class women had little choice but to turn to a host of community lenders, tallymen, pawnshops and street lenders to provision their homes, but unlike the culturally honoured masculine building societies and friendly societies, these systems were at best, understood to lack credibility; at worst, serve as handmaidens of frivolous consumerism and exploiters of women's naivety. In many instances, women had little choice but to turn to unrespectable credit lenders to maintain the respectability of their families. While the many male debtors in fiction found moments of sympathy and redemption, Gustave Flaubert's condemnation of Madame Bovary for her excessive spending and inability to adhere to the norms of thrift that regulated her gender.

Nineteenth-century women were legally denied the right to enter into financial contracts, though they were the principal consumers of the household and this situated them in a profound contradiction. Rappaport (2000) and Finn (2003) vividly show how these contradictions began to unravel in nineteenth century court cases. Retailers demanded payment for the goods women acquired on their husband's proxy credit. When husbands refused to pay, judges unable to charge women (defined in law as noneconomic subjects), tended to uphold the rights of husbands, to the of consternation retailers. Hire purchase, which secured credit on the value of the good, offered a solution to the conundrum, and the chapter concluded with hire purchase expansion in Britain via American piano and sewing-machine sellers. The cult of domesticity established in the nineteenth century, the gender and class relations that animated it, and the institutions that financed it had a profound impact on the formation of Britain's late modern consumer culture.

Chapter 3 discusses how Victorian thrift was recast in the early twentieth century. The Bloomsbury group depicted thrift as an agent of imperialism, patriarchy, and class subordination preventing ordinary people of the nation from enjoying their rightful due to the beauty and bounty of their labour. John Maynard Keynes argued that domestic consumption was the saviour of the nation. He championed domestic automobile production as a way to disentangle Britain from its imperialism and its thrift habits that ill-suited modernity. Credit was refocused from a tool for imperial trade to a means of kick-starting the domestic market. A new modernist ethos emerged in which delaying enjoyment into the future was replaced with an emphasis on enjoying pleasures of consumption and aesthetics in the here and now. Virginia Woolf advocated not only that women should have a room of their own, but their right to decorate it, and wear fashionable clothes within it. Hire purchase underwrote a booming trade in furniture and appliances.

The British government endorsed the importation of American-style automobile financing to replicate the phenomenal success of American consumer culture. US automobile producers, Ford and General Motors, colonized the British market with their cheap cars (Harvey, 1989), financing and marketing techniques (Marchand, 1998). Yet, ambivalence followed the introduction of foreign financial instruments. Domestic institutional, moral, social, historical, and geographic obstacles stood in the way of replicating American mass car-financing in Britain. Utility companies and retailers played a greater role in socializing credit in the early twentieth century than automobile manufacturers. Still the internationalization of British hire purchase pointed to a new type of finance. As George Ritzer said, although little commented upon, the importation of American financial instruments deserve debate because they have the potential to embed American systems of rationalization, modernism, and consumerism, as much as if not more than Hollywood films or Disney cartoons (Ritzer, 2001; 1995).

While the two World Wars encouraged people to direct their savings towards the survival of the nation, and rationing curtailed the cult of domesticity, after theWWII historians document how a massive housing boom and New Town developments began to reconfigure older community leisure and consumption practices onto more individualized patterns. While critics derided the New Towns and the loss of the working-class neighbourhood, many women reported contentment with their new homes and embraced modern conveniences. The easing of credit restrictions in 1958 saw new appliances steadily stream into homes. Showing how firmly embedded the thrift ethos was in British culture, the acquisition of durable goods was frequently justified as prudent. Parents gifted major appliances to children for their future. Appliances entered the home by way of the logic of 'reversed thrift' where monthly payments for a new cooker, fridge, or washing machine were justified as an act of saving for the future, while cleverly enjoying material goods in the present (Olney, 1991). Cooperative movements too blurred the line between spending and saving by rewarding consumption with dividends redeemed later. As Martin (1991) points out 'what is most striking is the *persistent coexistence and confusion* of the two ethics' – production and consumption (Martin, 1991, p. 426).

Chapter 4 explores the banks' gradual reorientation towards the consumer market in the 1960s. For close to 200 years, the banks encouraged a focus on large-scale short-term credit, best suited for the needs of the state, industry and wealthy families. The state nationalized the banks for a time in 1946 to combat inflation. These experiences, combined with the long tradition of aristocrats taking up banking careers and the banks' status-based structures, led bankers to view themselves more as civil servants or guardians of the commonwealth, than sellers of mass financial services. In this paternal role, bankers believed it was their duty to prevent consumers from using credit for the acquisition of what they deemed were luxury goods.

After WWII, as war debt reduced, public sentiment demanded a better life after turmoil and austerity lost its noble sacrifice, policy-makers conceived of a banking system that might serve the interests of mass consumption. State legislation covering hire purchase in 1938, 1954, 1957, 1964, and most importantly the comprehensive consumer credit legislation of 1974, was drafted to protect consumers, to bring credit providers under the control over the government, to fashion the law in accordance with everyday credit practise, and democratize and equalize the treatment of credit consumers. This involvement of the state in credit markets is noteworthy because, it can sanctify, legitimate, and contribute to the institutionalization of modern credit instruments and practices. As McManus notes, 'A government licence is a better guarantee from the point of view of both trader and client; it is a valuable stamp of approval' (McManus, 1975, p. 73).

As the banks refocused their attention towards everyday consumers during the 1960s, they turned their attention to the 'unbanked'. The once middle-class-bound banks reached out to the remaining 76% of the population. They offered checking accounts and car loans, over-drafts, and debit cards modelled on the American success with these services. Change in banking culture was signified in the expansion and new branch layouts, the embrace of consumer-oriented technology, friendly attitudes towards consumers, and attention to market research and advertising. It became discriminatory to assess credit worthiness upon gender, ethnicity, and class. Bankers no longer deemed it their business to advise consumers against the acquisition of luxury goods on credit. Born of a hope that people would invest in their well-being and social mobility, the new political rhetoric, which advocated the accelerated flow of capital to consumers, dovetailed neatly with the reorientation of the banks as convenient points of access to ready cash.

Chapter 5 traces the banks in the 1980s when Margaret Thatcher, viewing the banking practices as still too antiquated and elitist, encouraged another reworking of banking structure. In her political addresses between 1951 and 1990, Thatcher stressed the importance of investment in forging the enterprise culture and homeowner democracy she deemed necessary for the renewal of the country. Thatcher loathed that domestic and foreign corporations looked beyond the City of London for better investment capital deals and felt that regulation curtailed the services bankers could offer, and actions they could undertake; thus contributing to the banks' un-enterprising character. Cutting the red tape and unleashing competition into the financial sector, Thatcher believed, promised to discipline Britain's gentlemanly bankers and encourage them to forge an even more efficient, consumer-orientated and innovative financial sector. Changing regulation opened the banks to domestic and foreign competition in 1986. Money – the most abstract and yet material of all commodities – went to market.

The regulatory change was coined the 'Big Bang', which aptly summed up this profound transformation of the British financial sector. American banks seized upon the opportunity, bringing their marketing approaches, financial methods, and technologies, which had proven so popular within their own peculiar financial system, into the square mile of the City. In the competitive swirl of global finance, profits, and market expansion hinged on encouraging as many members of the public to take on as many profitable financial services as possible between public and to the banks targeted the working poor, immigrants, the young, and especially women in intensive marketing campaigns. As Ralph Samuel cleverly pointed out, this modernization and internationalization of the banking sector was sold to the public by Margaret Thatcher's appeal to Victorian values including self-reliance, the importance of private property and the domestic sphere, and the idea of thrifty housewife (Samuel, 1992). Part of the deep cultural appeal of these values was how they ironically lay wast to traditional credit restrictions. Computers allowed detailed record-keeping and diagnosis of the most profitable banking services. Reports highlighted the obvious: consumer credit and mortgages were, quite literally, licences to print money.

Deregulation allowed the banks to offer mortgages, once the preserve of building societies. Private homeownership was the keystone of Thatcher's emerging ideology of enterprise culture. The legacy of a propertied class, nineteenth century slums, two world wars and hard-fought politics to improve the conditions of the working classes, and returning soldiers, shaped a distinctive property market in Britain. In 1979, 32% of the housing stock was state controlled (Mullins et al., 2006, p. 36). Council houses posed an obstacle to Thatcher's property-market dream, thus she rhetorically recast state housing from a social benefit to pawn a slumlord state played to limit people's freedom to control their own environments. Linking this rhetoric to practice, Thatcher's right-to-buy legislation created a private market for state housing. This legislation, combined with banking deregulation, made the homeowner and mortgage market in Briton more expansive than at any time in history.

Forced to overcome their shyness about selling financial services, the banks used television advertising and direct marketing campaigns to hawk overdrafts and credit cards like soap and beer. Advertising messages repositioned the banks from institutions promoting savings to ones profiting from debt. Advertisers presented new credit products as an easy and convenient means of negotiating one's lifestyle in a competitive money market. Where once the advertisements encouraged audiences to save for their children's education, vacations, and home refurbishment, post-Big Bang notions of convenient access to credit, management of finances for maximum return, and utilizing funds for individual wish fulfilment were layered on top of the old rhetoric. Consumers were empowered within these advertisements, encouraged to reject inconvenience, to look for the best price, and to live in the moment instead of wasting time delaying immediate pleasures for those in the future. Taken together, the financial advertising of the closing decades of the twentieth century articulates a sense of entitlement.

Credit was readily available to finance any lifestyle, and advertising suggested that to not take advantage of this instrument was to be old fashioned and committed to senseless acts of self-denial.

Britons neither passively, nor ignorantly imbibed the rhetoric of either Margaret Thatcher or bank marketers. Access to mortgage and consumer credit made sense to people on an experiential and wider cultural level. Britain's culture of private homeownership dates back to the Magna Carta, but the nineteenth century was when some of the most enduring cultural messages and practices of home were forged. Property fused with social mobility, and Victorians cast the home as a sacred sanctuary. Yet, only the most wealthy could afford to fulfil the homeowner dream. This changed after WWII, when impatient for the good life, mortgage lending and bank loans accelerated providing many consumers access to a middle-class lifestyle: Home ownership grew from 48% of the population in 1970 to 70% in 2006 (Mullins et al., 2006, p. 36). Margaret Thatcher reminded Britons that private property gave them the right to 'live their personal lives in the environment of their choice' (Thatcher, 21 May 1975). The opportunity to express one's social and individual self through the domestic sphere was deeply seductive.

Financial services helped unleash this pent-up demand. The banks were confident to extend credit to those with a toehold on the property ladder. On the public's side, a collective faith in rising property prices bolstered people's willingness to take on more debt. The volume and craft of financial services' advertising expanded and refined. Financial ads made up for 10% of overall media expenditure. Mindful of their 'boring' reputations the banks utilized extensive budgets to secure top promotional talent. The banks associated themselves with celebrities, articulated their grandeur with panoramic shots of a galloping black stallion, and tried to convey their authenticity through shaky street-shots of 'everyday people'. Bank advertisements presented credit as an accepted modern convenience, and banks as lifelines for contemporary existence. The advertising and marketing of financial instruments post-1980s aligned with the long held interest in domestic aestheticization that accompanied home pride. While, cars, TVs, and appliances in every home had been ready signs that consumerism was spreading to the masses in the 1950s, by the mid 1990s the intensified beautification of housing was funnelled through the ancillary industries of furnishing and gardening, and reflected in the expanded lifestyle media (Chaney, 2002; Szmigin, 2006; Taylor, 2002; Brundson, 2003). Between 1971 and 2006 the volume of spending on goods and services increased two and a half times (Office of National Statistics, 2008).

And whether stylizing a home or decorating the body in a new outfit for a night out on the town, credit cards became the preferred tool for lifestyle maintenance and advancement. By 2007, there were 67.3 million credit cards, 5.7 million charge cards, and 71.6 million debit cards (APACS, 2007). Credit cards averaged 2.4 per person, however this was minor compared to the US, where the average is 12.7 credit cards per person (US Census Bureau, 2008). Still, Britons held a third of all unsecured debt in western Europe (Marsh, 2006). Cash became passé and credit cards the preferred, thus normalized, medium of financial exchange. It is now impossible to engage in lifestyle activities such as booking a hotel room, obtaining tickets to a concert, or shopping online without a credit card.

To economists who read consumer confidence indexes like tea leaves, it became clear that consumer lifestyles forged in the domestic economy were the engines of economic growth. Recognizing credit and mortgages as the golden geese that laid successive quarters of wealth generation, New Labour was loath to deviate from the more open consumer market shaped by conservative politics in the 1980s. As the staggering public war-debt diminished, a personal debt problem emerged. Private property, retail, and consumer finance market expanded, while per capita savings declined. Personal debt grew to £1.457 trillion in 2008, exceeding the Gross Domestic Product, the total value of all goods and services produced that year (Bank of England, 2008). In short, Britain was spending beyond its means.

Chapter 6 explores how British broadsheets constructed these transformations in their public debates about personal finance in the closing years of the twenty-first century. Besides reporting economic indicators, the press provided potent parables about personal finance, offering advice, relaying morality tales with heroes and victims, dupes and scapegoats. Journalists exposed troubling banking practices and held politicians accountable for keeping the banks honest. Some stories, such as debt-related suicide, set off key public and political debates and contributed to policy discussion and change. I examine how British broadsheets firmly placed personal debt on the public agenda.

Chapter 7 presents how journalistic discourses presented the anxieties underlying the consumer-led boom via three intertwining themes. The first theme gave space to politicians to celebrate the consumer-led economy and debate the important role that the management of personal finance played in its maintenance. The transformation of the financial markets contributed to the rebirth of consumerism of the post-1980 period in Britain (Lee, 1993). Homeownership grew from 10% at the beginning of the century to 70% at its close. Ready mortgages and credit allowed for wider participation in the cult of domesticity, as two thrids of the GDP was accounted for by the house renovation, retail, and service sectors. At no other time in history had the fate of the nation hinged so profoundly on the individual consumer's decision to buy a new pairs of shoes, upgrade their kitchen counter-top to granite, visit an acupuncturist, or ritualize their morning with café-bought cappuccino. New Labour, who stressed the importance of consumer choice and equated social welfare with a strong economy, did much to support the expansion of a consumer economy in Britain. With annual GDP growth running at close to 3%, Britain ranked among the most prosperous (if not egalitarian) economies and fastest growing of all European nations (Economic and Financial Indicators, 2003). Blair's government was loath to make serious interventions in the financial marketplace, out of fear of disrupting the expansion of the consumer economy and stalling its creation of jobs.

A second theme highlights how the banks' marketing was taken up as an exploitation of hard-pressed consumers. Journalists documented human-interest stories detailing the anxiety that accompanied mounting debt loads in millennial Britain. In the pages of the *Times* and the *Guardian*, economists began to question whether easy credit and low mortgage rates were worth the economic risk they posed. Critics asked whether extracting undue usury from poor people had sponsored the fantastic profit of the financial industry and the lifelong enslavement of a generation of aspirant students and homebuyers. Clearly modern audiences do not passively accept banking messages. Consumer complaints directed to OFSTED testify that people are sceptical and critical of banking advertising. Still the banks' privileged access to the media and control over the financial industry make it difficult to ignore their contribution to money meanings.

The third discourse constructed by journalists focused on the role of the troubling contemporary financial consumer. The media, morally condemned consumers for their exaggerated sense of entitlement, for not upholding their financial contracts, for ignoring the virtues of thrift and productive debt, and engaging in a hedonistic drive to bankroll excessive celebrity lifestyles on someone else's tab. The press highlighted what they described as dangerous new financial attitudes emanating from the young and women who engaged in 'champagne lifestyles' they could not afford. Because the evidence showed that older males held the lion's share of debt and were most likely to declare bankruptcy, press accounts of such attitudes were better understood as the working through of a taboo, than a credible reflection of women's personal financial practices.

Chapter 8 turns the focus to how the preferred remedy for the attendant anxieties stemming from the personal financial market became the subject of therapeutic discourses. Conservatives and New Labour agreed that markets provide the best means of fulfilling the public's genuine interests because of the priority accorded in them to consumers' free choice. The individual consumer was thought best able to assess how much debt he or she could manage. Consumer culture came to hinge upon how well consumers manage money – that is, how carefully they balance income with spending, expectations, and aspirations. Blair weakened the bankruptcy laws and referred the troubled debtor to credit counselling services. Where once evictions, debtors prison, bankruptcy courts, and community shaming rituals had been the cultural humiliations served upon those who could not manage their finances, millennial Britain addressed financial struggle therapeutically. Debt counselling business boomed in the wake of the subprime "melt down" as the percentage of borrowers three months in arrears rose steadily. Counselling services increasingly became advocates of the indebted consumer, taking over a role once played by church and community.

Medical researchers, too, have joined the chorus, linking financial problems to a host of ailments: alcohol and drug abuse, obesity, sleeplessness, depression, headaches, panic attacks, and ulcers (Furnham et al., 1995). Divorce heightens financial anxieties, it seems, because resources are fought over as household incomes split – usually at a point where consumer outlay increases for childcare and the maintenance of two households (BBC News, 16 October 2006). OFSTED research in 2008 showed that as their debt grew, many became depressed about their inability to manage their accounts effectively – at their inadequacy as economic subjects. Young adults especially, found making their means and aspirations meet, increasingly difficult. These studies reported that even children were touched by financial angst: 22% ten-year-olds and more than 30% 15-year-olds reported regularly worrying about money (OFSTED, 2008). Clinical case studies suggested women, in particular, financed consumption beyond their means to impress peers and assert independence from family members, despite inevitable domestic, social, financial, and criminal complications (Glatt & Cook, 1987).

Since the 1980s, psychological professions have debated whether shopaholism and its accompanying consumer debt load should be listed as a specific mental disease in the Diagnostic and Statistical Manual of Mental Disorders. Some psychologist have even reported success treating the malaise with psychotropic medication. Up to 10% of the population was thought to be afflicted by the illness, and growing numbers of the public, particularly women, self-identified as shopaholics.

The chapter concludes with an examination of Sophie Kinsella's (2001, 2002, 2003) shopaholic novels and suggests that the pleasure of the novels may lie in part in the way they humanize the pathological debt-ridden shopper. By building an embattled but resilient financial consumer, Kinsella's novels strike a deep cord with their readers, most of whom are women. These books trace the life cycle of Becky Bloomwood, a young British woman, who moves through early career, marriage, life abroad, and motherhood. Bloomwood's significant appetite for consumer goods and her considerable shopping talents results in a life constantly upset by financial strife. In response, Bloomwood engages in an endless and comical array of justifications for her excessive shopping habits and poor financial management. Bloomwood also reveals a style of consumption that is no longer rooted in the modernist ethos of artistry and grace, fuelled by ever-changing fantasies borrowed from Cinderella mythology, celebrity lifestyles, and fashion runways. Domesticity is but one of Bloomwood's many fantasies. A new pair of shoes are more the object of her obsession than a man. Thus, critics of the books have noted that they challenge traditional romance, but replace it with the romance of the marketplace. No matter how disastrous her financial plight, somehow, Bloomwood always manages to right herself, frequently because her debt is swept away on the white charger of good luck, or the support of family, friends, and lovers. Still, she is caught in a cycle readers identify with. Credit, the tool that allows Bloomwood to actualize her fantasies, is also the tool that continually points her back to the hard reality of the balance sheet, which she in turn continually attempts to evade.

The conclusion considers the limits of Britain's financial fantasy life.

1
Prudent Investment and Modest Consumption

Margaret Thatcher's attempt to create an 'enterprise culture' marks a crucial turning point in British history (Curran & Burrows, 1991; Heelas & Morris, 1992; Hall, 1988). Steeped in the neoliberal ideology of unfettered markets and private property rights, her government's policies fomented a radical departure from the British politics preceding her time in office. As Anderson notes, her 'one hundred new pieces of legislation which laid the foundation for this enterprise culture sought to reduce the state's role in public services, privatize public corporations, and discipline unions to foster business innovation and ultimately expand the economy' (Anderson et al., 2000, p. 8). But reformation of the marketplace was a means to an end: her goal was to create 'a new culture – an enterprise culture' that rewards the entrepreneur and 'breeds a new generation of men and women who create jobs for others instead of waiting for others to create jobs for them' (Thatcher, 8 February 1984).

Thatcher refused the artificial demarcation between economic and cultural policies. She took inspiration from the work of Adam Smith, who she proclaimed 'got the answers right' because he was a professor of moral philosophy – not economics. She bragged therefore that as a politician 'you do not do well in economics, you do not do well in standard of living, unless the spirit of a people has revived' (Thatcher, 8 February 1984). Thatcher saw GDP growth as a by-product of the spirit of the nation. To address this spirit she undertook political revivalism. Her economic speeches regularly invoked a curious blend of mythical Victorian petty bourgeois values – hard work, thrift, sacrifice for the future and self-reliance – which she believed forged the proud and strong nation of shopkeepers from which she had descended (Anderson et al., 2000, p. 16).

Yet her Sermon on the Mount speech in 1988, made it clear that her political views were also profoundly shaped by her 'strict Methodist up-bringing'. As she readily confessed 'I believe in "Judaeo-Christian" values. Indeed my whole political philosophy is based on them' (Thatcher in Anderson et al., 2000, p. 13). Wealth creation, according to Thatcher, is required for carrying out God's work and receiving his glory. 'How could we respond to the many calls for help, or invest for the future, or support the wonderful artists and craftsmen whose work glorifies God, unless we had first worked hard and used our talents to create the necessary wealth?' Celebrating family values, Thatcher asked her audience to 'recall that Timothy was warned by St. Paul that anyone who neglects to provide for his own house (meaning his own family) has disowned the faith and is "worse than an infidel"' (Thatcher, 21 May 1988).

Following the logic of Adam Smith, Thatcherism first set out to release the pent-up energy of the petty bourgeoisie as the engine of new wealth. What she added to Smith's liberal belief in the power of market exchange was the importance of focusing on British moral character in her attempt to move Britain 'from a dependent to a self-reliant society – from a give-it-to-me to a do-it-yourself nation. A get-up-and-go, instead of a sit-back-and-wait-for-it Britain' (Thatcher, 8 February 1984). Her cultural strategy especially targeted the unemployed through the Enterprise Allowance which provided weekly benefits to the unemployed – but only if they started a business (Thatcher, 8 June 1988). In its wake, small businesses (especially cafes and fashion boutiques) expanded, raising the number of self-employed individuals in five years from 9 per cent to 12 per cent and leading Thatcher to enthuse that finally 'the spirit has returned to Britain' (Thatcher, 8 June 1988).

But Thatcher's proposal for an enterprise culture involved much more than simply convincing the unemployed to start a small business. The second pillar of this strategy was the privatization of council houses. Thatcher saw public housing as obstacles preventing the poorest citizens from expressing a fundamental aspect of their British character: the drive for private property. Homeownership was waved as the magic wand that gave people a prized 'sense of independence, of self-reliance, of individuality'. Thatcher frequently paid homage to the sacrifices people made to acquire property. Importantly, she suggested that the reward for homeownership was the publics' right to 'live their personal lives in the environment of their choice'. As she explained, 'if we have our own home, for instance, we don't have to rely upon the State or the local authority to provide one for us. If we have savings we can tide ourselves over hard times on our own resources. And we are much more likely to be responsible citizens if we have possessions to look after, because we are answerable to ourselves for their upkeep and we are the first to suffer if we fail in our duty' (Thatcher, 1 September 1959).

For Thatcher, having and paying for mortgages exemplified the spirit of enterprise because families that own property work harder, 'save their money', 'forego some immediate pleasure or luxury' and delay gratification (Thatcher, 21 May 1975). House-holding, she claimed, had a calming influence on people by focusing their attention on pragmatic domestic concerns instead of radical socialist ideas and violent crimes. United by a shared interest in maintaining high property values, house-holders watched out for one another and kept their neighbourhoods in order. The privatization of state housing, she proclaimed, was therefore the best means of expanding market democracy and restoring Britons' pride.

The deregulation of banking and mortgage sectors was the third pillar of enterprise culture. To achieve her goals she had to undo the last vestiges of protectionist regulation of Britain's financial sector. Her attack on the banking system was an attempt to shake up the congenitally uncompetitive and snobby gentlemanly bankers. Bankers from around the world were allowed to invest, to take over, and to merge with British banks. Her policies also permitted the banks to expand their consumer credit options and get into the mortgage market – long the preserve of building societies. 'Gone are the controls which hampered success', she proclaimed in 1986. 'The City's growing confidence and drive owe a good deal to young people. Its vast new dealing rooms are run by the young. People who made it not because of who they know or what school tie they wear, but on sheer merit. That is the kind of society I want to see' (Thatcher, 10 November 1986). Competition, faith in new technology and liberalized credit rating systems enabled the banks to loosen their traditional lending strictures and profit from the expansion of new financial services.

Thatcher's homilies about hard work were far from new moral sentiments in Britain. This brief historical overview can hardly do justice to the many cross-cutting and multilayered threads which are woven into British economic history, yet, in some ways, Thatcher's attack on gentlemanly banking and loosening of the British household's purse strings run counter to some of the most enduring discourses surrounding debt, saving, and the prudent management of personal finance. Amid the present credit crisis it is apparent to us that the 'big bang' did produce ready access to mortgages and consumer credit. Thatcherism legitimated a revived use and understanding of consumer credit that stimulated the economy through debt. Successive governments could do little more than gently tinker with it after she left office. The impact of her neoliberal ideology on British society has been widely debated by political economists and historians; yet the part played by Thatcher's deregulation of personal finance has received far less attention until very recently. In what follows, I set out to outline the ways that the public discourses on personal financial relations were being rewritten throughout the modernization of Britain.

Thrift as character

Part of the appeal of Thatcher's rhetoric was how it connected to a set of values associated in British culture with growth and democracy. Historians would recognize in Thatcher's appeals the spectre of the work ethic that Max Weber identified as key to the formation of British capitalist culture. Weber traced the work ethic back to the rise of the Protestant middle class who in the seventeenth century began to struggle for power and legitimacy against the Catholic land-owning aristocracy (MacKinnon, 1988). Weber linked the productive forces that underwrote industrial capitalism to a 'type of feeling which is closely connected with certain religious ideas' (Weber, 1958, p. 53). The Protestant sentiments of work and thrift described in Weber as the Spirit of Capitalism offers the best cultural explanation of the factors motivating the accumulation of wealth. Overrepresented by lower-middle-class shopkeepers, the Protestant ideals of asceticism and doing God's work on earth, said Weber, motivated the capitalist entrepreneur. Work was a divine commitment to the faith, serving as 'the most powerful conceivable lever for the expansion of that attitude toward life' (Weber, 1958, p. 172). More than a moral duty, people strove through labour to fashion a cultural and personal sign of goodness. Catholic worship of idols, heavenly rewards, and predestination did not provide the same motivation to industrial productivity as a Protestant sense of providential investment for a class anxious about falling down, and eager to climb the ladder to heaven and status through the accumulation of wealth.

As the moral force of usury faded under Bentham's legal attack on its legitimation, Britain's industrial revolution dawned. Between 1780 and 1830, a refined division of labour, coupled with the application of industrial technology, and expansion of domestic and international markets reshaped social relations and brought new attitudes towards business. Religion, according to Huggins, continued to play a role through the nineteenth century in articulating Christianity as a way of life. For middle-class men who wished to join the social elite of their town, attendance at the right chapel, wealth, involvement in charitable or philanthropic affairs, and the holding of public office became a mandatory route to reputation. Reviewing mid-Victorian diaries or private letters, Huggins noted how often the entries seemed 'dictated by rules of propriety and lacking in spontaneity, with few personal confessions or mentions of non-respectable behaviour'. In his view, 'respectable public behaviour was underpinned by fear of pressure from church, neighbours, friends and family within these communities'. But respectability was not simply a matter of personal integrity, but a performance motivated by the promise of social advancement. Maintaining one's respectability paid, while losing it became surrounded by the fear of social failure (Huggins, 2000, p. 587).

Personal finance was intertwined in these ideals for, as Protestantism spread and the British cast their eyes to the future rather than heaven or hell, their interest in saving, the value of thrift, frugality, efficiency, and educating one's self for the future intensified. Thrift became a yardstick upon which personal consumption was observed and morally evaluated. The charge of deviance befell the spendthrifts who squandered funds for self-gratification and the debtor who lacked self-control. Temptation and idleness required exorcism as they thwarted the productive drive. Gambling and excessive drinking, unremarkable practices within traditional culture, became vilified and linked to financial ruin. Correct consumption, thrift, temperance, and self-restraint marked moral respectability and social standing.

Adhering to protestant values required considerable discipline, but its popularity lies in its democratic impetus. Its promise was that contentment would visit those who, regardless of class, practised the values of hard work, self-reliance and thrift (Kinmonth, 1980, p. 537). Moral respectability rather than inherited privilege assured one's standing in the community because, according to Protestant doctrine, 'The rich man and the good poor man both must pursue their callings in order to provide for the legitimate needs of themselves and their families and neighbors' (Seaver, 1980, p. 48). The faithful were also united in their opposition to greed 'for rich or poor alike greed perverts all just relationships: Greed is the universal solvent, finally destroying 'any sound comfort in God, for no man can serve two masters' (Seaver, 1980, p. 49). The poor had always practised thrift out of necessity, using every scrap of material and leftover food (think of how many recipes utilize stale bread), but it is questionable whether individuals felt 'good' about their acts of frugality. The cultural change in meaning was how the middle classes brandished thrift as a self-conscious ideal: The squandering of material gain was wasteful because it needed to be reinvested for the future (Howe, 1975).

Throughout the nineteenth century Christian writers set out to explain the wonders of hard work, temperance, self-reliance, and thrift. Samuel Smiles became one of the most famous town criers of Victorian values. Smiles waxed lyrical about the wonders of thrift, propriety, and self-restraint in his incredibly popular books. *Self-Help*, which appeared in 1859, was reprinted three times in its first month of publication, and by 1901 had been to press 50 times. Smiles' work was widely read in the US and translated into Dutch, French, German, and Danish (Richards, 1982, p. 52). Smiles insisted upon self-reliance. He constructed the state, as a cold, distant, and clumsy institution, incapable of serving individual happiness or solving the conflicts between competing individuals in the market. Only free individuals could decipher their own needs and produce their own pleasure or pain. Smiles 'was confident that all disputes in society could be solved by educated debate and agitation' (Morris, 1981, p. 92). Reasonable and self-disciplining individuals, not violence and class-warfare, were the proffered way to securing greater wealth for all (Morris, 1981).

Self-reliance was intertwined with notions of saving and prudent investment. Although savings institutions, established in the late eighteenth century, offered chequing accounts and annuities to a wider population, they were not taken up by the wider public (Hewitt, 2006). The members of the church and civil society took it upon themselves to socialize thrift to the wider public, and offer them the means for carrying out the habit. Religious figures who had once taken pity on the plight of the poor also propagated self-reliance by popularizing the ideals of prudent investment. Rev. Henry Duncan founded his first penny savings banks for the indigent and working classes in Scotland in 1810 because they were a way of spreading the virtues of thrift. Penny banks encouraged anyone over seven to deposit and withdraw funds. Children were urged to tithe for their future by saving in the present. To welcome them, the banks proclaimed how the 'smallest amount of money was not too insignificant to be saved nor was the most obscure bit of land unworthy of cultivation' (Straus, 1920, p. 196). Noticing the popularity of the penny banks' movement, an act of Parliament in 1817 regulated the formation of banks. Sanctioned by the state, the number of savings banks swelled. By 1818, there were over 200 savings banks spread throughout England, Scotland, Wales, and Ireland (Pratt, 1830).

Beverly Lemire (2004) documents how Sunday school networks took up the task of preaching the gospels of saving, which by 1850 boasted two million members. In 1846, a Sunday school teacher insisted that the school-based banks 'often saved whole families from destitution' (2004, p. 30). Thrift was well established in the elementary school curriculum by 1870 (Lemire, 2004, 2005). The cause spread into the mainstream school system. Birmingham inaugurated penny banks in their board schools in 1876 and by 1885 could claim 68 such branches with 9000 accounts. The Manchester School Board was also among the earliest to approve the opening of School Penny Savings Banks in three schools in 1877 and their numbers grew by 1885 with 136 School Penny Savings Banks holding more than 12,000 accounts.

Other savings institutions and movements took up the thrift. By 1860, £42,000,000 were invested in savings banks by over 1,500,000 depositors in the UK who received varying rates of interest from £4 11s. 3d. to £3 5s. 0d per cent. The state further legitimated the savings field with its construction of Post Office Savings Banks in 1861, 'a fund and assurance office for investing savings of the poor' that was ignored by the mainstream banks. In 1861, 2535 Post Office Savings banks accumulated £1,698,000 (Chadwick, 1861). The omnipresence of these savings institutions goes some way in explaining why the Victorian period has been dubbed the age of thrift.

Accommodation and acrimony

In 1832, any man able to accumulate the requisite £10 to qualify could vote. In short, political franchise depended upon financial accumulation. As a result, parliament filled with businessmen who pursued policies that best served their class interests. The newly enfranchised successfully advanced their interest in wealth accumulation. Reflecting on the impact of these changes over the century, Herbert argues that a sense of 'unbounded prosperity' gripped early Victorian culture. The solid and fixed relations structured by property wealth gave way to 'new ones based on the liquidities of manufacturing, commerce, speculation, and credit'. As Walter Bagehot remarked in 1880, the special genius of the system was its ability to rush speculative capital with mercurial swiftness to whatever sector of the economy offered a chance of profit (Herbert, 2002, p. 196).

The growing affluence, which tended to circulate through a limited number of hands, encouraged criticism. Karl Marx protested loudly against the new forms of speculative investment analysing the exploitive class relations of the industrial economy. His writing has provided a powerful voice of opposition to the forces of nineteenth-century wealth generation by mustering the puritans' moral warnings about greed to attack the ascendant industrial bourgeoisie. The expansion of the money economy guided by speculative investment turned the feudal world upside down, he argued, 'confounding and confusing' the established character of nature and humanity. 'It transforms fidelity into infidelity, love into hate, hate into love, virtue into vice, vice into virtue, servant into master, master into servant, idiocy into intelligence, and intelligence into idiocy' (Marx, 1859). Marx's patron and writing partner, Fredrick Engels, argued that accepting the money economy as natural, the bourgeoisie had themselves become inhuman and alienated from their fellows: 'The middle classes in England have become slaves of the money they worship. ... Their sole happiness is derived from gaining a quick profit. They feel pain only if they suffer a financial loss' (in Herbert, 2002, p. 311–12).

In *The Power of Money* (1844) Marx calls money both a visible divinity and a common whore. It is the visible divinity, the bond of all bonds, he argues, because it has the power to shape all things in an industrial economy and empower men beyond their true capabilities. 'That which I am unable to do as a man, and of which therefore all my individual essential powers are incapable, I am able to do by means of money.' It is the common whore because although it allows the purchase of anything, in buying we are alienated from our essential nature. In this sense alone, money is a 'truly creative power'. One can be 'bad, dishonest, unscrupulous, stupid, but because money is honoured' so too are those who possess it. While money can seemingly wash away the greed of the capitalist, what it really represents is his ability to create more wealth in his own interest.

The working class in Britain did not heed Marx's call to take up revolution, and why not is a question that occupied critics on the left for decades. According to Smith, a deeply rooted cultural pragmatism in Britain shaped an accommodationist instead of a revolutionary politic. The working class fragmented into 'numerous associations, inextinguishable prejudices and loyalties', which could not be neatly corralled around 'one single pattern of affections or hatreds, or one single class relationship' (Smith, 1941, p. 409). Common sense dictated that it was better to seek change within the known rules of society than ushering in an entire new playing field of unknown rules. This position was bolstered because capitalism created a space for franchisement and an expanding middle class, thus 'multiplied its defenders'. Members of this new class popularized reform after 1832 through humanitarian movements that drew upon 'the work of Bentham, Mill, Dickens, Disraeli, and Carlyle' and according to Smith had a greater influence on the working class than Marx (Smith, 1941, p. 407). Political action through parliament became the preferred means of change. The parliamentary idea permeated the political notions of the working class. Meanwhile, the Labour Party and trade unions succeeded in establishing a long series of laws to protect the accumulated rights of labour (Smith, 1941, p. 416). Impervious to revolutionary ideologies, the British worker preferred cautious pragmatism (Smith, 1941, p. 417).

Still, as Christie Davies' wonderful essay on the construction of the capitalist entrepreneur in popular culture suggests, notions of the thrifty individual circulated widely in Britain as the butt of many jokes. Considerable awareness surrounded the thrifty accumulator who was portrayed in a respectful light at the same time as being ridiculed as the inhuman miser for his inhumanity and lack of gift circle generosity (Davies, 1992). The romantic stories of Charles Dickens, circulating widely in newspapers in the nineteenth century, arguably earned more of a hold on the popular imagination than Marx's political pamphlets because they appealed more to accommodation and nostalgia for the days of the gift circle than radical revolution.

The law continued to enforce the prerogatives of those with money to invest, as debtor's prison, until 1869, welcomed members of all classes unable to pay their debts. Charles Dickens took up the torch handed on by Defoe to become one of the most powerful Victorian advocates of social and political reform. Dickens' hatred of the treatment of debtors was personal. His privileged childhood came to an abrupt halt when his father, who amassed bills through social entertaining, was sentenced to debtor's prison. At 12, the young Dickens found himself at hard labour in a boot factory. The emotional bitterness the experience generated in Dickens towards a family, community, and state that refused to come to his aid, was a constant source of inspiration for his writing. His *Little Dorrit* addresses the topic of debtor's prison directly and provides one of the most vivid renditions of its horrors in modern literature:

> Like a well, like a vault, like a tomb, the prison had no knowledge of the brightness outside, and would have kept its polluted atmosphere intact in one of the spice islands of the Indian ocean.
>
> (Dickens, 1885, p. 2)

It is described as a place of darkness, where the light of reason, forgiveness, and grace were incapable of shining. But it was not simply the people in debtor's prison who were enslaved, according to Dickens. The widespread obsession with trying to advance socially through expensive status competitions placed people in a prison of their own making. The message in many of his financial fictions is the same: the industrial economy extracts the greatest of pain from the most innocent and good, but no one seems to care. He warns of the social disgrace that befell those who slipped down the social ladder. An example of his financial advice is found in *The Old Curiosity Shop*, in which little Nell Trent, who nurses her grandfather with devotion and kindness is cast out on the street where she eventually dies after being forced to gamble borrowed money, when a spendthrift son-in-law and Nell's bother wasted the grandfather's fortune. The cautionary tale proclaims the importance of financial respectability and offers reasons to fear debt. The spendthrift can bring down an entire family. Respectable people struggled to avoid the moneylender and the workhouse (Thompson, 1999/2000).

Dickens' work is known as much for the social commentary woven into its plots, as his richly drawn characters: small helpless children were forced into thievery because of poverty; amicable spendthrifts brought innocents in their families to ruin; misers turned their back on the plights of the poor and disabled. For Dickens, fortunes were less a source of liberty than a force that socially disconnected people by making them arrogant and thoughtless. It took considerable psychological resources to maintain pecuniary respectability. Herbert's analysis of Dickens's literature, notes the unconscious forces that trouble the minds of those obsessed with thrift and productivity. Most of Dickens' characters, from Scrooge to Micawber, suffer from neurotic symptoms which would seem to have been in epidemic proportion in the age of nervous tics, psychosomatic disorders, 'self-torment', 'depression and dyspepsia'. Dickens thus brought to light the psychological pains of debt more vividly than the systemic forces of social inequality.

Yet nineteenth-century culture humanized not only the debtor but also the moneylender, resolving the conflict in the idea of plutocracy. The psychological anxiety of achieving the norm of financial stability was acknowledged but this did not disrupt the idea that accumulated money was the measure of a man's character. Linda Rozmovits argues that the critical acclaim of Henry Irving's production *Merchant* which played at the Lyceum Theatre in 1879–80, in which Shylock 'in all but the most literal of senses, wins the trial' (Rozmovits, 1998, p. 62), demonstrates how nineteenth-century Britain became more plutocratic.

The Victorian period fostered growing sympathy for those who gained wealth through prudent investment. The staging of the play portrayed Shylock not as a vengeful Jewish usurer, but as a respectable trader swindled out of his rightful repayment of a legal and binding contract. This reinterpretation of the morality surrounding credit and debt was an unprecedented success, running over seven months, and viewed by an estimated 330,000 people. To those who watched this reinterpretation of the tale, money contracts were a matter that had to be honoured – regardless of race or creed of the lender (Rozmovits, 1998). Respect for the productivity of money did not discriminate: thus, the play spoke to a new moral order that increasingly made space within Britain's plutocracy even for the once contemptible Jewish moneylender. While most commentators acknowledge the importance of Marx's critique of greedy capitalists, less attention has been devoted to the ways that the privatization of property, the commodification of labour, and the expansion of banking also reframed the discourses on personal finance in the nineteenth century.

The self-interested moralizing of the bourgeois plutocrat also chaffed against the long held dominion of the property classes. Industrial wealth accumulated outside the agrarian economy threatened the privilege that those of good breeding had become accustomed to. Inheritance, breeding, and education no longer assured riches in an age where shrewd businessmen of humble backgrounds made sums rivaling the courtly classes. In reaction, according to Nicholas Cooper, as early as the Georgian period, the property class brandished 'their membership of a class that was distinguished by its behaviour, its growing responsibilities, its increasing education and its members' awareness of belonging to a recognisable and exclusive elite' (Cooper, 2002, p. 296). A new humanist ethos of civility reworked the medieval codes of courtliness to announce class legitimacy. According to Cooper, civility was 'frozen as rules of politeness and good breeding'.

Taste and judgement became tools for creating distance between the property and industrial classes. Unable to bar industrialists from advancing economically, old-money elite staked the rhetorical deck to ensure they had the upper hand in the game of social honour. Manner, sensibility, and attitude towards money became the pawns in struggles for class legitimacy (Carter, 2002; Langford, 1989; Davidoff & Hall, 1987). Industrialists who made their money from organizing labour quite rightly valued hard work, efficiency, and productivity. The property elite mocked this incessant drive to 'do', 'make', 'hurry', and 'accumulate', declaring it ill of nature, harried, and mechanistic.

The historian Martin Johnes argues that British landowners also tried to create exclusivity, by cloistering around particular leisure pursuits, such as archery clubs, that resurrected an ancient, outmoded hunting technology to mark class boundaries and legitimacy (Johnes, 2004). The bourgeois character was subject to ridicule. The property class avoided public discussion of wealth and with personal bankers and credit lines they never had to touch a shilling, thus enabling the new industrialist to be defamed as money grubbing, dirty, and obsessed with filthy lucre. The old elite argued the industrialists' worship of liquid assets and stock options fostered dizzy, fragmented characters lacking the stabilizing influence of property. By enacting a refined performance of politeness and disinterest the industrialist could be cut down for their abruptness, loudness, and rudeness. The industrialists' liberal emphasis on individual interest was designated greedy and self-obsessed when juxtaposed with the noblesse oblige and social duty to 'the people' of the landed classes.

Still for every act of class distinction, every snide dismissal, every ounce of wounded pride, there was a counterforce of class accommodation and emulation. What else could explain the reason why so many industrialists, having made considerable wealth, retired to the countryside to take up the life of the squire? So, too, would many industrialists try to advance their offsprings' position by sending them to public schools to be educated as gentlemen, rather than by teaching them the ropes of the family business. While they may not have liked the industrial class much, the profits from property rents earned by the old-money elite certainly were not diminished that much by the rise of the industrial class. The law of contract strengthened the position of the property classes who could use it to enforce their lease arrangements. The dissolution of usury prohibitions coupled with new opportunities to expand rental profits through reinvestment was clearly welcomed even as the bourgeois values were mocked.

Towards a democracy of debt

Since the closing decades of the eighteenth century, enclosure laws forced rural families off the land imposing harsh consequences for those without tenure to land (Kowaleski-Wallace, 2000). We are familiar with the account of how people flooded into the factories and mines desperate for a steady income in the industrializing economy. But, limited housing stock and few jobs created extreme social hardship for the mobile poor. Political concern rose as massive migration strained the village parishes, the primary centres of giving to the poor. Fear of crime and poverty in overflowing cities, led the church to proselytize about Victorian morals of thrift and respectability to the poor and the young. In short, 'the working classes did not need to be told by the middle class that family life was important, that honest toil was better than loafing, or that saving for a rainy day was sensible' (Thompson, 1981, p. 189).

Since E. P. Thompson's research, it has also been clear that the working classes brought their own cultural resources to consolidate their position in the age of industrialization – which partially aligned them with a pride in work, frugality, and a concern for public reputation. However, Thompson argues, this does little more than suggest a coincidence of purpose and of values on the part of some of the petty bourgeoisie and the working classes. It does not show that these values, and the institutions that embodied them, such as burial clubs and friendly societies, were alien impositions on an unimaginative or reluctant working class.

Nowhere are the many ironies surrounding the diffusion of the middle-class virtues of prudence, thrift, and productivity into the working-class communities better illustrated than in the area of personal finance. As is well documented, well before the industrial revolution peasant communities had established non-contract traditions of wealth sharing, such as charitable potlatching, gift circles, Christmas saving clubs, labour pools, and friendship trusts. During the early industrial period, those informal financial arrangements existing in working-class communities were gradually forged into important institutions of personal lending and savings. One of the first to do so was Miss Priscilla Wakefield's 'Friendly Society for Women and Children', which got its charter in 1798, emerging from the well-established working-class practice of saving in the summer for the Christmas season. Hardly surprising then that in 1797, when Jeremy Bentham tried to promote what he called Frugality Banks to instil self-reliance in the poor, they met with little success, for it was more intent on spreading morality and forestalling state intervention, than in providing the means for the poor to improve their lives.

In the early nineteenth century, however, working-class lending was mostly organized by and for men in the artisan classes. The vast majority of lending arrangements took place in the pubs because they were readily available and cheap places for men to meet. In the pubs, men largely shared the company of other men, creating the trust and familiarity necessary for money exchange. Some of the rituals associated with working-class drinking, for example the buying of rounds, can be understood as gift circles which functioned as exercises in community trust building, by knitting males into relations of reciprocity of financial obligation. Established as Friendly Societies, they often gave themselves exotic names – Ancient Foresters, Loyal Shepherds, Hearts of Oak, Buffaloes, and even Druids – nostalgically beckoning the mystery of ancient tribal associations, seductive to their modern male clientele. For this reason they were largely forged around masculine breadwinning pursuits, such as providing funds for the purchase of tools, sickness benefits, insurance for workplace accidents, strike pay, and burials.

According to Johnson, while most writers worry about the friendly societies' alignment with trade union movements, organizing trade disputes was of secondary concern to the pragmatic everyday needs they serviced. For example, the friendly societies had provided protection to the poor against the enclosure laws. The Rose's Act of 1793 protected members of friendly societies from being evicted from the land. They provided 'life assurance and sickness benefits' (Johnson, 1988, p. 38). They outfitted workers for employment. In many sectors of the industrializing economy, workers were self-employed with piecemeal work arrangements enduring well into the twentieth century. Coal miners, steel workers, builders, and even those working in manufacturing were expected to purchase their own equipment and uniforms. Expenditures for acquiring and maintaining the tools necessary to work one's trade were considerable, therefore, preparing people for labour was one of the central services of friendly societies:

> For working people in many types of employment, at all levels of income purchased goods and services not (or not simply) for immediate satisfaction, but to enable them to participate (or participate more effectively) in self-employment.
>
> (Johnson, 1985, p. 40)

Given the creed of self-reliance and working-class pride, the Friendly Society's funeral insurance was a particularly attractive advantage of membership saving many from the disgrace of not being able to pay for their loved ones' funeral. Working-class communities had long traditions of self-reliance which extended to burying one's own family members. Yet the historical work of Hurren and King (2005) suggests that the onus of paying for the paupers' funeral was a burden on the families of the poor who found that the burial rituals expected were far from spartan.

The shame associated with a pauper's funeral loomed large in Victorian culture stimulating families, communities, and parishes to do all they could to avoid having the dead bear the stigma. Hurren and King (2005) document the heroic efforts on the part of bereaved families to find the financial resources to carry out burials in accordance with well-established and expensive ideals. Officials found it difficult to ignore the 'appeal cajole, negotiation', and threats of the poor for respectful treatment of the dead; therefore did all they could to enable the family to provide for a respectful funeral. The emotions triggered by pauper funerals, and concern for women and children left destitute after the death of a breadwinner, also carved into the Poor Laws a willingness 'to pay allowances to the families of those bereaved for some time after the funeral' (Hurren & King, 2005, p. 327). Therefore, the popularity of the friendly societies stemmed from many of the pragmatic and emotional needs of communities they promised to address. By 1892, there were 6.8 million members in a friendly society. Almost every English family was protected in either one way or another through membership in a provident, friendly or insurance association. These institutions became symbols of respectability. As Bailey notes, next to turning out in one's Sunday best, nothing signalled working-class respectability more than membership in a friendly society (Bailey, 1979, p. 342). The state looked favourably upon the friendly societies, too, because they helped the poor help themselves. Celebrating their spread, the state protected the activities of the friendly societies from competition; but fearing that the working classes would exploit members of their own community, it also denied them the right to make profit.

Banking for the working classes was enthusiastically supported by the middle classes 'to provide the means by which the lower orders might come to make provision for themselves, thus achieving the dual aim of lessening the burden of the poor rate and becoming more prudent and sober working men' (Bailey, 1979, p. 340). Yet the records indicate that the friendly societies were community banks: they rarely expelled members or denied services to those behind on their payments, so profit was probably not their modus operandi. Surpluses were splurged on charity acts and celebrations that brought people together through 'a wide range of social activities from sports and concerts to education'. In many communities the local football team was outfitted by the friendly society. Large certificates honouring the friendly societies' good deeds were hung in the pub for others to see. Johnson suggests that friendly societies competed with one another in communal potlatches that manifested the wealth of the whole community (Johnson, 1985,

p. 39). Charitable benefits without a sermon helped to popularize their social events.

These working-class-traditions sullied their reputation in the eyes of the temperance movement. As Bailey notes, 'The beer drinking customary at many friendly society meetings threatened the respectability on which independence was predicated' (Bailey, 1979, p. 347). However, representatives 'defended public-house meetings on the grounds that they offered respectable opportunities for fellowship and an innocent conviviality (Cordery, 1995, p. 51). And although middle-class temperance movements argued that holding friendly society meetings in the pubs encouraged drunkenness which stripped men of their work ethic, friendly society meetings in the pub also enabled the matching of worker to job, suggesting the pub could enhance employment and work productivity as much as it instilled anti-work ethic values (Crompton, 1975). As Bailey notes, although traditionally grounded in tribal feasting, drinking, and competitions of honour, friendly societies were modernist in their outlook, advocating a version of middle-class respectability by offering public lectures, libraries, and reading groups. Working-class culture in its adaptation to an urban industrial setting was more additive than substitutive. What outsiders chose to see as anomalies were its normalities: to members of the friendly society the concurrent pursuit of 'thinking and drinking', 'virtue and vice' represented not so much a conflict of value systems as a reconciliation (Bailey, 1979, p. 341). For example, he notes how the working class climbed 'into the sober garb of the Sunday suit' and 'read the books on offer', but this did not stop the customary visits to the pub or the hawking of the suit on Monday to tide the family over the week (Bailey, 1979, p. 342).

Building societies: Home sweet home

In 1775, Richard Ketley, a pub owner in Birmingham, organized a group of friends and clients into a society that saved money to help each other purchase a home. The idea of this society was simple: people deposited money into savings accounts that provided interest. Rising wages and more stable unionized working conditions helped support the building society habit among the working classes. Small and locally based, such early building societies were also gossip circles which took into account family circumstances when organizing payments. Relationships were terminated once all members of the society had a home. Based on his original idea, the number of homeowner-friendly societies reached 2000 by 1870, demonstrating the popularity of home finance as the motive to save and borrow.

Recognizing the importance of these friendly societies in helping working classes acquire property, in 1871 the Woolwich registered as the first permanent building society. This incorporation was soon followed by other national building societies, which constituted a crucial new force in the property market. Structured under the Act for Friendly Societies of 1763, building societies were legally prohibited from profit making, thus surpluses were ploughed back into the organization, increasing the trust of the community. Generous tax breaks and other government favours contributed to the economic health of the building society. With its funds secured by property, and the public's great propensity to keep up on their monthly instalment payments, the security of the building societies were assured. As Bab (1938) notes, 'bricks and mortar' would become the investment 'preferred by many over the more fluctuating value of other investments' (p. 61).

Building societies also gained acceptance among the working classes by focusing on the mortgagee's ability to pay principal and interest, regardless of the region in which one lived, their occupation, creed, or religion. Margaret Finn's masterful history of the character of credit in Britain argues that there were deeper implications of the regularization of lending and saving among the working classes during the nineteenth century. Contractual financial relations, according to Finn, made the name of the borrower, their family, and their standing in the community insignificant. At the bank, building society or investment house, their honesty, loyalty, integrity, respectability, and their social ties in the community were less important than their credit history, employment record, and assets. Loan contracts in banking institutions reduced the requirement of good character to the willingness and ability to pay back. 'Past record became more important than the reputation of the personal character'. Thus, moneylending was being rationalized, becoming more 'bureaucratic, abstract, calculable, and utilitarian' (Finn, 2003, p. 7).

The Victorians' growing interest in homeownership lies in its unique cultural history. Feudal law prohibited the alienation of the crown's title making private property the bulwark against wayward authority. Private property has been enshrined and protected in law and worshipped since the Magna Carta. As early as the thirteenth century those in power realized that providing people with sovereign control over a piece of land created one of the most powerful forms of binding social contracts. In an effort to quell peasant uprising, crown land was appropriated in the thirteenth century, packaged into smaller lots and sold at affordable prices (Pollock, 1986; Holdsworth, 1927; Moynihan, 1982). The home was in a real sense a man's castle, protecting him against the intrusion of the state, and more importantly, from the landlord.

In 1290 it became permissible for land to be alienated from the crown, but it was not until the Statute of Wills that the bequeathing of land to kin ensured that the full economic value and social mobility of landownership could be realized. The household also provided families something to leave their offspring. This passing on of property through the family represented a powerful means of wealth accumulation and social mobility. Reviewing the literature on homeownership, Harris and Hamnett concluded that the 'meaning of home ownership has usually been treated as self-evident: for most writers it is the unambiguous indicator of economic well-being, social mobility, and status' (1987, p. 173). The home lay at the intersection of a constellation of Christianly themes including family values, masculine pride, and the earnest attempt to better one's lot in life.

It is perhaps with these values in mind that in 1835 de Tocqueville suggested private homeownership rather than state transfer of funds as a way to solve Britain's pauper problem. Homes domesticated mobile labour, encouraged independent consumption over communal sharing, and ultimately fostered social cohesion over revolution. Samuel Smiles argued that homeownership tamed the revolutionary spirit:

> The accumulation of property has the effect, which it always has upon thrifty men; it makes them steady, sober, and diligent. It weans them from revolutionary notions, and makes them conservative. When workmen, by their industry and frugality, have secured their own independence, they will cease to regard the sight of others' well being as a wrong inflicted on themselves; and it will no longer be possible to make political capital out of their imaginary woes.
>
> (1881, p. 106)

Studies suggest that homeownership reinforced conservative political views. According to Hoyt: 'There is a natural sympathy between the values of property-holding and commitment to the Conservative Party' (Garrahan quoted in Hoyt, 1977, p. 127). Regular mortgage payments came to represent the hallmark of personal financial stability, the state of goodness on which the entire social system would focus upon. The ability to work to support one's family, most powerfully articulated by way of homeownership, became identified deeply with the discourses on manliness. Smiles used property as a metaphor to describe male character:

Character is property. It is the noblest of possessions. It is an estate in the general goodwill and respect of men; and they who invest in it – though they may not become rich in this world's goods – will find their reward in esteem and reputation fairly and honourably won.

(in Hadley, p. 12)

This new ideal of masculinity linked earning power to social respectability: birth, breeding, and refinement that had previously defined the character of the gentlemanly classes were eclipsed by the 'moral qualities, which marked the truly manly character' as someone who earned their place in society. To be a man called for the constant demonstration of productivity. As Tosh notes, manliness had to be earned, by mastering the circumstances of life and thus securing the respect of one's peers. It lay within the grasp of every man who practised self-help and single-minded discipline (Tosh, 2002, p. 458). Working-class men were not exempt from the pride that accrued to those who earned their respect through clothing their children and standing their mates to a round at the pub. Helen Bosanquet observed that breadwinners in the working-class boroughs of East London, who paid their rent regularly, were widely considered 'a good principled man' (1896, p. 220).

Financing the homeowner democracy

The traditional home, quite literally a man's castle, was a walled protection from a harsh state, tax-collecting monarch, and creditors during the nineteenth century, and was gradually remapped as a safe haven for a respectable family. Beginning in the early part of the century when Britain was plagued 'with continuing political unrest, the exigencies of poverty, brutality, pressing sexuality, disease and death were all too familiar', the home became a means for people to 'control their destiny through religious grace' (Davidoff & Hall, 1987 p. 358). The home symbolized man's ability to protect his family from the cruel uncertainties of modern life, securing the domicile's significance in Victorian culture. Property investment became justified by a sentimental rhetoric immortalized in the oft repeated solemnities: A man's house is his castle; Home Sweet Home; Home is where the heart is; East, west home's best.

Little noted during the Victorian period, homeownership was becoming a major driving factor in the democratization of credit and the expansion of financial institutions. Yet, despite their popularity, nineteenth-century building societies had at first only a marginal impact on housing provision in Britain. At the turn of the twentieth century, fewer than 10 per cent of working people owned their own homes. Well into the twentieth century, the working classes remained woefully underrepresented in the property market. Only the most elite craft labourers had homes, and most of these were outside London. Middle-class families also preferred renting homes to purchasing them in the nineteenth century. Between 1907 and 1911, 80 per cent of the population left estates of less than £100 representing only 4.57 per cent of the value of all estates (Williams, 1978).

One of the most common explanations of this situation has been that financial power in Britain remained concentrated in the hands of landed aristocracy who continued to control both the buying and building of houses and factories through leasehold arrangements that took centuries to untangle. These leasehold arrangements offered limited tenure but retained property rights in the future for the estates of the established property owners. 'The use of short-term, ninety-nine-year leases; the holding of the land under elaborate settlements and wills; coherent, controlled, and careful planning; a preference for high-class, residential tenants; concern for regular, secure income and long-term reversion rather than short-term, speculative gain; these are the common characteristics of urban estate development by "aristocratic" landowners' (Cannadine, 1980, p. 313). Summarizing the situation, Hobsbawm noted how the claim to property uniquely shaped the British economy: 'The political and social structure of Britain was controlled by landlords ... by a rather small group of perhaps 4000 people who between them owned something like four sevenths of the cultivated land. ... Such a degree of concentrated landownership was unparalleled in other industrial countries' (Hallsworth, 1996, p. 26).

The property class accommodated the industrialist class, according to Ingham (1834, pp. 19–23); yet, the industrialist bourgeoisie never achieved the same level of power as they would in America, in a country where property, retail, and finance remained the most privileged sectors of wealth generation (Hallsworth, 1996, p. 34). Rightly viewing land-ownership as a primary source of wealth generation contributed to the formation of a widespread culture of homeownership. Private home-ownership would emerge as a core value underwriting the householder economics that would dominate Anglo societies throughout the twentieth century. The expansion of homeownership in Britain continued to rise during the first half of the twentieth century from 15 per cent in 1915 to 35 per cent in 1938. Even if it lagged behind America by up to 20 per cent, homeownership provided the home base for British domestic consumerism. As Hallsworth notes, the common sense of homeownership is deeply rooted in British culture:

This fact [home as wealth] helped ensure the election of Margaret Thatcher in 1979 on promises of wider homeownership. Nationally, there is more activity associated with industrial property investment than with industrial enterprises as an investment. In Britain, the security of land values has always been the 'bottom line'.

(Hallsworth, 1996, p. 35)

Thatcher engaged in national and international politics, yet preached a deeply domestic rhetoric, centred on small business and the home. During the nineteenth century the house emerged as the clearest manifestation of a man's claim to financial respectability – a physical embodiment of his pecuniary standing, self-reliance, and productivity. Yet despite their seemingly egalitarian ideals, Victorian thrift institutions and the praise of private property consolidated patriarchy by proscribing women from borrowing money for their daily management of household finance. Until 1935, a woman's legal access to credit was through her husband's good standing in the community. The next chapter takes up the shadowed and contradictory personal finance of women during the nineteenth century.

2
Women, Home, Consumption, Lending, and Ill Repute

Chapter 1 suggested that Thatcher's revivalist politics drew strengths from moral principles that rooted the spirit of capitalism and deified self-reliance secured by hard work. But her rhetorical arsenal included the conjoined 'thrift ethos' that valorized provident investment and savings enabling people to purchase property and look after themselves. The thrift ethos became a favoured tool for attacking public debt. Thatcher saw the nation under siege by left wing politicians' inability to live within their means. The 'thrifty housewife' became the talisman Thatcher used to badger her political opponents. Only a housewife could bring order to the government's books, thrown into disarray by disorganized, childlike, spendthrift male state politicians. Drawing inspiration from her mother, Beatrice Roberts, dressmaking entrepreneur, who modelled the lessons of thrifty household (Thatcher, 1 August 1980), Thatcher regularly announced that government must be as mindful of the nation's purse as her mother was of the household's. 'Everyone, whether it's a housewife or a business, has to learn to live within a budget' (Thatcher, 8 July 1985). As she explained, 'You will never get a prosperous society unless you have people in power who manage well. Every prudent housewife plans the future, and it is similarly the job of the politician in economics to try to foresee and plan the future' (Thatcher, 14 December 1974). She warned the public: 'We must learn again the value of thrift. We cannot go on spending that which we do not earn' (Thatcher, 8 September 1975). And as she later bragged of her thrifty accomplishments, 'I can't help reflecting that it's taken a Government headed by a housewife with experience of running a family to balance the books for the first time in twenty years—with a little left over for a rainy day' (Thatcher, 25 May 1988).

Thatcher set out to discredit her political opponents' Keynesian economic policy, which advocated state investment to jump-start the economy. She noted that 'nations cannot go on consuming more than they produce, and that anyone who tries to avoid this elementary truth by the simple expedient of printing money may, for a while, give himself the illusion that he is richer than he is, but will soon become a great deal poorer than he need be'. Printing money, according to Thatcher, caused inflation which debilitated the housewife's ability to service her family and thus oppressed her spirit. Inflation, said Thatcher, reduces the value of savings, undermines financial agreements, stimulates hostility between workers and employers over matters of pay, encourages debt, and diminishes the prospects of jobs. Inflation for Thatcher was a moral issue not just an economic one (Thatcher, 4 March 1981). Her top political priority centred on containing the 'insidious evil' of the 1970s inflation with the antidote of thrift. Thatcher's policies therefore promised future prosperity by applying her mother's teachings to state finance. Thrift restored not rationality but morality to the market system. 'It's always sound, good housewifery and good sound budgetary policy to be economical', she intoned (Thatcher, 31 January 1975).

The meaning of home

During the ninenteenth century, as building societies perfected savings and mortgages to enable working-class men's acquisition of a house, personal finance and retail entrepreneurs focused on providing financial instruments to service the inside of the home and the housewife who oversaw it. The private domain emerged as a site of great economic importance, and in this chapter, I explore some of the paradoxical cultural narratives that underwrote the salience and value of domesticity. Appeals to thrift, sanctuary, family values, graceful expression, and self-transformation through beautiful decoration justified new levels of materialism and abundance. Advertising of the period romanced women in their role of consumers. I attend to how retailers institutionalized a fashion cycle in home decoration and personal appearance propelled by retail credit. Hire purchase networks extended through the financing of pianos and sewing machines, deeply significant objects of the period.

The domestic economy was shaped by paradoxical gender relations. Men's reward for working hard and paying the mortgage was a home sanctuary to retreat into from the harsh circumstances of industrialism. Women, excluded from full participation in industrial society, because of custom and patriarchal laws that prevented their acquiring credit until 1935, were invited to assume the social roles of homemakers, society women, and consumers. British culture romanticized women's role as mothers, housekeepers, and thrifty consumers. The female authors of popular home economics textbooks of the period reminded women of their power as housekeepers and the important role they played in the nation. Some went so far as to suggest that women's experience as manager of the households and children made them superior organizers to men. At the same time, these new relations sparked fears about the unleashing of women's consumptive appetite. Social reformers worried that families and the nation were on the road to ruin because women's lust for goods and financial naivety made them vulnerable prey for the peddlers of debt – tallymen and pawnshops.

Décor and gender

The best known narrative of the home cast it as a sanctuary where respectable men raised their families under the grace of god, buffered from market transactions, economic calculation, and rationalizing forces of modern culture. According to Davidoff and Hall: 'The well appointed home and garden were practical and symbolic shields to ward off the cruelties of the world' (Davidoff & Hall, 1987, p. 357). For artisan and tradesmen classes, especially with homes above their workplace, the homily of sanctuary implied buffering themselves from the constant pressures of productivity. Although it was a necessity, renting was considered inferior to homeownership because it failed to secure prudent investment and 'meant never being able to impress a personality on surroundings, intrusions of privacy, restrictions on hospitality and sudden notices to quit' (Davidoff & Hall, 1987, p. 257).

Much has also been written about how the Victorian home staged the interest in social comparison and the enactment of appeals to social distinction. As Davidoff and Hall suggest, the Victorian house displayed the owner's character and wealth, and more importantly; 'their taste and moral standing in a normative community increasingly concerned about both' (Davidoff & Hall, 1987, p. 358). As Burroughs noted, the pride of homeownership extended inside the home: "The corollary of pride in ownership is the care with which the owned item is used. ... A carefully tended plot of urban land can be a joy to the neighbours and passers-by as well as to the owners. Pride usually, though not always, leads to beautification – or at least to what the owners consider such (Burroughs, 1966, p. 12). This fateful link between homeowner pride and aestheticization stimulated much activity within Victorian culture. By the late Victorian era, the meaning of the home transformed from a family shelter and workplace into a private sanctuary appropriately provisioned for comfortable living and raising a family (Cohen, 2006).

What is deeply significant about the narratives of home was how they invested the home with the power to shape and socialize individuals. Religious narratives spilled in through the front door of homes, flowing through their parlours, reception rooms, and children's bedrooms. Thrifty self-reliant Victorians, weary of ostentatious public Catholic cathedrals of worship, cast the home as a site of private worship. An architectural planner in 1891, recognized the home as the natural site of goodness because it 'requires no elaborate creeds, its worship is the simplest, its discipline the gentlest, and its rewards are peace and contentment' (Newton, 1988, p. 214). In 1913, G. K. Chesterton wrote of the Victorians: 'Theirs was the first generation that ever asked its children to worship the hearth without the altar' (Briggs, 1988, p. 214). Household objects, both useful and decorative, came to serve as a robust medium of social communication. Drapes and furniture, after all, are not only commodities lodged in economic transactions of market exchange but also meaningful goods used in a cultural system of structured social relations, values, and ritualized social interactions converging around domestic lifestyles. Besides providing pawns for status competition and serving as markers of respectability, objects became a means of articulating graceful spiritual enlightenment.

Class and gender struggles played out in the Victorian parlour. Pursuing home decoration began as an amateur pursuit for upper-class men who set a tone for interior design that others competed with and played off against. Cohen (2006) notes how the decorator manuals and magazine ads they carried in the early nineteenth century primarily addressed upper-class men because they oversaw most of the purchases for the home – especially the furniture. Sutton-Ramspeck draws attention to how male novelists, Dickens', *Bleak House* and *Our Mutual Friend*, Trollope's *Dr Thorne*, and George Paston's *A Writer of Books*, place men in charge of establishing and furnishing the private realm which their wives thereby adopt (Sutton-Ramspeck, 2004). Accounts suggest that gentlemen practiced home decoration with an entitled sporting spirit, displaying the trophies gathered from the empire in their homes. The popularity of collections explains the abundance of books in the library, art in the smoking room, buffet for displaying china in the dining room, and weapons in the armoury. The home was less a sanctuary than a museum and source of education, as male homeowners tended to tour guests round the home describing where and how the displayed objects were acquired. The objects on display served to be admired and stood as emblems of male taste and character. The Victorian gentleman's professional reputation and social standing connected to the mannered display of goods and fashion in the home.

It was within the middle-class home that women inherited the mantle of home décor by way of a complex set of circumstances. Shannon's study of men's conduct literature of the period suggests, middle-class men's reluctance to embrace the home decoration hobby was not due to lack of wealth, education, or cosmopolitan sensibilities, rather due to popular cultural messages that associated excess attention to detail in dress and décor with the 'dandy's idle status'. Decorating clashed with middle-class productivity ethos. Shannon notes, 'antagonism toward effeminate behavior accelerated during an age in which rugged masculinity and athleticism were enthusiastically celebrated by popular culture'. Paying too much attention to interior design threatened to subject men to accusations that they were weak and womanish. Another blow to decoration as a masculine pursuit occurred after Oscar Wilde's 'gross indecency' conviction in 1895, when interior design, decorating, and shopping – cartoons depicted shop clerks mincing about – were rendered not simply feminine, but also homosexual activities (Shannon, 2004, p. 613). The codes of masculinity did not include an interest in drapery or vases of flowers on the table.

As cultural discourses chased men out of the kitchen, Victorian customs and trade unions restricted the sectors where women could make money. Economic historians suggest the expanding productive capacity of the common wealth conspired with the cultural ideal of the sole male breadwinner resulting in a situation where women's contribution to the household economy was at best ignored, at worst debased (Wilson, 2005/6). The working-class men who constituted 80% of the population, earned wages 'so low or so uncertain that they would not support a family unless supplemented by the earnings of wives and children'; thus it is estimated that about 30% of women worked full time (Burnett, 1974). The Census of 1851, for example, indicated that industry employed 2.8 million women and girls over the age of ten, providing a 'vast reservoir of labour, necessary for an expanding though immature economy whose fluctuations demanded additional workers at one time, fewer at another' (Davidoff & Hall, 1987, pp. 48–9).

Still a 'cult of domesticity' constituted women's proper role as a subservient, virtuous, and pious wife and mother (Feeley & Little, 1991). This Victorian ideology changed broader cultural norms about the relations and roles of both men and women, ultimately affecting individuals in all classes (Feeley & Little, 1991, p. 746). As Cook notes, work outside the home associated masculinity with the self-interested, instrumental world of market relations, leaving the domestic realm of women and children as the 'refuge' of moral life under the care of women in the roles as wives and mothers (Cook, 2004, p. 33). The laws and ideological formations dividing the home and the labour market around class and gender lines were much stronger in Victorian Britain than they are today (Vickery, 1993).

Sutton-Ramspeck's fascinating study of the influential nineteenth century housekeeping literature penned by Ward, Grand, and Gilman captures a sense of the active construction of women's roles. The female authors of home economics textbooks embraced female roles and pressed them into political service towards women's emancipation (Sutton-Ramspeck, 2004, p. 20). In the hands of Grand, Sutton-Ramspeck argues, the humble act of housekeeping becomes poetry, elevated to the status of masculine creativity: 'The broom wielding New Woman housekeeper is conflated with the godlike writer-creator in masculine traditions who separates light from darkness in order to "enlighten" the benighted masses, creating a universe out of chaos and humans out of dust'. Given that women spent their days in the home, they felt confident in advancing the argument that they were best qualified to dictate its design (Sutton-Ramspeck, 2004, p. 106). Control over décor and housekeeping became a means for a 'reimagining of the relations between the aesthetic and the practical, the individual and the familial, the private and the public, the traditional and the innovative, the scientific and the artistic' (Sutton-Ramspeck, 2004, p. 108). The making of a beautiful and sanitary home was asserted as a 'political act' (Sutton-Ramspeck, 2004, p. 108).

Home economics textbooks reminded the hard-working middle classes of the moral importance of decorating according to the principles of thrift and utilitarian prudence. Grand proclaimed clutter free, fresh, and cleanable homes superior to cluttered, dusty homes of the aristocratic dandies. She advocated the inclusion of objects of useful beauty, art for man's sake, instead of attention grabbing displays of useless art for art's sake (Sutton-Ramspeck, 2004, p. 115). Catherine Beecher's *A Treatise on Domestic Economy* (1841) also praised plain style décor, and received praise from Sir Arthur Conan Doyle as a book that contained 'more wisdom to the square inch' than in 'any work of man' (Briggs, 1988, p. 248). Quaker tables, ladder-back chairs, and simple clean white walls exemplify the aesthetics of many middle-class Victorian homes. Thrift and cleanliness commingled in the plain style.

After the publication of Chadwick's Sanitary Report in that linked disease and hygiene, a cult of cleanliness spread throughout Victorian Britain and into the home. Soap became the first branded consumer item. By 1844, labouring families in London spent roughly half of the amount they spent on rent on maintaining the hygiene of the family – one third of that on cleaning products (Church, 2000, p. 30). Home economics textbooks quoted nurses as experts in the correct layout for the home: promoting a hospital aesthetic for the home as a way to ensure maximum health. Florence Nightingale's pioneering work, *Notes on Nursing* (1860), emerged as another authoritative source for women on how to fashion a healthy home (Church, 2000, p. 27). The sanitary plain style was asserted as morally superior to the excessive interiors of the wealthy and the cluttered and cramped ones of the poor.

Yet, the thrifty plain style competed with other cultural assumptions that valued romantic self-expression. Artistic home decoration became associated with curative properties and cultural refinement. Beautiful art objects expressed moral grace at the same time as they spoke of the owners' pride in artistic self-expression. Art on the wall, sculptured and painted vases, patterned rugs, china, and portraits of ancestors abounded. The movement recognized interiors as socializing agents that could bring about self-transformation: Painting one's walls and studying the form of furniture became acts of grace, which 'humanized' the amateur home decorator (Cohen, 2006, p. 97). To minimize gender conflicts, and recognizing that men and women required distinctive forms of socialization, the Victorian middle-class home was divided into masculine and feminine domains. 'Drawing rooms, for example were regarded as feminine and usually decorated with 'spindly gilt or rosewood, and silk or chintz,' while the dining rooms, considered masculine, required 'massive oak or mahogany and Turkey carpets' (Langland, 1992, p. 295).

According to Higgins and Langland, women's role as decorators privileged them as key filters and transmitters of the ideology of appropriate standards communicated through appearance, conduct, and domestic management. Responsible for the socialization of children, women 'defined appropriate protocols for children's behaviour, or the acceptability or non-acceptability of acquaintances' (Huggins, 2000, p. 587). Langland argues that women became master controllers of cultural codes and discursive practices: making, applying, and following the class rules of fashion, décor, and etiquette (Langland, 1992, p. 299). Carefully tending to fine distinctions of look and conduct, women, says Higgins, 'subtly defined and demarcated the boundaries and internal divisions of middle-class life'. Because she watched, every middle-class woman knew others watched her, and thus disciplined her activities out of fear of social disapproval (Higgins, 2000, p. 587). Women played an important role as guardians of class boundaries.

The good Victorian middle-class woman was encouraged to assume responsibility for charitable acts outside of the home. According to Higgins, while men drew the rules of politics and labour, women shaped 'the rules of propriety, decorum and morality, and exercised control or influence over the behaviour of their children'. In 1839 Sarah Ellis put the matter succinctly: 'Society is to daughters of a family, what business is to the sons' (quoted in Langland, 1992, p. 291). Men devoted discretionary income to support their wives' management of social questions. And as Cook notes, middle-class women played an important role in progressive social movements such as 'child-saving' as well as contributing volunteer work in the community and church to help the poor (Langland, 1992). Beeton's guidebook advised women to reach out to the working classes, 'advising and instructing them, in a pleasant and unobtrusive manner, in cleanliness, industry, cookery and good management' (quoted in Langland, 1992, p. 296). Extending beyond their church role as missionaries of the gospel, women were invited to assume an active role in shaping society.

Their role as mothers was especially empowering for women. Ward, Grand, and Gilman 'portray motherhood as a means to effect social change'. The idea that the hand that rocks the cradle rocks the world, presented women as not simply equal to men, but superior. Men may protect the nation's borders and bring home pay packets, but women held a more awesome responsibility: 'as mothers of men' they 'have the capacity and responsibility to help society evolve, to raise its moral tone' (Sutton-Ramspeck, 2004, p. 91). Sutton-Ramspeck draws attention to the numerous ways the female authors she studied infantilized men, suggesting in the home men required women's care and organization skills as much as children. Ward's *Elizabeth's Campaign*, according to Sutton-Ramspeck, constructs women as endowed with an 'organizing gift' that prepares them to run not only households efficiently, but also 'manage a large estate, feed an army, protect a nation and lead a great change in society as a whole (p. 148). It took a woman to provision, organize, and morally uplift the childish state of men (Sutton-Ramspeck, 2004, p. 63).

Financing the home

Legally men held dominion over family property: 'As the owner of the family's property, he was considered to have legal duty to maintain his family and was assumed to have direct knowledge of all familial consumption' (Rappaport, 2000, p. 51). Male responsibility extended to purchasing or paying the rent, as well as all expenses and debts incurred provisioning and maintaining the family home. It was the middle-class male's solemn duty therefore, to pay for everything or provide his wife with money for the purchases necessitated for the family. A sense of responsibility for his familial property propelled the house-proud male back into the labour market. His respectability depended on it: continual work and debt was the price he paid for his family's public respectability. Financing the home fuelled productivity.

Provisioning according to their station and decorating, furnishing, and maintaining their home according to a sliding normative order of class expectations and taste meant that, by the 1860s, the Victorian middle-class home was hardly private and no longer austere. Large picture and bay windows allowed light in and made the insides of homes visible to neighbours and those who passed by, revealing the plush décor and rich fabrics that draped, covered, and carpeted the Victorian home and its highly ornate woodwork. Middle-class women, given scope to choose many kinds of fashionable decorations, covered their interiors from ceiling to floor in doilies, flowered wallpaper, frames, mirrors, craft objects, art, and furniture: the home became a space for artful display of woman's taste, identity, and prowess. The Victorian middle-class domestile spoke generally of a growing sense of pecuniary entitlement settled onto the discourse of thrift. The cloak of respectability was also a straightjacket of growing financial responsibility.

Regardless of class, women bore the burden of domestic provisioning and had to work within the means made available to them. According to Vickery, few women enjoyed an undemanding life free from constant labour: 'The vast majority of middle-class housewives coped with heavy housework and quarrelsome servants, while simultaneously struggling with the nervous art of creative accounting' (Vickery, 1993, p. 389). Controlling middle-class husbands or those with limited earning capacity or a taste for gambling and drinking posed a particular problem for women. But, for Victorian moralizer Samuel Smiles, it was not men who did the troublesome spending in the house. Smiles warned men of the spendthrift women lurking about waiting to bring financial ruin and humiliation to men's homes. Smiles advised men to search for a thrifty woman who would maintain a respectable home and family:

> There can be no thrift, nor economy, nor comfort at home, unless the wife helps; – and a working man's wife, more than any other man's; for she is wife, Housekeeper, nurse, and servant, all in one.

If she be thriftless, putting money into her hands is like pouring water through a sieve. Let her be frugal, and she will make her home a place of comfort, and she will also make her husband's life happy – if she do not lay the foundation of his prosperity and fortune.

(1885, p. 158)

Ironically, men often feathered the nest with elaborate decorations in the hope of attracting thrifty brides, knowing that though nominally powerless, the Victorian housewife played a crucial role in the manifestation of domestic respectability.

Thrift rivalled beauty as a virtue. While she was not honoured for her labour, the thrifty woman who minded the cost of things, mended socks, sheets, and shoes, made meals out of old bits of leftovers, and gathered medicines from the fields was idealized. Valued was the wife who devoted her energies to the care of the family and put something aside for a rainy day. Yet, the definition of utility and thrifty consumption was never fixed. Norms for middle-class consumption steadily increased. In 1830 women read *The Family Exchequer Book* that taught them a system of domestic bookkeeping (Lysack, 2008, p. 93). By 1856, according to Krista Lysack's study of Victorian women's writing, Walsh's *The Manual of Domestic Economy* enforced norms. It outlined how much a middle-class family should spend, and detailed in charts appropriate expenditures for housekeeping, including not simply bread and butter, but also 'Italian goods, Beer, Wine and spirits, candlery and washing'. Adding to this 'carriages and horses, rent and taxes, and amusements', the cost of a respectful middle-class home was £1000 annually. This sum Lysack argued, outstripped most middle-class incomes.

Middle-class women: The circuits of shopping

A significant retailing revolution occurred between 1860 and 1914, which made available goods to meet the norm of a respectable middle-class household. Significance of the retailing revolution that occurred between 1860 and 1914, which made available goods to meet the norm of a respectable middle-class household. The establishment of 'large-scale department stores, the massive expansion of the popular press in the form of inexpensive books and periodicals, and the rapid development of increasingly sophisticated advertising techniques', the formation of retail districts and supporting leisure, increased 'awareness, availability and affordability of fashion and furniture (Shannon, 2004, p. 597). The new shopping districts had a profound impact on consumption habits (Rappaport, 2000; Bowlby, 1985; Nava, 1996).

Although going to market was part of a wife's daily routine, late Victorian shopping became a means for middle-class women to stay busy in a respectable way. The department store's opulent interiors, theatrical window displays, entertainment, as well as the inclusion of streetlights, and public toilet facilities solidified the practice of shopping as a respectable leisure activity. Retail outlets, shops, and showrooms providing new opportunities to view, learn about, and discuss household management. Janet Walkowitz points out how the shopping districts organized furniture and fashion to compliment women's role as house-keepers: 'The expansion of the retail revolution in the second half of the century extended this decorative role to a larger segment of middle-class women, who increasingly played a more visible and central role as con-sumers and managers of household expenses' (Walkowitz, 1998, p. 5).

The retail sectors institutionalized clothing and fashion cycles. Fashion played a pivotal, if under acknowledged, role in the British industrial revolution (McKendrick et al., 1982). Textiles were as important as ore. New technologies and imperial lines of trade, which expanded the availability of cloth, profoundly influenced women's lives. Fashionable clothing also became a crucial marker of public respectability, as it was a way to display taste (Davidoff & Hall, 1987). Women judged one another by the cut of their clothing in a knowing way, for they were frequently handmade. According to Church, 'There were increasing numbers who regarded themselves as "respectable", who at least on occasion, indulged in expenditure on appearance, both of the person and the home' (Church, 2000, p. 637). On Sunday, even the most entrenched resistance to fashion unravelled under the intensified social pressure to appear fashionable. The church professed the growing belief that Jesus preferred a smartly dressed worshipper. Building upon these cultural impulses, a brisk fashion cycle operated during the nineteenth century. Increasingly, clothing shops appeared cheek and jowl to furniture makers and depart-ment stores in the West End. Fashion sense was now constantly commu-nicated through women's magazines, through an expanded advertising press, on the streets where different classes mingled, and in the shop windows. Poor women learnt about the fashion habits of the wealthy while acting as servants in homes (McKibbin, 1978, pp. 193–4). Fashion cycles fuelled appetite for new and novel goods, challenging the princi-ples of 'making do'. Women dared to admit that they 'did not like things to last' (Briggs, 1988, p. 248). These developments would call for further adjustments to the definition and principles of thrift.

The cult of domesticity obscured both the deep class and sexual logics, which bifurcated domestic provisioning and problematized its daily finance. A market society makes the pre-requisite of domestic consumption, money, available to those who have work or draw credit. The female shoppers' purchase of fashion and furnishings for the Victorian household have been more visible to historians than the vast networks of finance that enabled their acquisition. Because, law forbid women and children from entering into credit contractual agreements until 1935, Finn highlights the great contradiction that surrounded women's place in the consumer economy:

> Denied the ability to enter into binding economic contracts, married women of the Victorian era were nonetheless fully responsible for securing the goods, which supplied the daily needs of their households. Thus, while prevailing legal norms circumscribed their economic agency, prevailing social expectations required them to exercise considerable economic initiative.
>
> (Finn, 1998, p. 129)

Most middle-class housewives received an allowance, but also bore the responsibility for thriftiness, being accountable to their husbands for utilizing their allowances in appropriate ways. Of course, family financial arrangements varied greatly. Some men dictated strictly how funds were to be apportioned. Others had difficulty understanding why women could not make their allowances go further. For example, the sale of domestic appliances was slow in Britain because many men felt it was their wife's duty to keep the house clean with her elbow grease. Far from tyrannical, many men were pleased to offload decisions about consumption onto their wives. Typically, men and women shopped together, particularly for large items, and women no doubt exerted some influence over purchase decisions. In spite of patriarchy, in practice Victorian women exercised their own prerogatives in home decorating and its financial management.

Loeb's study of Victorian advertising found a promotional rhetoric populated by strong female characters, challenging the common view that depicted women of this period as reticent, passive vagabonds of their husband's charity. Victorian women in both classes exercised considerable influence over household matters, particularly furniture and decoration. Although constrained by her husband's purse strings, women found ways to exercise their power. According to Loeb, 'she could, for example, emphasize her superior understanding of taste, status, or utility as applied to the domestic sphere, appeal to the flexibility within the family budget (often carefully crafted from her own reading of domestic economy manuals), or she could suggest that a particular purchase would bring her special pleasure' (Loeb, 1994, p. 34). Advertisers, acknowledging the shift in gender relations, no longer made direct appeals to men, but targeted luxury goods to men as a means of pleasing their wives.

Advertisers could attempt to manipulate, husbands could limit the funds available, but the ultimate decision (to buy or not to buy) was usually hers. As a consumer ideology of choice and of pleasure proliferated, women were empowered in the marketplace. They gained a new form and degree of economic control and they became arbiters of new social values including gender (Loeb, 1994, p. 34).

Retail credit and hire purchase

As Smiles implied, the idea of familial standing implied that a man had to trust in the wisdom, thrift, and respectability of his spouse. Practically, because he was frequently absent from home on work and leisure, it was impossible for husbands to supervise all domestic affairs as the law demanded however much he might feel it was his prerogative. The law recognized the need for women to acquire goods for the home, and therefore allowed them to proxy for their husband's account and enter into credit transactions for 'necessary goods'. There was a dynamic mutuality at stake in the cult of domesticity: women in practice traded on a man's respectability, undertaking credit agreements under the man's proxy and signature. While most women conformed to their roles, resourcefully shouldering the financial burdens of domestic consumption as thrifty housekeepers, part time labourers, and financial stewardesses of community debt, some women's refusal to play the role of the thrifty consumer exposed the limits of the proxy credit system.

Challenging legal cases revealed an anomaly in gendered personal financial relations – an avid female shopper with no ready means of credit. By deeming the female consumer as 'inherently un-credit-worthy', these legal traditions influenced retail and family history. The custom of extending credit to customers was widespread, practiced by everyone from corner shops in working-class neighbourhoods to elite retailers. Legal troubles relating to lending practices were somewhat controllable upto the mid nineteenth century because the debt relations undertaken by both middle class and working class were personal. Middle-class women knew their local merchants and merchants knew the family.

But as middle-class women began to make more extensive use of their husband's accounts to acquire goods from major retailers in the fast expanding West End shopping districts of London in the closing decades of the century, relations changed. At first, many of the new department stores welcomed people onto their books because it increased the turnover of goods, but as the number of accounts swelled, the ability to ensure 100% payback became more tenuous. In reaction, some major department stores refused to offer credit, focusing their marketing effort instead on the lower prices they achieved through economies of scale. Others, unfamiliar with the husband's reputation, sometimes relied on the newspapers for information about the financial viability of those to whom they lent. They began to keep blacklists naming women whose husbands had publicly removed their proxy by way of an ad in the newspaper.

While they represented a minority, Erica Rappaport's evidence of court cases between 1860 and the early twentieth century suggests that some women disobeyed their husbands: cheating retailers of considerable sums in the process. Documenting these disagreements between female shoppers, shopkeepers, and husbands, Rappaport notes widespread use of consumer credit within middle- and even upper-class families. When retailers called in their chips on women's mounting debts, women justified their shopping 'by claiming status as the family's consumer and defining consumption as a rational legitimate economic act' (Rappaport, 2000, p. 49). Men countered that they had not authorized their wives to purchase the products. Shopkeepers found themselves in the middle of a massive legal and social contradiction. Looking at the cases as a whole, Rappaport found that the law and courts defended paterfamilias over the rights of the commercial class:

> Regardless of the husband's social class or the amount of debt, the legal system buttressed his economic authority against the dangers of credit, advertising, large luxurious urban shops, and itinerant hawkers of finery.
>
> (Rappaport, 2000, p. 49)

According to Davidoff and Hall, the husband's responsibility for his wife's debt began to be called into question as early as 1860, yet it was not until the twentieth century that a legal definition of women's rights to own property and enter into contracts was established to solve this problem. In the meantime, the laws governing women's credit remained unclear creating discord, publicly in the courts and privately in the home.

With no clear legal solution to the problem, cultural narratives had to work doubly hard to contain the contradictory relation of finance. The uncertainties surrounding credit drew women's purchases into ever-greater suspicion for undermining the social and economic power of men. This was particularly so when the goods they acquired were deemed luxuries or fashion items. 'Whatever the precise locus of these financial and emotional conflicts, they ultimately turned upon a pervasive fear that the expanding consumer economy had unleashed female desires that could financially ruin both husbands and shopkeepers' (Rappaport, 2000, p. 49). Popular culture regularly represented women 'as voracious, compulsive shoppers who overwhelmed both shop workers and their husbands with their insatiable desire for goods'. A popular joke that circulated among drapery and department store staff asked: 'When is a woman not a woman. Answer: When she attends a sale' (Shannon, 2004, p. 600). Popular discourses pathologized women as kleptomaniacs and satirized them (Abelson, 1989). Men who cowered in the face of their wife's seemingly insatiable demands for new dresses and fancy objects for the home, were chastised as hen-pecked roosters; 'Molly husbands and squaw men' (Shannon, 2004, p. 58).

Fearsome scapegoats circulated to calm the moral upset that surrounded debt and unthrifty consumption. The image of the female debtor that circulated in literature of the period was far from wholesome. Although Margaret Finn concluded in her review of eighteenth and nineteenth century literature that novels largely humanized the male debtor, this was not the case with *Madame Bovary*, published in France in 1857, but quickly translated and read widely in Britain. In this story, Emma Bovary, a female debtor, is condemned to a horrible and shameful death: suicide by arsenic poisoning. This tale of a bourgeois housewife who marries for respectability and brings her husband to ruin due to her adulterine and spendthrift ways, provided a cautionary tale appropriate to the modernizing sensibility of the high Victorian consumer economy. The novel expressed something deeply conflicted in the new notions of domestic life.

Emma Bovary exemplifies the insatiable woman. Despite a moderately successful husband and a lovely child, she rejects the 'boring countryside' and 'inane petty bourgeois, the mediocrity of daily life'. Her passions could not be contained and her desires 'made no difference between the pleasures of luxury and the joys of the heart, between elegant living and sensitive feeling' (p. 66). Unhappy in her marriage with Charles, and her affairs with both Rodolphe Boulanger and Léon Dupuis, Emma turns to a more reliable source to satisfy her desires, consumption. Monsieur Lheureux, a cunning draper, peddling fine goods and finance, arranges for Emma a power of attorney over her husband's estate. She draws down the estate in lavish spending sprees and accumulates promissory notes from Monsieur Lheureux. Flaubert carefully lists her consumptive digressions in detail:

> She bought herself ostrich plumes and Chinese porcelain and travelling chests; she borrowed money from Felicite, and Madam Lefrancois, from the proprietess of the Croix Rouge, from anybody, anywhere. With the money she finally received from the Barneville sale, she paid off two bills; the other fifteen hundred francs just melted away. She took out fresh loans, and so it went on!
>
> (p. 255)

Elder Madame Bovary, who Emma and Charles call upon many times to salvage them from Lheureux, finds little sympathy for Emma's spending and reviles her refusal to behave as a proper wife to her son by exercising faithfulness and thrift. Examining Emma's purchases, which the elder Madame Bovary must pay for, she channels the voice of thrift:

> Couldn't you have managed without a carpet? Why had you to recover the armchairs? In my day, there was only one armchair in a house, for one elderly – at any rate, that was the case in my mother's home, and she was a most respectable woman, I assure you. Not everyone can be rich! There's no such thing as a fortune that can't be frittered away! I'd be ashamed to pamper myself the way you do! ... Nothing but finery and frippery!
>
> (p. 244)

Although Emma tries sometimes to account for her finances, 'she would come up with such outrageous totals that she found them impossible to credit. Then she would begin afresh, soon grow confused, drop the worldly enterprise, and think no more about it (pp. 255–6). Emma's powers of repression prove no match for the logic of the market and its reality principle that demands payment. Lheureux provides Emma with the opportunity to acquire, maintain, expand, and even hide her debt, yet, when he calls in his chips and refuses to show her mercy, a sense of marketplace justice makes it difficult to read him as a conniving loan-shark. Flaubert tips the weight of blame on Emma's shoulders in the pages where she begs Lheureux to give her one more chance and prevent her fate in debtor's prison, offering herself as recompense:

'Losing her nerve, she pleaded with him; she even pressed her lovely long, slender hand on the shopkeeper's knee... To which Lheureux responds: Don't touch me! Anyone would think you're trying to seduce me!' (p. 61).

Emma's shameful act of prostitution to get out of her debt defies cultural notions of the good woman, making it difficult for readers to sympathize with her. Faulbert offers Emma only one escape, to take her own life, a cowardly act on its own, but one that is made worse because it leads her husband into sorrow, financial ruin, and leaves her daughter alone in the world with no inheritance. Madame Bovary is correctly recognized as a modern character in her refusal to adhere to the roles and norms of her gender: faithful wife, caring mother, and thrifty consumer. Flaubert offers no simple placation for modern desires that attempts to find satiation in the expanding fields of consumer culture and personal finance.

Hire purchase and the financing of domesticity

The growth of hire purchase in the second half of the century suggests that a technological solution for addressing the legal obstacles surrounding gender and finance worked alongside as the normative regulation advanced in cultural discourses. Hire purchase, stretching back to Roman homeownership, had a long history among elite jewellery and furniture sellers, who had faith in their wealthy clients' ability to eventually settle the bill. For a little money down, and an agreement to pay a service and monthly instalments, individuals acquired goods that would have required years of saving. Because it secured credit on the value of the good, hire purchase provided retailers a way out of the troubles of keeping spendthrift women on the books. Hire purchase brought a new level of abstraction to lending, by avoiding the security of the merchant's knowledge of familial respectability. This credit instrument also blurred traditional class distinction in consumption. Not only did working and middle-class consumers make use of hire purchase, but it also facilitated mass consumption.

American piano and sewing machine manufacturers perfected the techniques of mass hire purchase in the British marketplace, beginning in 1850. American style hire purchase was first tested on the sale of a quintessentially British consumer object, the piano. Into the piano poured the ideals of gentility, civility, gender, and social advancement. The piano, which took considerable dedication to learn, also captured the Victorian middle class's drive for self-development and active use of time. As E. P. Thompson noted, in mature capitalist society all time must be consumed, marketed, put to use; it is offensive for the labour force merely to 'pass the time' (Thompson, 1967, p. 91). 'In their own lives the middle class were committed to self improvement by going to concerts, buying sheet music and performing it at home' (Taylor, 2002, p. 69). Rev. J. R. Haweis felt that the instrument socialized women in helpful ways: as Latin grammar strengthened a boy's memory, so 'the piano makes a girl sit upright and pay attention to details' (Briggs, 1988, p. 248). Husbands and fathers supported the diversion of funds to the piano for their wives and daughters (Leppert, 1992, pp. 111–12). Pianos served as an aid for marriage, particularly marrying up the social scale (Lin, 1996; Stenberg, 1998). Swaddled in their fineries, young middle-class women tickled the ivories for the enjoyment of house-guests, many of them potential suitors. The piano acted as a modern dowry, an investment parents made in their daughter's social advancement through marriage. In this context, the piano according to Briggs became 'a sacred object, 'a household god' (Briggs, 1988, p. 248). The piano, installed in pubs, churches, schools, and hotels, was available to uplift the amateur player, regardless of class. Piano marketers promoted the instrument's civilizing capacity to the poor. 'What is a home without a piano?', was one of the advertisements noted on a wall in London's poorest East End by Charles Booth.

One of the largest businesses in London, Broadwood pianos, employing 300–400 craftsmen, produced 2500 pianos annually, still could not meet the demand. The cost of a piano, roughly the annual income of a clerk or schoolteacher (50–60 guineas), was prohibitive for most. American manufacturers challenged British piano production not simply with their machine made pianos, but the three-year payment plans they offered in 1850. Middle-class families could acquire a piano over time. The sale of pianos under hire purchase witnessed some of the most important legal precedents of lending, because many of the instruments sold were of poor quality and broke before they were owned outright. Still nothing dampened the consumer's enthusiasm to acquire a piano for their home. Sales climbed rapidly (Parakilas, 1999). Networks of hire purchase spread.

By the turn of the century the place of the piano in the middle-class home was so secure that architects created an indented area in parlour walls with a 'piano' window above, which allowed light to shine down on the keys. Hire purchase enabled many working-class people to acquire the instrument for their home. A South Yorkshire miner told the Select Committee on Coal in 1873 that people's homes had 'more pianos and perambulators in recent years and that the piano was not exceptional' (Briggs, 1988, p. 248). The piano, in terms of practical application, was a wholly useless object, but socially it proved exceptionally important. The sale of this luxury good on credit marks an important transition in consumer culture and personal finance (Ehrlich, 1990). Instalment payment was well established in the housing market, but its use for consumer goods signalled a significant change.

The domestic production of fashion

Similar success followed the sale of sewing machines on hire purchase plans. Unlike the piano, clearly designated as a luxury good, the sewing machine was nested within conflicting attitudes towards mechanization and women's work. The making of clothes, the mundane task of women for centuries, was, within the more affluent middle classes, elevated to a prized craft skill expected of the thrift conscious British housewife. According to Briggs, 'Needles figured prominently in the Victorian imagination' where they were associated with the gentle female art of needle work. The quilts, crocheted and embroidered items spun by the hands of women, daughters, and aunts, became 'some of the most coveted of Victorian things' (Briggs, 1988, p. 205). The American sewing machines produced by Isaac Singer in some people's minds, 'threatened to make hand-needlework one of the lost arts'; but for most women, Singer's treadle sewing machine, showcased at the Paris World fair in 1855, was godsend that eased the time-intensive burden of hand-stitching. The machine become the darling of Europe. British working-class women justified their purchase of sewing machines as a prudent way of improving the quality and efficiency with which they made family clothing, and perhaps enabling them to take in extra work to help with the bills. For the middle classes, the sewing machine was more than a symbol of thriftiness. It implied the craft, skill, and pride she took in her sartorial efforts. In this sense, the sewing machine had a dual symbolic character blending thrift with fashion ability.

The cost of the machine was beyond what the middle class could pay for outright, and was unthinkable for working-class women. However Edward Clark, Singer's partner, and lawyer, solved the problem with a hire purchase plan which allowed those with small incomes to acquire a Singer. The machine cost about $125 and could be paid off for $3 per month. Coffin notes: 'Without the development of credit the sewing machines would not have entered into the working-class market' (Coffin, 1994, p. 754). The financial bonds that hire purchase formed wove the household into the national economy in important new ways (Coffin, 1994, p. 757). Other manufacturers and retailers, who by the 1860s began to perfect the use of hire purchase as a marketing tool, offered special deals: first and last month's payments were waived, arrangements with no money down were made, and goods were delivered for free. Although they did so according to their own tastes, credit allowed working-class women to fashion respectable households like the middle class.

Financing the world of goods: Working-class women

The vast majority of the working class and large segments of the middle class simply did not have the means to purchase big-ticket items outright. Mindful of the demands of the public gaze and the uncertainty of men's wages, most working-class women shouldered the weighty load of thrifty domestic consumption. Early studies of the working poor, undertaken by Charles Booth in London, Seebohm Rowntree in York, Maud Pember Reeves in Lambeth, and the Liverpool Economic and Statistical Society on Merseyside, revealed that 'on average, over half the total expenditure of poor urban workers in these areas went on food, while rent took twenty or thirty percent, fuel and light accounted for nine percent of expenditure, and clothing between three and seven per cent' (Johnson, 1988, p. 31). Meanwhile, rates of pay for the working man increased in spurts and starts. The disproportional amount of funds devoted to food in the nineteenth century suggest women had to engage in highly creative accounting to nourish the family, shoe the children, and avoid the disgrace of going out into public in a dated dress of rags. They did so by relying on the network of credit institutions that permeated working-class neighbourhoods.

Although they lived in an age that strongly advocated looking forward, the harsh economics meant that most working-class families lived in the shadow of constant debts (Johnson, 1985). Horrell and Oxley argue that the friendly societies did little to ward off the adverse economic circumstances faced by many nineteenth century families. In times of economic adversity the first line of defence remained women's labour, kinship, and community ties (Horrell & Oxley, 1999). Demonstrating the point, Horrell and Oxley explore a cabinetmaker's careful documentation of the family's incoming and outgoing expenses to reveal that the cabinet maker was not the sole supporter of his family (Horrell & Oxley, 1999, p. 33). Faced with mounting debts following the death of his first wife, his second wife Fanny, toiled for five years to re-establish the family's financial solvency. Fanny took on extra work even through pregnancy, moved house to lessen the rent amount, 'tended to the lodgers that the family kept in their home' and helped the family make do on less. Children too would make financial contributions to the family. Their earnings provided a form of pension (Horrell & Oxley, 1999, p. 35). Cases like this were the norm, according to Horrell and Oxley. During times of crisis 'informal strategies', particularly women's labour and thrift, aided families more than friendly societies (Horrell & Oxley, 1999, p. 36).

As the case above suggests, diverse systems of lending emerged in working-class neighbourhoods that banking networks ignored. The centuries-old act of saving in the summer for the Christmas season continued within diddlum clubs, a kind of cooperative bank, where people saved by purchasing tickets redeemed at specific retailers. Women frequently organized these clubs selling tickets to other women in the community to earn extra to support their own Christmas hampers (Taylor, 2002, pp. 29–30). Diddlum clubs enjoyed a greater social respect because women managed the transactions by and for other women and it involved the esteemed practice of giving. So too did significant numbers of unemployed single women occupy their spare time collecting rents and savings and providing small loans. Taylor finds a 'wide spread existence of local female street moneylenders, and they remained a feature of many of the poorer working-class districts, at least up until the Second World War'. A typical example is given by a Southampton docker's daughter, who remembered, 'Every street had its resident money lender, usually a woman who charged "outrageous rates of interest"' (Taylor, 2002, p. 48). Female lenders often operated out of their home providing money to other women for family expenses, while male lenders tended to operate out of public houses lending men money for 'drink and cigarettes' (Taylor, 2002, p. 52).

The corner shop was one of the first ports of call for working-class women looking to make it through the week. According to Hosgood, 'Successful small shop keeping demanded an investment by the proprietor in the social life of the community' (Hosgood, 1989, p. 438). The corner shop charged more for its goods, to insure the administration of credit cards and bad debt. Some shops provided inferior goods which they allowed well-known regular customers to purchase at low cost on credit. Larger outlets were less likely to modify practices or give working-class customers any credit. From the point of view of a mother with no funds to feed her children, the convenience, long opening hours, and flexible credit terms offered by these corner stores proved invaluable.

Benson notes that many remained loyal customers to corner shops because they believed their repeat business would build goodwill with the owner who would extend credit in the future (Benson, 1996, p. 89). These bankers of the poor had a great deal of economic power within the community, it is true, yet 'they also recognized that in times of hardship they had a certain obligation to provide either a credit lifeline or preferential treatment to regular customers' (Hosgood, 1989, p. 439).

The pawnshop was another important source of credit that nineteenth-century women widely used WWI. The wealthy used pawnshops when they found themselves involved in lengthy court cases; however, the working classes made up the majority of the customer base and frequented them often. According to Minkes, pawnshops emerged in poor industrial districts and rapidly became essential in the context of precarious working-class incomes and absent social safety nets (Minkes, 1953, p. 15). Like the corner shop, families appreciated the convenient location of the pawnshops in their communities (Minkes, 1953, p. 10). Typically the pawnbroker had to hold the taken item for one year. The individual pawning the object received a part of the market value minus service charges. If the individual did not return to purchase the good at full, then the pawnshop auctioned it off. Pawnbrokers also sold new goods, sometimes pawned by manufacturers to raise funds.

For many, pawning was a routine of everyday life meshed with the cycles of paid work. Truck laws legislated weekly cash payment of workers. Pay packets arrived on Friday and were spent over the weekends – including drinks at the pub and tithes at the Church. Monday and midweek therefore became the prime pawning days. 'The heavy pledging day in a period of rapid turnover of loans is Monday. … The heavy redemption trade is met on Friday and Saturday' (Minkes, 1953, p. 17). Women pawned household objects and clothing to obtain liquid assets for medicine or rent. As Stallybrass notes, there was a deeper lesson about poverty implicit in this tenuous hold the working-class family had on fluid goods: the prized jacket or dress served not only as a cloak of respectability, but also as a source of liquid cash in emergencies. 'What little wealth they [the poor] had was stored not only in banks but as things in the house' (Stallybrass, 1998, p. 202). Carried out regularly, pawning called for face-to-face contact, negotiation, and time to examine the goods. Pawning thus formed strong connections between pledges and proprietor. Women referred to pawnshop owners as 'uncle' and 'pop', rhetorically bringing them into the family. The pawnshop proprietor's relationship with women drew suspicion. To protect women's financial virtues, the state, until the mid 1980s, set a national interest rate ceiling of under 35% APR for over a century.

Prior to mass transportation, a host of individuals provided door-to-door financial and retail services and also upset cultural ideals of propriety. Rubin's study documents the reign of the tallyman before the formation of the permanent department store. 'Pack' or 'tally' men arrived at provincial railway stations daily carrying 'drapery goods, wearing apparel, coals', small household items, and hardware including 'thimbles, umbrellas, china figures' (Rubin, 1986, p. 208). Tallymen helped people acquire larger furniture items such as cupboards, beds, and subsequently, entertainment objects such as pianos and gramophones. However, clothes, and later, patterns for making clothing, were a particular staple of the trade. Records suggest that up to half of the tallyman's trade was the sale and financing of men's apparel. Yet, the tallyman's clients, according to historical accounts, appear to be exclusively 'women consisting principally of the wives of labourers, mechanics, porters etc., servant girls and females of loose character'. Women in the 'more respectable classes' were said to have had little need for tallymen, most likely because they had other means of acquiring credit and goods, or were affluent enough to purchase goods outright (Rubin, 1986).

Dating back to the seventeenth century, the tallyman sold goods on credit. Acting outside of literate culture, the tallyman eschewed formal contracts, in favour of tally sticks, 'well-seasoned ash, birch or beechen' sticks to record financial transactions (Rubin, 1986, p. 207). Tallymen recorded acquisition and payment by marking two sticks; one given to the customer. Records suggest the tally trade was extensive and lucrative. For example, Rubin references a witness to the Select Committee on Manufactures in 1833 who said tallymen visited families 'one in three weeks' (explaining the other tallyman moniker 'Johnny Fortnightly') and 'one half of the population [of Lancashire]' acquired their clothing during these visits. There were up to 20 tally firms in Manchester. An average client list might include, for example, 360 customers in Stockport and 1100 in Manchester, gathering on average 'half a crown every three weeks from each family (Rubin, 1986, p. 208). 'An estimate at the turn of the century suggested there were 3,000 firms in the tally trade employing directly and indirectly 21,000 workers' (Rubin, 1986, p. 214).

Rubin documents the moral upset excited by tallymen suspected of using their charm and eloquence to sell poorly made, overpriced goods to gullible women or poor mechanics. Depictions likened the tallymen to a drug dealer, who displayed initial charity and thoughtfulness, but later expected exorbitant amounts of interest from those who could least afford it. The stereotype was a cold individual who did not flinch at the misery his fancy baubles on credit brought to families. Charles Booth felt women were unable to resist the tallymen's charms: 'Their [tallymen] power of talk does it. Wives left at home all day, dull; along comes a tallyman with an oily tongue; they like a gossip, and don't have the chance of seeing many men, so they talk and then buy' (Rubin, 1986, p. 209). Helen Bonsanquent described the tallyman thus,

> [a] still more insidious exponent of credit is the tallyman, who finds an occasion for exploiting the future of his victims in every conceivable article, both of necessity and luxury. Of course his success depends upon the skill with which he can magnify the delights of immediate acquisition, and minimise the pains of payment.
>
> (Bosanquet, 1896, p. 225)

The moral fear the tallyman provoked moved the government to instate the Pedlars' Act of 1871, which required peddlers and hawkers to obtain a licence to operate (Rubin, 1986, p. 210). Rubin argues neither legislation nor the expansion of department stores in the 1870s halted door-to-door trading. Members of the working class who lacked the funds to purchase goods at department stores and whose ability to travel was limited continued to rely on the tally trade well into the twentieth century (Rubin, 1986, p. 206).

The Providence bank also went from door-to-door exchanging funds for tokens that women used to purchase things at various shops. Meanwhile, truck laws outlawed the practice of paying workingmen in tokens instead of cash to prevent the offloading of inferior goods at high prices. Its equivalent, from the Providence bank, crept in through the front door of domestic consumption. Working-class women who redeemed taokes for frequently inferior goods, paying more for them than if they used cash, were aware their practices were not economical, but justified them by claiming they appreciated the personal attention and convenient door-to-door services of the Providence bank. Women also claimed that the weekly visits by the bank's representatives reminded them of the need to save or pay their bills.

New moralities of debt: The politics of taste in the age of respectability

Working-class households did not lack pride and the art of beautification that followed it. Even during the 1840s when working-class wages were meagre and work sporadic, housing interiors in coal-mining communities were reported as routinely clean and 'typically showy and costly'. Some of the other items found in homes included mahogany chests, four-post beds, and an eight-day clock within walls. Coloured prints and lithographs hung on the walls. Victorian women, of all classes, showed a particular fondness for drapes. Johnson notes, 'pointed distinction[s] were drawn by the inhabitants by their labours in colouring their doorsteps and windowsills with hearthstone, planting window boxes', and putting up the all important lace curtain, a community flag of respectability (Johnson, 1988, p. 34).

As working-class wages rose in the second half of the nineteenth century, mass consumer objects, previously the preserve of the upper middle class, began to appear in working-class households too (Fraser, 1981). Hire purchase promised to equalize the processes of credit, offering all classes the same opportunity to amass debt. Using credit, 'by 1873 many Yorkshire miners had expensive objects like pianos and sewing machines in their home. Men wore machine-made watches from Switzerland' (Church, 2000, p. 637). By the turn of the century, interest in home appearances was thoroughly entrenched within working-class culture. 'The instinct of house pride seems almost never wanting. ... Some attempt at ornament is always made and colour prints, photographs, and dust-collecting knickknacks often abound in houses from which the more pawnable articles of useful furniture have been stripped' (Johnson, 1988, p. 36). No doubt, these trends were an indication of the scrimping, planning, and saving in the penny banks that characterized the mindful management of the family budget as well as the growing use of various forms of credit.

Society ladies, at the end of the nineteenth century, became deeply concerned about the way working classes used credit to manage their lifestyles. McKibbin outlines the work of Mrs Helen Bosanquet, Miss M. Loane, and Lady Florence Bell. They all studied the socially excluded and were more interested in psychology and culture than statistics (p. 176). Mrs Bosanquet, the daughter of a Unitarian minister, was an educator and charity worker. Miss Loane, the daughter of a Royal Navy captain, became a superintendent of district nurses. Lady Bell, married to industrialist Hugh Bell, a magistrate in Middlesbrough, felt it her duty to inspect the lives of that town's working-class. The working-class women, they documented, did not seem to practice the ideas of thrift and self-reliance that these commentators expected of them. While Mrs Bosanquet felt the wealthy needed to donate funds to elevate the poor's tragic situation, by and large middle-class reformers viewed debt as an individual's fault. The working class appeared unable to engage proper self-restraint. As Johnson notes: 'In many middle-class eyes the pawnshop a credit-granting retail outlet and the post-1918 growth of hire purchase represented the antithesis of those sturdy individualistic and prudential values that underpinned the Smilesian virtues' (Johnson, 1984, p. 86).

In 1896 Helen Bosanquet published her study 'The Burden of Small Debts' in poor working-class communities in the East End of London in the well-respected *The Economic Journal*. She concluded that the credit in the commercial world had seeped into everyday life. Debt was a common practice and private indebtedness was widespread (Bosanquet, 1896, p. 213). In her view, thrift had become 'old fashion'. She set out to 'objectively' explore the advantages of credit provision for the general public (Harris, 1990). She found none. Detailing lending organizations and practices, she documented 82 loan societies in one of the poorest neighbourhoods of the East End of London. Bosanquet estimated that East London was 'the very Paradise of indebtedness' with one in three families in the red. She pitied the small businessman, who she felt bore the price of the working class's inability to control their debt. She noted that the Shoreditch Country Court registered 12,600 cases of small amounts, the highest being £50, from such individuals as the general shops, tallyman, and savings and loan companies (p. 226).

The practice known as the 'Monday to Saturday', where people pawned their clothes during the week then reclaimed them on Sunday for church, was recognized as a 'common' and 'degrading custom' (Bosanquet, 1896, p. 218). She drew attention to inequalities between middle- and working-class lending provisions. While the small neighbourhood stores provided easy credit, the larger shops in middle-class shopping precincts insisted upon cash (Bosanquet, 1896, p. 219). She felt that funeral establishments profitted from poor people's vulnerability by refusing to lend for small-scale funerals. Only funerals of £25 or more were financed contributing to the grand scale of the East End funeral, as people used the money for 'mules, footmen, feathers and paul' (Bosanquet, 1896, p. 221). Bosanquet was perplexed why people held the pawnshop proprietor in great esteem, viewing him as a 'tradesman or even philanthropist'. She noted that the pawnshop dealer was hardly an altruist charging 24% interest and assuming no risk because they possessed the object and had complete security.

Unable to understand working-class pride, distrust of strangers within the community, the reformers became frustrated by the unwillingness of people to accept their help. Reformers read people's refusal to speak, look them in the eye, and sensitivity to criticism as signs of their vulnerability.

Lacking social graces and reason, reformers worried that working-class women would form highly 'personal' relationships with the door-to-door lenders. Miss Loane believed woman's relationships with the tallyman was 'morally tainted'. Lady Bell was 'disgusted' by the way the working-class housewife could not control her wants before him:

> If she had a penny in her pocket, she will be quite ready to spend it on the first thing that comes within her en, as she stands at her door. It may be a 'tallyman' who comes along with something to sell on the hire system a worsted shawl, perhaps, a workbox, or even a gramophone, but whatever it is the woman buys it simply because it is suggested to her.
>
> (McKibbins, 1978, p. 181)

Middle-class reformers readily asserted their own impeccable measures of self-restraint while accusing others of greed and pretentiousness. Mrs Samuel Barnett observed:

> In most rooms there is too much furniture and there are too many ornaments. ... I have counted as many as seventeen ornaments on one mantelpiece—three, or perhaps five are ample. She who aims to be thrifty will fight against yielding to the artificially developed instinct to possess.
>
> (Johnson, 1988, p. 37)

Blinded to notions of systemic social inequality, the reformers constructed psychological and biological stories to explain the working classes' financial choices. In their snapshot studies, Victorian matrons deemed the working classes habitual borrowers, for whom debt was not a temporary occurrence, but a 'plan of life' (McKibbin, 1978, p. 224). Bosanquet associated the working-class debt cycle to their lack of appreciation for property values, their present mindedness and their need for instant gratification. She admonished them for their 'hired goods' which, she claimed, had 'none of the steadying effect of genuine possessions'. Goods were 'light come light go', and working-class women were like 'spoiled children with too many toys' unable to appreciate what they had, always searching for something more novel (Bosanquet, 1986, p. 221). Women 'revel in the possibilities of sewing machines and bangles' (p. 221). Women struck Bosanquent as senseless. Why, she thought, would they pay £8 for a sewing machine on hire purchase that cost less then a pound to construct, and would not cost more than 4 or 5 pounds if paid in full. The goods were too readily available and acquired for a very short period. No sooner taken home than taken back to the store.

Bosanquet felt the poor were delusional, living life in a fiction, believing they owned goods on credit when they did not. 'To furnish on the hire system is perhaps as unsatisfactory a way of housekeeping as can be desired; even the furnished lodging has more of a reality about it'. Women, she proclaimed, were dangerously devoting more money to 'things' and the maintenance of 'things' instead of the welfare of the family. They 'magnify the delights of immediate acquisition and minimise the pains of the future payment'. Those that succumbed to the convenience of credit, she condemned as hopelessly lost in the present: unable to borrow prudently with 'an eye to future profit' instead borrowing to satisfy 'present convenience' forgetting about future loss. Accounting and 'real value' were not part of their calculus. People lived under the pall of debt as 'half a man' because their future was not their own. The reason why the working class was indifferent and filled with despair was that their clothing was in hock, taken at any moment, and the landlord meddled in their affairs. They were not free. Rather, by indulging in credit, one 'sold himself into slavery from which there was no escape' (1896, p. 225).

Even Engels read the decorations and fashion consciousness of the working-class woman as a negative omen, because he took it as representing a working class that was selling out to middle-class values. The cult of domesticity was redirecting and suppressing revolutionary drives: 'The most repulsive thing here is the bourgeois respectability, which has grown deep into the bones of the workers' (Church, 2000, p. 638).

Like the middle classes, working-class women did their utmost to remain fashionable in their appearance. Yet the reformers also condemned them for their efforts to join in these public displays of respectable fashion. Miss Loane saw the poor as 'martyrs to fashion'. Styles of dress spread like cholera between the middle and the working class. However, the middle classes judged the latter's preference for more 'godish' and 'bright' cloth to be coarse (McKibbin, 1978, p. 189). Whether encouraged by emulation, interclass competition, a thirst for novelty, or a felt need to keep up with the times, middle-class reformers reviled against the widespread imitation of middle-class fashion. Where fashion was concerned, the poor were not resentful of what other women had, but in great admiration of upper-class styles.

> In a town where there are both rich and poor the dress of the latter will invariably follow that of their well-to-do neighbours; the fashions

spread like an epidemic from high to low, repeating themselves in poor materials with all extravagance of cut and colour accentuated.

(Bosanquet, 1896, p. 221)

The evidence left by these social reformers provides insight into both the class divides of consumption and its moral condemnation. According to Tratner, buying 'on credit in the nineteenth century had been a sign of laziness, weakness, and lack of energy' (2001, p. 29). Reformers deemed working-class consumption immoral, wasteful, and excessive, as sumptuary laws appeared to move into normative discourse. Some historians challenge these assertions of the extremes of working-class dependence on credit, pointing out that the historical record has 'tended to overestimate working-class consumption, underestimate working-class saving and overlook working-class investment' (Benson, 1996, p. 98). So too is the idea that lenders hoodwinked women an exaggeration. Women used available sources of credit to make their lives bearable. Benson argues that working-class debt is best understood as a rational act of 'thrift in reverse'. Workers purchased luxury items such as 'furniture, clothing, domestic utensils and ornaments in the summer, which they pawned off one by one in the winter to help tide over the bad time' (Benson, 1996, p. 88). People invested in objects instead of savings banks. Possessing objects brought more joy to joyless lives than money, while being convertible into cash when necessary.

Conclusion

Nineteenth century Britain experienced unprecedented wealth creation. The middle class, and especially the working class, began to imagine an ever-expanding prosperity that gave them the confidence to defer payment into the future. Personal financial networks increased. Although they enjoyed less than full participation in the labour market, within the home, women did contribute significantly to the formation of the consumer economy as managers of domestic consumption. A Victorian woman's experience of shopping was both liberating and constraining: she found expanding domains of pleasure and self-expression at the same time, she felt the constraints of her limiting financial circumstances tightening around her. To make ends meet, women turned to a variety of credit sources available, and for the most part, even working-class women, used them mindfully: to keep the children fed and the creditors from the door. Women's control over the domestic budget was a lynch pin in the formation of Victorian capitalist markets.

The law cases over women's financial culpability exposed the contractions underwriting the role that women played in supporting the cult of domesticity.

The repackaging of the house as a romantic refuge of self-development powerfully fuelled the importance of the house in the economy. The private home, was not all that private, but open to the surveillance of social reformers as well as neighbours, setting into motion the decoration of interiors to maintain respectability and advance social status. Religious discourses informed thrift but also legitimated artful consumption as a source of divine grace. Home goods also served as important economic resources for maintaining the working classes. Pianos, sewing machines, clothing, and furniture were 'fluid savings', which held value that could later be liquidated as required. Material objects netted into the thrifty ideals of investment in the future. The rhetoric of thriftiness had a Janus face. On the one hand the careful calculus of making limited means meet and increasing aspirations required skilled savvy. On the other, the requirements of decorative furnishings and fashionable clothes, social niceties, and relaxation for the family issued a siren call to a broader vista of respectable social display and judgement.

The divided world between the productive and consumptive realms of the household; between breadwinning men and spendthrift women; between public wealth and personal consumption; between family respectability and domestic finance; never existed. These gendered spheres were profoundly interwoven. This is not to imply that these realms were equally valued or empowered. Under the institutions of productive thrift, the friendly and building societies were held-up as cherished bastions of the working-class community's resourcefulness and self-reliance in financial matters. The home became a vessel of masculine pride and an emblem of the prudent attitude to credit that enabled men to achieve it. Yet the middle classes, unwilling to extend the growing empowerment they were enjoying in domestic and marketplace spheres to other women, deemed the instruments of saving and debt that evolved around the working housewives' everyday borrowing morally suspect. The acquisition of objects for the inside of the home on credit at the corner store, clothes and trinkets for the family acquired through the pawnshop, the tallyman, or the street-lender, and labour-saving appliances achieved by hire purchase, were simply the necessary instruments of household management. The novel financial arrangements pioneered by the Singer sewing machine and American piano-makers augured in a different system of domestic finance. This new trajectory for the mass production and distribution of furniture and appliances to the working class blended utility with demonstrable respectability, functionality with fashion, and accomplishment with cultural capital.

Margaret Thatcher's political rhetoric above drew strength from the nineteenth century feminist debates that sought to establish the importance of housekeeping roles not just in the kitchen but in the public sphere. She ignored the rising levels of private debt housewives necessarily accumulated to maintain their respectable and thrifty households.

3
Hire Purchase, Home Furnishings, and the Cult of Domesticity

The ideal of domestic respectability that valorized private homeownership and thrifty consumption among the bourgeoisie was abundantly evident in the public discourses of the Victorian Era. So too, the primary business instruments for financing this growing cult of domesticity, mortgages, hire purchase, and retail credit, became more regularly used by the general public. Yet, despite the increasing wealth that accompanied the expansionism of the British Empire, at the dawn of the twentieth century, life was still marked by relative hardship and scarcity for many working-class families. Homeownership remained the preserve of the upper and suburban middle classes, and reticence towards acquiring debt, especially for luxuries and indulgences, remained a questionable practise among all classes.

The widespread sales of sewing machines and pianos on deferred payments, however, suggested a widening space for domestic consumerism emerging that presaged greater acceptance of personal debt. This chapter explores some of the emerging discourses about credit that, from the turn of the century on, encouraged the expansion of personal and state debt as a way of spreading economic well-being in Britain. The economic writings of John Maynard Keynes with his rally call: 'let goods be homespun ... and, above all, let finance be primarily national' (Esty, 2000, 179 p. 8) provided both a new way of understanding debt and consumerism, as well as political economic policy to support a modern orientation to the marketplace. Keynes attacked Bentham's *laissez faire* capitalism as 'the worm which has been gnawing at the insides of modern civilisation and responsible for its present moral decay' (Mini, 1996, p. 100) because it encouraged foreign instead of domestic investment. Keynes worried that Britain was 'drifting into financing port improvements, housing electrical developments, etc., abroad at lower rates of interest, while forgetting simpler projects at home. Yet it is not true that there is nothing at home which wants doing'. The 'roads had to be adapted to the needs of the motor car, homes had to be built, the advantages of electricity had to be brought to everyone, large sections of cities were decrepit and ready for rebuilding', he pointed out (Dow & Hillard, 2002, p. 28). In a letter to the *Times* in 1924 he proclaimed: 'The conditions for free markets success has disappeared' (Mini, 1996, p. 102). He argued, 'Domestic returns were as good as foreign ones, risk was lower and domestic investments were socially better: not only did they provide home employment but if a domestic investment fails the nation retains the investment (a popular housing project, the Underground of London, etc.) while in the case of foreign investment all is lost' (Mini, 1996, p. 102). Keynes encouraged a new sense of nationalism.

The nineteenth century imperial economy, in Keynes' analysis neglected the needs of the British population. He attacked the paradox of thrift produced after WWI by advocating a liberalization of demand. Opposing the Bank of England's economic policy that constrained consumption, Keynes became the godfather of public debt. He advocated funnelling investment into national markets to fight recession. Keynes' monetary policy objective was to stimulate the circulation of capital by emphasizing consumption (demand) as an important factor in the equation of economic growth. Hardly an advocate of Communism, or even Socialism, Keynes committed himself to providing every able citizen with gainful employment, not simply as a moral duty, but in a pragmatic belief that employment and spending bolsters growth. Employing people during difficult economic times increased their purchasing power, said Keynes, equating to higher consumption levels that would spin off into new businesses and advance the entire economy.

Other modernizing voices joined Keynes' call for the nation to support consumer demand. Also finding the Victorian thrift ethos limiting and loathsome, Keynes' friends in the Bloomsbury group promoted his rallying cry for the normalization of credit as a means of democratizing consumption. Leonard and Virginia Woolf became notable polemicists for modern consumerism, although their justifications for expanding consumer credit were more poetic than political or economic. Leonard advocated cooperatives as a modernizing institution because consumers saved more by consuming more, whereas for Virginia they gave value to women's role as domestic managers and highlighted the part that style and aesthetics played in mass marketing to female consumers, rapidly becoming the major buyers of clothing, furniture, and durables.

Against the backdrop of this more consumerist rhetoric, advertising and retailing encouraged working-class women to modernize their homes. While the department store Titans of Oxford Street played their role in the advance of credit, utility providers proved more important. Women began to rethink their allegiance to the utilitarian black gas cookers rented from the gas companies favouring the stylish white ones that could be acquired through hire purchase: in so doing they were normalizing indebtedness as a part of prudent domestic management.

America's mass consumer culture impressed some British economists. In the early twentieth century economists, politicians, and manufacturers became increasingly aware that financing homes and automobiles, two of the largest investments a person made in their lifetime, contributed to more rapid turn over of commodities and growth in the consumer economy (Olney, 1991). Cars proved an ambiguous test case of Keynesian ideas about the role that consumer credit plays in the expansion of national consumption. The reclassification of automobiles from luxury, to everyday item also illustrated the progressive erosion of the thrift ethos. Britain had its own automobile sector, but the industry grew slowly until the introduction of American style marketing of cars on deferred payment purchases. In what follows, I also trace the role that style and credit play in the American car marketers' move into British automobile sales. Although there were a number of reasons why British car purchases failed to match the dizzying heights achieved in the USA, by 1939 close to 75% of all cars in Britain were acquired using credit. By the end of the twentieth century the profits for financing an automobile were greater than making and selling them. In 2002, while GM lost $5.2 billion (US) manufacturing vehicles, its financing arm GMAC earned $9.8 billion selling loans, insurance, and mortgages (DeCloet, 2005).

Fashion, furniture, and femininity

British homeownership rose during the first half of the twentieth century from 15% in 1915 to 35% in 1938. Between 1880 and 1939 new housing projects appeared in many major cities. Workers in the expanding white-collar and service sectors happily took up the affordable mortgages that the state encouraged financial providers to offer. New homes, however, contributed to changing domestic relations, which in turn altered consumption and credit patterns. Men, who once worked in or near their homes, now took the train to work. Leaving early in the morning, they returned in the evening. Women's responsibility for housekeeping and home décor continued to grow, as did their handling

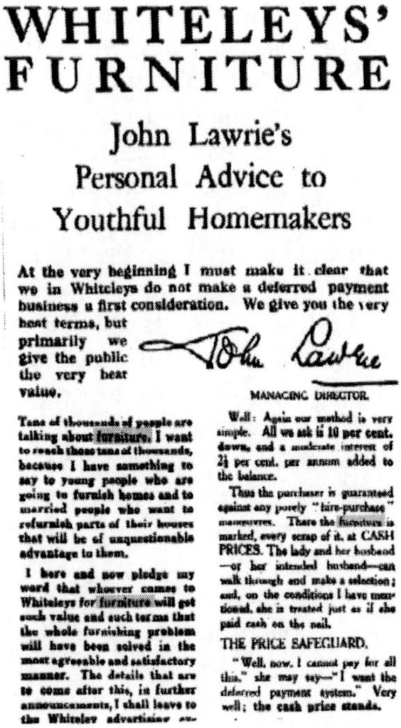

WHITELEYS' FURNITURE

John Lawrie's
Personal Advice to
Youthful Homemakers

At the very beginning I must make it clear that we in Whiteleys do not make a deferred payment business a first consideration. We give you the very best terms, but primarily we give the public the very best value.

[signature] John Lawrie

MANAGING DIRECTOR.

Tens of thousands of people are talking about furniture. I want to reach these tens of thousands, because I have something to say to young people who are going to furnish homes and to married people who want to refurnish parts of their houses that will be of unquestionable advantage to them.

I here and now pledge my word that whoever comes to Whiteleys for furniture will get such value and such terms that the whole furnishing problem will have been solved in the most agreeable and satisfactory manner. The details that are to come after this, in further announcements, I shall leave to the Whiteley advertising an-

Well: Again our method is very simple. All we ask is 10 per cent. down, and a moderate interest of 2½ per cent. per annum added to the balance.

Thus the purchaser is guaranteed against any purely "hire-purchase" manoeuvres. There the furniture is marked, every scrap of it, at CASH PRICES. The lady and her husband —or her intended husband—can walk through and make a selection; and, on the conditions I have mentioned, she is treated just as if she paid cash on the nail.

THE PRICE SAFEGUARD.

"Well, now, I cannot pay for all this," she may say—"I want the deferred payment system." Very well; the cash price stands.

Figure 3.1   Whiteley's furniture ad addressing homemakers.

of personal finance and presence in the workforce. By WWII, 'Apart from their neatly arrayed collections of pipes and pottery, men's part in domestic decoration – if indeed they had one at all – reduced to do-it-yourself home repair' Middle- and working-class housewives used consumer credit, variously called instalment plans, deferred payment schemes, and hire purchase to acquire white goods and furnishings that advertisers promised would make their lives more conformable and convenient. In an ad for *Whiteleys' Furniture*, managing director John Lawrie forsakes, 'purely hire-purchase manoeuvres' preferring to speak of a 'deferred payment' purchase. The 'lady and her husband – or her intended husband', he claims, can make a purchase for the ticket prices shown in the store. And, if she says, 'Well, now, I cannot pay for all this' she may say I want the deferred payment system' at 10% down and 2.5% annually paid in interest on the cash price, he explains. Although furniture retailers, as this ad suggests, felt obliged to euphemise the language of consumer debt, they had few qualms about offering it and understood well the demand for beautiful objects for the home.

The Bloomsbury Circle

Others joined furniture advertisers to refashion the nineteenth century thrift ethos. Certain aspects of modernism played a decisive role in articulating new cultural sensibilities that helped structure mass consumption. While many voices played a role, the Bloomsbury group, in particular Virginia and Leonard Woolf's support for their friend J. M. Keynes, was significant because they advocated the modernization of British consumerism. Like Keynes, the Woolfs argued that thrift was the handmaiden to war and colonialism, not a virtue. Thrift denied Britons the pleasures of domestic consumption. The Bloomsburys' political concerns differed from the Fabian society, trade union, and suffragette movements of the time, which tended to blend Puritanism with Socialism. McClymont noted how early twentieth century leftist politics focused on disciplining 'individual existence through moral exhortation forged a world of severe ethical standards and strict cultural frontiers. This was grounded in an almost overwhelming preoccupation with work and by an indefatigable belief in the possibility of good money; one which explicitly rejected the interrelated evils of unearned inheritance, dishonest acquisition and, above all, gambling' (McClymont, 2008, p. 25). In contrast, the Bloomsbury group, protected by economic and educational privilege, challenged the strict sexual and thrift mores of Victorian culture and hence its foundations in political economy. Although they wielded their cultural capital like a sword, Bloomsbury channelled their bourgeois attitudes towards domestic life through a modernist vision promoted to wider public. Radically, consumerism and credit played a key role in their vision of the future.

Virginia Woolf and her husband, Leonard disagreed on many issues, but united in their praise of cooperatives as the means of ensuring collective consumer and producer empowerment. Cooperatives institutionalized the profoundly modern idea that linked spending with saving. The original impulse for the cooperatives stemmed from labour politics. In 1844, 28 workers, mainly weavers, created the Rochdale Equitable Pioneers' Society 'to provide food, goods, and education facilities for their fellow' (Johnston, 1897, p. 2). Angered by middlemen profits and the sale of inferior goods to the working classes at high price the cooperative movement forged for the 'purpose of securing in the purchase of commodities advantages impossible to be obtained by one, through an equitable division of the profits derived from their purchases' (Stein, 1933, p. 428). The weavers turned the knowledge of collective powers gained through their experience of guilds and unionism in production towards the task of organizing consumption cooperatively. They assigned a fixed interest rate and distributed profits to co-op members based upon sales, thus cutting out the middleman by establishing a direct link between supplier and consumer. Popular and nationally based, cooperatives challenged the thrift ethos with dividends that rewarded acts of higher consumption (Furlough & Strikwerda, 1999, pp. 94, 96). Leonard Woolf thus saw in the cooperatives the possibility of building a new moral foundation for the national economy. If thrift, as he believed, was at the root of imperialism (Glendinning, 2006, p. 27), then the cooperative movement was the road to modernization. Studies documented the embrace of the cooperatives by the working class. By 1881, 971 co-ops had 547,000 members; between 1881 and 1900 the membership tripled and by 1914, a further doubling of membership occurred (Kelly, 1998). By the late nineteenth century the cooperative movement was 'a gargantuan enterprise of 1,127,000 members whose shops did a business of $160,000,000 each year' (Hall, 1939, p. 127).

The Women's Cooperative Guild, of which Virginia Woolf was a leading member, introduced novel political issues onto the agenda including 'fair prices for all consumers through collective bargaining, for adult suffrage, the reform of tax and divorce laws, peace and military disarmament' (Trexler, 2007, p. 876). For Mrs Woolf the cooperative movements incubated a feminized consumerism: Ignored by unions, women curated domestic spaces, managed household finance and the shopped for their families. Women appreciated that co-op goods sold at a reasonable price, were undiluted, not tampered with, or under weight. Research suggested popular concerns that the co-ops encouraged impulsive and frivolous spending by rewarding consumerism with dividends were unfounded. Women used dividends, earned through the act of consumption, in thrifty ways to help pay the rent, save for Christmas, children's education, or to acquire a cherished item for the home (Stein, 1933, p. 429). Again, consumption and the old practice of prudent investment were intertwined, not antagonistic (Stein, 1933, p. 432). Consumption was a duty not a sin. So too did the Bloomsbury group voice a unique modern sensibility which made consumption, credit, and Oxford Street retailers central agencies providing women and the working classes self-fulfilment, their right in a modern society.

The aestheticization of consumption: women and the art of making a home

While the aestheticization of the home had been linked to the grace of God in the nineteenth century, many commentators agree that

Virginia Woolf's writing popularized the Bloomsbury vision of a secular aestheticized consumerism. According to Jennifer Wickes, Virginia Woolf's writing gave as much 'voice and representation to the everyday market albeit through different genres and emphasis on different institutional formations' as political writers and theoretical economists (Wicke, 1994, p. 12). Woolf's writing imagined Britain's future unfolding in the shopping districts of Oxford Street because the glittering abundance showcased in these stores, their emphasis on fashion, exoticism, and theatricality challenged the Victorian aesthetics that valued goods for their durability and utility. The transient sensibility of the shopping district, the colour, energy, and ever-changing windows were to her 'hopeful' assaults on history (p. 15). Woolf celebrated Oxford Street department stores such as Selfridges as the 'modern aristocrats' who anticipated the future of domestic consumerism. Even more radically, she applauded the 'courage, initiative, and audacity' of department-store owners in reaching out to the common, female, shopper (p. 14). Mass-oriented department stores challenged the old order of patriarchy and access to goods constrained by class. Consuming, claims Wicke, is at the heart of Woolf's narratives because 'the market is perceived to be a shadowy common room within which acts of much creative magic or transforming potential can be performed' (Wicke, 1994, p. 21). Amid the throng of shoppers 'consuming (a synonym for "saving less") was stripped of its stigma' (Wicke, 1994, p. 22). Like Marianne, the symbol of the French Republic, the women shopping in the West End were for Woolf foot soldiers of a new revolution taking place in the nation. The Victorian economy dominated by the male vista of the ever-productive and self-regulating machine, in Woolf's writings, is rearticulated as a reflection of women's creation of beauty – a field of 'fluidity', 'play', and 'disorder' (Wicke, p. 15).

However difficult it is to summarize Woolf's fluid and unconventional novels, what is clear is that her work rejected the progressive chronology of the nineteenth century narrative substituting a fluid struggle for subjective freedom against societal restraints. Characters like Orlando transcended morality, moved through nonlinear time and blurred gender lines. Mrs Dalloway, trapped between the masculine world's mores of hoarding and investing, offers a 'magical solution to this antinomie— sacrifice through spending' (Tratner, 2001, p. 21). Mrs Dalloway's tireless devotion to shopping and entertaining gives expression to the housewife's valuable contribution to the circulation of wealth through domestic consumption. There is almost a sense of duty ascribed to her mindful pursuit of beauty, pleasure, and civility (Tratner, 2001, p. 118).

While the Victorian novel protagonists triumphed in a struggle to be true to themselves in a morally restricted world, the modern hero, according to Michael Tratner, quested 'for hidden desires, for alternative selves' that could bring pleasure (2001, p. 43). According to Tratner, Woolf's modernism was rooted in an unconstrained stream of consciousness style that conveyed an openness to experiences and feelings and a willingness to explore the possibility of multiple selves. This modern discourse sought to distance individuals from the binding practices and habits of the past and encourage the embrace of the new and the ephemeral. Role playing and fantasizing brought people into new relations to objects. Potential is not ossified in the relations of the past, but exists in the 'momentary' and the 'everyday'. Structures are not fixed, but 'a liquid terrain of experience, choice, agency, or desire exquisitely sensitive to all the ripples that play across its surface' (Tratner, 2001, p. 44). In the modern world the expanding shopping districts, media outlets, and artistic lifestyles offered new templates for achieving desire.

Importantly, these sensibilities were modelled in the domestic sphere in the Bloomsbury sisters' interior design reflected a sense of beauty, play, and fluidity, devoted not to god, but to self-expression. In 1904 Sir Leslie Stephen's daughters Virginia and Vanessa began refashioning 46 Bloomsbury Square in a 'less familiar version of modernism' that included colourful drapes, rugs, curtains, and round cushy chairs (Reed, 2004). This, and the Lake District home, Charleston, became canvases for aesthetic expression and play. The group of extraordinary artists and intellectuals that assembled in these interiors prompted widespread interest.

For Tratner the contribution of artists, like the Bloomsbury, to the modern cycles of consumption was found in a sphere beyond their popular essays and novels. The group infused goods with new meanings and thus, according to Tratner, addressed the problem of marginal utility at a time when economists had begun to recognize consumer ennui as a serious obstacle to continued economic growth. Plentiful and unchanging goods bored consumers, thus failed to deliver to them the same levels of pleasure as goods new and full of possibility. According to Tratner, artists aided the turnover of goods because 'Artist's re-appropriated discarded goods and used them in new situations to recharge tired goods with novel symbolic means as a means of revitalizing the desire of goods'.

Still, Woolf's embrace of shopping in 'Oxford Street Tide' and of aestheticization by way of consumption was not without reservation, and veiled elitist fear of mass consumption (Carey, J. 1992). Woolf also saw London's most famous shopping street as garish, gaudy, a place where 'the buying and selling is too blatant and raucous' (Tratner, 2001, p. 113).

The interaction of taste and the marketplace delighted and chilled Woolf. The new retailers were constructing a society freed for 'creation and fertility' and encouraging the wider public that unending beauty is 'within the reach of everybody' (Tratner, 2001, p. 116). However, the seduction of the glimmering consumer marketplace threatened to distract people from seriously reflecting upon its consequences (Tratner, 2001, pp. 116–17). The market also failed to '[educate] the mass to a higher standard of aesthetic sensibility'. Thus, Bloomsbury suggested organizations to protect consumers from the magical spell of the marketplace that the masses were blinded towards. Critics, such as Raymond Williams, viewed this type of paternal protectionism as little more than an extension of the patronizing discourses of nineteenth century social reformers. As a fraction of the upper class, the Bloomsbury group's opposition to thrift, said Williams, 'relates to a lower class as a matter of conscience: not in solidarity, nor in affiliation, but as an extension of what are still felt as personal or small-group obligations, at once against the cruelty and stupidity of the system and toward its other-wise relatively helpless victims' (Williams, 2005, p. 155). Despite its seemingly progressive stance, emphasizing the freeing aspects of consumerism meant little within conditions of immense systemic inequality and where elites like Virgina Woolf continued to feel entitled to draw limits on others' consumption, while blithely denying any on her own.

The little black gas cooker: style and utility in the mass market

Hire purchase sellers exploited the turmoil surrounding modernist consumer politics, extending to consumers the ability to acquire goods immediately rather than saving for a deferred future. It granted consumers immediate pleasure, and gave the working-class access to deemed luxury goods. Consumer credit facilitated a higher and quicker turnover, thus was crucial to the extension of the modern fashion cycles. Yet, in practice, lingering cultural concerns about debt and the acquisition of luxury goods curtailed the use of hire purchase. Sean O'Connell (2004) argues that the growth in consumer credit in the twentieth century was as essential to the formation of consumer culture as 'the moving assembly line was to mass production.' But, because the extensive use of consumer credit transgressed the lingering Victorian moral norms of pecuniary respectability, O'Connell states 'for many individuals, credit or its partner in crime – debt – were not simply economic concepts but represented a moral state'. Lord Beaverbrook writing in the *Daily Express* suggested that the stigma on credit lingered longer in the UK as 'the

British public is slow to adopt a plan which the American finds so useful and attractive'. His explanation is that both 'an innate conservatism of temperament' and the 'idea that purchase by instalments is not quite respectable' restrained the acceptance of hire purchase for many household goods. The discourses of thrift also remained rooted in British working-class culture. Historian Judy Giles conducted interviews with working-class women married in the 1930s, discovering that their narratives of the past valued thrift and derided indebtedness. The former was associated with mature femininity and good household management, the latter with immaturity and irresponsibility of the wayward male (Giles, 1992).

Utility companies became an unlikely impulse for overturning conservative attitudes towards hire purchase. While Americans celebrate Ford as the mass marketing king, in Britain utility providers deserve that crown. Utility providers began to think about the mass market earlier than other big-ticket merchants. Their interest was shaped by a modernist engineering ethos and by their being publicly owned. Since modern utilities provided the nation with tools to enhance their cleanliness and health, social reformers supported instead of criticized these companies' marketing practices. By 1933, roughly two-thirds of the electrical distribution, 40% of the gas supply, four-fifths of the local transport services, and 90% of the water undertakings, all of which had become essential resources, were overseen by publicly owned and operated utility companies (Dimrock, 1933). Utility companies' strong union ties forged their allegiance to the working classes. Mandated by the state to forego marketing principles of selling to only the most lucrative customers, utility operators treated their markets more as a mass, differing from many private retailers who continued to target consumers based on class. Thus, while in the US private automobile manufacturers promoted the idea that cheap automotive fuel was a citizen's right, the right to cheap natural gas for the home, to this day animates, Britain's collective consciousness.

The sales of the black gas cooker, designed for working-class households in 1875, offers a telling example of how the design of household goods became interwoven with new methods of payment. Introduced in the mid-nineteenth century, natural gas was a magical substance whose fires subdued both the dark and cold damp life of Britons. Academics draw attention to the direct role gas played in the formation of British consumer culture; the way the introduction of gas street lamps reduced crime, made women feel more comfortable walking in public spaces thus contributing to the expansion of London's West End shopping networks. But in the home the wonders of gas seemed even more miraculous. The gas cooker quickly ignited. Conveniently, it required no trips to the dirty woodpile or coal bin. The powerful modern taboo against dirt and disease may well have helped secure this clean burning appliance's place in people's hearts and minds. Yet, until the last quarter of the nineteenth century, only the wealthy could afford to cook with anything but wood or coal. Gas piped into the household was a status symbol.

While British manufacturers continued to offer working classes their lower cost inferior goods, utility companies were among the first to think about their sales in mass-market terms. The mass consumption orientation that utility companies adopted had less to do with altruism than the economics of a resource distribution industry. Although there was a constant supply of gas people purchased gas in seasonal patterns. Gas pipes were a fixed cost but volume was king; profitability increased when more gas was being used through the same infrastructure. One of the obvious ways of regularizing the flow of gas was to make it available for more uses, and in more venues – for lighting, heating, and cooking. Besides lighting the public streets, gas companies in 1875 decided to expand supplies to the domestic sphere, targeting the tool most important for sustaining the family cooker. The industry started its domestic trade with the assumption that consumers would buy gas cookers out right: 'Given a free choice, there is no question between buying and hiring. Gas companies would much rather the customer was the owner of the whole of his appliances' (Goodall, 1993, p. 547). The gas company correctly intuited the middle class' interest in owning a gas cooker. The wealthy quickly adopted the appliance, the infrastructure for domestic gas expanded, and interest in this modern alternative to coal grew.

Soon the middle-class market was saturated with gas cookers and this target population proved insufficient to increase the usage of gas. Despite their interest in this cleaner fuel and time-saving technologies, few working-class households had the means to purchase the stoves. Gas companies considered how they could get the working classes to cook with gas (Goodall, 1993, p. 556). Because utility companies understood themselves to be suppliers of fuel and not manufacturers or retailers of household equipment, they did conceive that hire purchase could solve the problem of affordability. Instead, following the advice of a municipal councillor, with first-hand knowledge of his constituents' daily lives, the gas companies tested the working classes' propensity to pay back their debts. While they could not pay all at once as the wealthy did, the councillor assured the gas company that if they provided stoves as part of a rental service included in their gas contract, people would make the regular rental payments.

The councillor was correct; the working classes dutifully paid rent in exchange for the cooker. By 1905, about 42% of gas cookers were privately owned, mostly by the middle classes. In a bid to expand the market, the gas company accepted assurances that customers would willingly acquire stoves paid for as part of their metered gas bill (Goodall, 1993, p. 547). Twenty years later gas cookers adorned most kitchens in urban England – half owned privately, the rest obtained through rental arrangements. In urban neighbourhoods gas cookers became caught up in the discourse of modernization. People argued that the gas cooker brought economic benefits and social esteem. The ownership of a gas cooker came to represent 'as good a mark of respectability as keeping a gig' in working-class communities: the tallyman was even more generous to gas cooker homes for he saw the family as a better credit risk (Goodall, 1993, p. 544).

The mass marketing vision of the utility operators was imprinted upon the stoves they made. Similar to phone companies, these public utilities not only built and maintained the pipes and tanks that channelled the gas through the city, but they also retained responsibility for the production and maintenance of cookers. Cookers were as endpoints in the household use of gas, not household appliances. Victorian concern with thrift may have guided the design which combined work-like pragmatism and minimal costly replacements and repairs. The gas companies' interest lay in increasing the flow of gas, and their profit. The men who designed the black cookers understood little about women's cooking experience, or their interest in kitchen décor. They therefore designed this household fixture for low cost, durability, and maximum functionality. Like Ford's mass produced model T, the utility stove came in one colour, black. The cookers lived up to their purpose. Virtually indestructible 'many of them were still in use when the industry was nationalized in 1949, some surviving until natural gas conversion between 1967 and 1977' (Goodman, 1993, p. 556).

By the 1930s, electricity providers began to compete for the market. Susan Bowden's historical study of the electricity companies, focused on the interwar period, documents their introduction of credit facilities to expand markets, encourage people to use more electricity, and win market share from the gas providers (Bowden, 1990, p. 52). Few people could purchase electric cookers, water, and space heaters at the time. 'In 1936, 75 per cent of the population's weekly income was £5 or less. Refrigerators cost 25 per cent; cookers 15 per cent and electric fires 1 per cent of a manufacturer's average annual earnings' (p. 61). Suppliers also believed that the public was unwilling to switch from gas to electricity without incentives (Bowden, 1990, p. 55).

People rented equipment, according to the Welwyn Electricity Company, because they preferred not to shoulder 'the responsibility of ownership of apparatus which they could not understand' (Bowden, 1990, p. 63). According to Bowden, the electricity companies correctly understood the conservatism in the marketplace. Consumers, particularly women, saw little reason to switch electricity, mainly because their gas cookers were economical and durable (Bowden, 1990, p. 64). To shift this attitude, the electricity companies used hire purchase to encourage people to acquire new modern appliances. The uptake of hire purchase schemes with local authorities was rapid, with 25% offering hire purchase in 1929, as compared with 84% in 1934 (Bowden, 1990, p. 55).

Manufacturers marketed the new cookers aggressively in women's magazines, swaddling the gleaming white stoves in the powerful rhetoric of modernity. The shiny new electric white goods became the status symbols of modernity and cleanliness achieved by going electric. In contrast, after WWI the black gas cooker's cast iron solidity seemed dated among the space age lines of the chrome and aluminium appliances of the electric age. 'The old black cookers supplied on rent became "out of joint with fashion and desire" the utilities concluded' (Goodman, 1993, pp. 555–6). Middle-class women expressed their growing sense of domestic empowerment with new white cookers. Working-class women not wanting to feel that they were leaving their children behind on the times added the white cooker to their home. Hire purchase gave working-class women the ability to acquire white goods they could not dream of owning if they had to pay for them outright. The impact of hire purchase was dramatic. Field's analysis shows that the overall proportion of customers with rental appliances especially within the working classes, dropped dramatically by 1930 (Goodall, 1993). Hire purchase emerged the financial instrument of choice for decorating the home with stylish furnishings leading Simonds to declare in 1940 that 'the whole business of hire-purchase agreements which is now for good or evil, a necessary part of our social life' (Simonds, 1940, p. 238).

American automobile financing, British roundabouts

John Maynard Keynes, with nationalist sensibilities, kept a keen eye towards America. American car manufacturers' efficient production techniques and aggressive global marketing impressed Keynes, as did the US' ability to organize its mass production distribution systems in the interest of consumers. Keynes also felt the US had an advantage because they produced more statistics to base their economic decisions upon and made bold use of financing tools. Keynes championed the formation of a British automobile industry to replicate that of the US. The British appetite for autos was clear, it being the biggest European market for autos before 1914. Keynes was aware of the importance of linking financial and industrial policy. The core idea of his famous work *The General Theory of Employment, Interest and Money* (1936) suggested that bringing financial and industrial sectors closer together would propel rising standards of living. Yet, his plans for a mass automobile market in Britain failed during his lifetime, mainly because he neglected to appreciate that cultural values were as important as industrial ones. The banks refused to follow Keynes' rally into the luxury goods credit market.

The British car market was highly attractive to Henry Ford who found British consumers receptive to his automobiles in 1908. London consumers prepaid for 400 Model Ts even before they arrived in London. Building on this early import success, Ford opened its first British dealership in 1910, followed by a production plant a year later near Manchester. By 1913 about 6100 cars rolled of Ford assembly lines (Laux, 1963). The Model T became the best selling car in Britain, claiming 30% of the market in the 1920s. GM followed Ford into the British market, shipping assembled cars to Europe for sale. Since the cost of shipping was prohibitive after the war, GM opened its own production facilities, and in 1925 purchased the British car company, Vauxhall. In 1931 Ford opened a massive plant in Dagenham Essex (Ford of Britain, 2008).

Despite clear demand, Labastille suggests that American car finance companies entered with trepidation into foreign markets viewing them 'as something complicated and mysterious'. They felt indigenous moneylenders had the upper hand (Labastille, 1932, p. 209). These companies worried about difficulties in collecting funds, due to the longer terms of credit customary in the UK. Throwing caution to the wind, in 1919 Continental Guaranty of America created a British subsidiary, United Dominions Trust (UDT) dedicated to the handling of credit sales for motor cars. By 1929, the company ran hire purchase schemes for Austin, Chrysler, Crossley, Darracq, Dodge Bros., Essex, Fiat, Hudson, Lea Francis, Morris, Renault, Rhose, Singer, Sunbeam, Talbot, and Wolseley (Bowden & Collins, 1992, p. 125).

Bowden and Collins provide a case to demonstrate the extra ordinary ambivalence the Bank of England held towards consumer credit during the interwar period. Concerned with reviving the economy after WWI, the Bank of England 'determined upon a most unusual course – to encourage a particular form of financial innovation by singling out the leading market operator for specially favoured treatment' (Bowden &

Collins, 1992, p. 126). They selected UDT because of its track record for prudence. Although the Bank of England wanted credit to stimulate the economy, the bank insisted that UDT privilege business undertakings in national interest. UDT was to ensure that credit supported the acquisition of the 'necessary and useful', not 'consumer's indulgence in luxury products'. Finally, UDT's activities were not to clash with those of other credit institutions (Bowden & Collins, 1992, p. 128). This union promised to ensure that consumer credit continued to operate largely outside of the banking sector, as it always had, and that American financiers faced little competition financing growth in the automobile market.

Recognizing the growing importance of independent consumer finance for its future, in 1919 GM also launched a subsidiary called The General Motors Acceptance Corporation (GMAC), dedicated to managing the company's instalment sales (Flugge, 1929, p. 151). In 1925 GM extended its in-house deferred payment schemes to Britain. GM experienced an immediate reward with a 'tremendous volume of motor sales between 1925 and 1929' (Labastille, 1932, p. 211). The initial attraction of these credit businesses to auto makers was to smooth fluctuations in demand (Bowden & Turner, 1993, p. 252). Labastille argues that GM believed that their aggressive financial marketing techniques also contributed significantly to increased car sales. By 1928, hire purchase financed 60% of cars sold in the UK. Still, moral stumbling blocks inhibited car credit expansion. According to Gordon's analysis, banks that lent credit readily to industries, believed it out of the question to lend directly to consumers. Gordon suggests bankers saw consumer-spending as part of the economic problem, certainly not its solution. As a result, non-banking institutions handled the growing hire purchase credit transactions that rose from less than £1 million in 1920 to more than £15 million in 1939.

The authors of the Macmillan Report placed the fault for the post-war depression on lack of productivity and consumers who lived beyond their means, with lack of 'concern for the morrow' (Scott, 2002, p. 195). Schwartz, in 1936, argued against those who viewed hire purchase as a magic escape from the contradictions of the capitalist economy (Schwartz, 1936, p. 183). Refusing Keynes's demand economics, Schwartz argued that hire purchase had not revved up economic growth but retarded it by funnelling wealth through intermediaries some of them foreign (Schwartz, 1936, p. 185). Schwartz suggested that rising prices were the result of retailers clawing back defaulted loans. The implication: good, honest, people of thrift were footing the bill for the carelessness of spendthrifts. While Schwartz agreed that credit was a powerful instrument, he supported the banks' decision to curtail the use of credit in the industrial sector, because, industry would more wisely utilize the investment to purchase useful and productive things that benefited the entire community. Schwartz argued that only the individual consumer not the wider community benefitted from consumer purchases, thus, consumer credit was a problem for the economy: 'Instead of a factory or a modernized plant or a fleet of lorries the community has a number of motor cars and pianos; instead of a screw in a ship a saxophone' (Schwartz, 1936, p. 195).

The reluctant marketing of car debt

The lingering moral shame that surrounded consumer credit, according to Bowden and Turner added pressure on some financial providers to make the practice appear respectable. This, the authors suggest, explains why some credit arrangements for car financing were written in favour of the elite, not the mass. For example, in October 1929, Gibson Jarvie, Managing Director of UDT, stressed the importance of creditworthiness and respectability in the decisions about financing consumer car purchases. UDT concluded that business ownership, marriage, and children were the signs of creditworthiness. Yet, very few members of the working class met all of these requirements, let alone one of them. The requirement of 25% down, although lower than down payments in the US, was still 'prohibitive for the majority of the [British] population'. Automobile payments in the 1930s accounted for between 27 and 58 percent 'of the annual income of the average salaried household' (Bowden & Turner, 1993, p. 253). Thus, it is no surprise that the 1930s automobile market was confined to the upper classes who purchased high-priced cars, and upper-middle-class professionals who preferred smaller less expensive cars, for they were the only two groups who could receive credit (Bowden & Turner, 1993).

The social shame surrounding consumer credit, according to O'Connell, explains why in a sample of car manufacturers' advertisements placed in the magazines *Autocar* and *Motor* between 1919 and 1938, hire purchase options were mentioned in only 4% of them. Given that by 1939 up to 70% of car purchase in the UK were through hire purchase, he speculates that perhaps retailers (and their customers) had moral qualms about talking about consumer credit for what seemed like luxury goods. His study finds that throughout the British automotive sector car dealers maintained 'a very discretionary marketing of hire purchase'. Generally speaking the car industry felt that mention of hire purchase schemes should only be placed in the footnotes of trader's advertising or suggested behind closed doors in a sales room. As O'Connell states, 'To do otherwise would jeopardise business with cash customers. Eleven years later the same magazine was still writing of the "old-fashioned but powerful prejudice against hire purchase on the part of the very class of people who are most justified in employing it"' (O'Connell, 2004). Motorists, like the car industry, O'Connell suggests, appear to have taken great care 'to conceal their use of hire purchase'.

Yet in a survey of display ads found in *Times of London* between 1910 and 1939 for cars built by General Motors or its subsidiary Vauxhall, over 10% (33 of 300 ads reviewed) made reference to deferred payment or credit arrangements available. The headlines for a Buick ad from the early 1920s, for example, boldly claimed: 'Your car is part of your home. Get it the same way'. The pitch draws a parallel between hire purchase and mortgages claiming, 'Houses, and even large estates, are obtained out of income. Why not motor cars?' The advertising text suggests GM marketers deflected the moral taint of hastily buying before you can afford to, with the legitimacy of homeownership: 'If you had waited till you could buy your home outright you might still be without one. But your home has brought you comfort and satisfaction. So would a car'. The ad concludes that the GM plan is like a club, which is financed by themselves and exclusive to their own clients. Thus, GM credit is presented as respectably, 'sound, dignified and economical'. However reluctantly, the practice of buying luxury goods like cars on the credit made inroads into the British moral economic of debt.

GM understood credit as a competitive advantage in the market, and did not shy away from aggressively promoting it to sell cars. Indigenous credit systems simply could not compete with GM's salesmanship. By 1938, dealers organized 60–70% of cars sold in the UK on instalment terms (Bowden & Turner, 1993, p. 252). According to Bowden and Turner, 'hire purchase credit transactions rose from less than £1 million in 1920 to more than £15 million in 1939. The terms of financing in Britain were even more favourable than the US, where financier expected larger deposits (1/3 on new; 40% on used cars) and balances to be paid off in as little as 12 months. In Britain, lower down payments and long contracts prevailed. The British economy and marketplace was always distinctive to that of the continent, but the embedding of American financial techniques further distinguished Britain's financial market from the rest of Europe. Those on the continent understood Britain as the best place to obtain good terms and conditions for automobile financing (p. 252).

Your car is a part of your home. Get it the same way.

IF you had waited till you could buy your home outright
you might still be without one.

But your home has brought you comfort and satisfaction.
So would a car . . . and you can acquire one as simply as
your home, without disturbing a single investment. You
can drive away a Buick-4 Majestic Tourer for £122 16s.,
the balance being divided into twelve monthly payments of
£24 8s. The General Motors plan, financed by themselves
and exclusive to their own clients, is sound, dignified and
economical.

*We will gladly give you full
particulars of the General
Motors plan of deferred
payments, and will demon-
strate the merits of the Car.*

Houses, and even large
estates, are obtained
out of income.
Why not motor cars?

Figure 3.2 General Motors ad Socializing Car financing by referring to the respectability of home financing.

Car markets proved an equivocal test of Keynes's ideas about state investment to underwrite economic expansion: to some degree the importation and promotion of US style instalment purchase schemes had a significant impact on the market for private cars in spite of the resistance of the British automobile industry, which refrained from promoting sales on credit. Still, many factors mitigated against private automobile ownership on a scale achieved in America, including the lack of roads, the prevalence of public transport, urban concentrations in addition to the general reluctance to go into debt for 'luxuries'. Although financing was attractive, British consumers shouldered much higher retail prices for domestic-made, foreign-controlled cars. Keynes's claims that credit would stimulate a mass-market car industry were disappointed; American style mass marketing simply didn't have the same impact in Britain. Despite the temptation of glossy new models, easy financing, or slashed prices, sales of cars beyond the middle classes did not parallel those in the USA (Bowden & Turner, 1993, p. 257).

According to Peter Scott, hire purchase remained a dubious option among the working- and lower-middle classes in the interwar period. People associated hire purchase with pretentious people who engaged in reckless indebtedness for the purchase of 'luxuries' to assert a social status beyond their means. Thus, people hid hire purchase transactions from neighbours, friends and, often, most family members (Scott, 2002, p. 196). This shroud of silence created a fertile ground for consumer abuse as unscrupulous snatch-back retailers reclaimed the goods for resale after borrowers had paid a sizable amount of the value (Scott, 2002). Hire purchase acquired a bad name. In 1938, the state set out to address these issues with the Hire Purchase Act. Whether the bill fulfilled its objective, to protect consumers, is questionable; but, the Hire Purchase Act created two clear, if unintended, consequences. First, without research evidence, small lenders came to bare the blame for consumer abuse. Yet, Scott argues small lenders were likely more socially responsible because lenders were 'tied to community mores and client retribution'. Big financial houses, like GMAC, known for their aggressive collection techniques, quickly distanced themselves from small lenders, highlighting how their large networks processed consumers more equitably. These circumstances resulted in the bill aiding greater monopoly control over hire purchase. A second unintended consequence of the Hire Purchase Act, was how state intervention legitimated consumer lending. If the state government regulated hire purchase, was it not clear that the practice was lawful and morally sanctioned, albeit within proscribed limits?

You've never had it so good: New towns, austerity, and class mobility in post-war Britain

Government expenditures mounted dramatically between 1939 and 1941 as financing the war effort became a great priority. To help pay the bill the government enforced an austerity ethos through banking, self-sacrifice, and rationing (Muller, 1913). Frugality was justified by patriotism and prudent savings channelled towards the contribution to victory. Having won the war, the British government faced an equally daunting task: to pay off the accumulated national debt. To shift the country from its war footing to mass peacetime prosperity, Keynes's ideas about mass consumerism began to underwrite Labour's post-war vision. Massive state investment funnelled into a social safety, health infrastructure, and a state housing policy. Nothing spoke more powerfully, to this moment of state control than the 1946 nationalization of the banking sector to combat inflation.

New towns: New consumerism

In the context of post-WWII, the attitudes towards debt, thrift, and consumerism shifting and turning since the ninenteenth century, experienced yet another layer of change. The early modernist celebration of debt exemplified in rhetoric of the Bloomsbury group may have helped ease some of the taboo that had surrounded personal finance, but the extension of a mass populous ethos, perfected during wartime, during times of peace underwrote significant changes in the institutionalization of debt. Welfare state provisions and growing wages shaped new lifestyles, creating a different set of desires and interest in such matters as leisure, convenience, home pride.

Welfare state policies ironically fuelled increased debt loads. Covering such areas as health, education, housing, and pensions, state programs replaced and secularized the Victorian charitable foundations, which had provided a limited and erratic social safety net. Money once socked away for family emergencies could be freed up for meeting and expanding upon daily needs. Further, work was more plentiful. The destruction of the country by war required a great deal of clean-up, and interest in large scale development projects was high. Weekly wages rose from 8.30 pounds a week in 1940 to 15.25 pounds in 1950. Pre-war hire purchase increased tenfold by 1950 (Clapson, 1999). People did not go into debt out of necessity, as was often the case in the nineteenth century, but because they imagined a future promising enough to be able to shoulder more debt (Clapson, 1999, p. 167). Britain's collective financial fantasy began.

Compared with the sins of war, hire purchase hardly seemed a sin. While consumer goods were acquired on hire purchase often caused anxiety to families (Taylor & Rogaly, 2007) and as Davies (1992) notes, in principle, in the 1950s, 'going into debt for purchases other than houses' remained an aversion, after experiencing the fragility of life during the war, it simply seemed silly to wait to enjoy the benefits of a fridge or carpet. A comfortable home was deemed important, creating sound property values in the eyes of friends, family, and neighbours.

The housing market, so important to the dynamics of consumer finance, expanded. Low cost housing provision, begun in earnest during the Edwardian period, increased dramatically after WWI; but, nothing compared to the political efforts to house returning soldiers after the second war. The stock of housing owned by the state rose from 10% to 25% after the war. The New Towns Act of 1946 set out to create a ring of new towns beyond the London Greenbelt allowing more working-class people to own a home (Hart, 1956). The state-subscribed living arrangements followed 'the popular urban terrace house arrangement that consisted typically of four rooms: two bedrooms in the upper part of the home, and a kitchen and parlour on the lower – two up, two down'. This housing style became the standard: 'Irrespective of the size of the floor area of the house, the organization of space followed the same pattern' (Kalliney, 2001, p. 110).

These homes further transformed older patterns of domesticity. Although family sizes of the middle classes had reduced since the mid-nineteenth century, small families of two children (who fit in the two-up-two-down model) became the norm in the post-war period. The keeping of kin and lodgers continued much longer in Britain than the US; for example, into the 1970s, in Britain 'some 25 percent of households [were] living with relatives' compared with 9% in the Unites States'; but the new homes favoured small family groupings. Tellingly, Clapson's research on women's experience of the New Towns found their interests refocused from the traditional street community to the privacy of their homes. The pleasures of private family life and consumption that began to blossom in the nineteenth century, became more widespread across all classes in the twentieth.

Into the new living an array of consumer goods entered, leading to the expansion of the domestic economy. Moving to the new towns brought 'many luxury recreational goods and labour-saving devices which rendered the working-class home a more comfortable place of relaxation, and television sets, record players, and functional electrical appliances, grew extensively in working-class homes from the mid 1950s' (Clapson, 1999, p. 346). Smaller family units give parents more time and resources to lavish on their children. The social advancement and contentment of one's children augmented older definitions of community respectability (Scott, 2006). Children increasingly motivated consumption. Many of the new commodities in the home were purchased under the pretext of 'gifts to the children'. It was common for mothers to give children clothes and shoes for their birthdays. Although not always appreciated by eight-year-olds, durable goods such as fridges and cookers became gifts. In short, the cultural impulse of providing a leg up for one's children, and older notions of inheritance served to break down the barriers of thrift (Scott, 2006, p. 36).

The Victorian devotion to cleanliness extended into the twentieth century New Towns. Domestic technologies grew in popularity along with women's full and part-time employment. Culture reclassified household appliances from a luxury to a necessity. Changes in shopping habits contributed to demand for technologies. Unlike London, the new towns had the space for American style supermarkets that spread after the war. Bringing butcher, green grocer, poultries, and bakers together under one roof, the supermarkets held attraction for women with time to shop. Although the new supermarkets refused to extend credit, as was the tradition in corner shops, they did over time happily accept credit cards (Boyd & Peircy, 1963, p. 34). Weekly instead of daily market shopping required larger fridges and storage capacities. To transport larger amounts of food and travel to the supermarket that was some distance from home made the car more a necessity. While the future was reflected in these changes, in 1955 more electric washing machines and bicycles were sold than automobiles (Downham & Treasure, 1956).

The new towns' young aspiring populations assumed the lion's share of hire purchase. 'Homes were the entrée into the consumer economy, linking up land speculators and builders, along with manufacturers of consumer durables' (Hoyt, 1966, p. 412). Household goods accounted for 50% of all hire purchase contracts (Boyd & Peircy, 1963, p. 35). Once people started paying for their home instalments, the next step – was to start buying durable goods the same way – was not such a drastic change. Hire purchase created a bridge upon which big-ticket durable goods and furniture entered the home. Scott finds it 'no surprise' that the new towns coincided with the expansion of material goods 'such as vacuum cleaners, refrigerators, and televisions. The furnishing of the home played a major role in the politics of hire purchase' (Scott, 2002, p. 201). Still, maintaining a modern lifestyle with heat, light, and transportation was costly.

Research confirmed for politicians the importance of hire purchase for the economy. An investigation by the National Bureau of Economic Research, in a longitudinal study (1929–41) 'ascertained that each change of 1% in the amount of national income caused the change of over 2–3% in automobile sales credit and 3% in credit used for purchase of other durable goods against deferred payments' (Einzig, 1956, p. 18). These findings confirmed that consumer's true discretionary income extended beyond their wages to include their willingness to use credit to buy now and pay later. A new Hire Purchase Act of 1954 sought to bring 'the 1938 Act into line with the changing value of money'. Four years later, as modern advertising expanded, the government introduced a Hire Purchase Advertising Bill that sought to prevent consumers from the guile of advertisements such as: 'Yours for £1' or 'Yours for 5s. a week'; but which failed to state 'what deposit has to be paid or how many payments will have to be made' (House of Commons, 1957). In a 1955 confessional article, Morrell outlines his experiences of working in a furniture company recording a significant difference in treatment between of working- and middle-class consumers. At the middle-class stores 'it was possible to buy comparable furniture on hire purchase at a total cost slightly below the cash price charged to working class customers'. Morrell estimated that 90% of working-class customers used the hire purchase facilities compared to 50% in the middle-class shop. In 1955, the working-class shop charged a 60% margin compared to 40% at the middle-class store. The store charged working-class customers over £2 the actual cost to open an application with the company (Morrell, 1956, p. 27).

Observing the new landscape, Harold Macmillan in a 1957 speech famously told Britons: 'You've never had it so good. In sheer material and credit terms, the lives of the majority of people were far in advance of that pre war'. In many ways this was true. The extension of credit was productive, generating growth in the British economy. Britain's hire purchase market was the largest in Europe. Retail stores increasingly competed to win consumers with the offer of hire purchase, which in turn increased the spread of this credit instrument. By 1961 the total hire purchase debt was estimated at £2.5 billion – a figure double the amount in 1958. 'Spending on credit had been transformed rather remarkably into a form of strength, a way to increase energy and even build capital' (Boyd & Peircy, 1963, p. 29). It was not the amount of money that one had in the bank that mattered but their ability to mass capital and have a sizable line of credit.

Still, while consumption and financing post-war increasingly appeared like that in America hire purchase and sales of goods never reached the same levels as America, a point that frustrated American marketers trying to sell their goods to Britons. American marketers entering the British market believed 'consumers abroad are much more reluctant to incur indebtedness'. Compared to the diverse immigrant populations of the US who embraced goods as toeholds to climb up the social ladder, the more homogeneous British community seemed resigned to their station in life. British culture, carrying the legacy of Victorian values, continued to suggest that social advancement and respectability had to be earned through honest exertion, the din of ones own effort and the sweat of the brow. Credit remained a non-respectable means of achieving respectability. British women, claimed the marketers, were more likely to replace a used item with another one exactly the same than to indulge in novelty. Boyd and Peircy noted that compared to the American consumer, marketers believed the British consumer lacked the desire 'to change and displayed a willingness to put up with no small amount of inconvenience – remaining wholly conservative tastes' (Boyd & Peircy, 1963, p. 35). Why, American marketer's bemoaned, would consumers not complain?

New lifestyles supported by credit

According to Taylor, traditional systems of local credit began to fade during the Edwardian period, as levels of prosperity, changing patterns in consumption and knowledge, and use of new forms of credit occurred. Many commentators highlighted the changing neighbourhood sense of community. Blumer (1985) noted, 'Most neighbourhoods today do not constrain their inhabitants into strong bonding relationships with one another' (p. 439). People no longer had to rely on one another in the same way or look to the street lender or butcher for a loan. State provisions replaced friendly societies and the meetings at the pub they initiated. New expectations of privacy combined with women's increased presence in the workforce dealt a blow to the door-to-door financial trade. According to Taylor (2002), younger generations resisted the old credit firms of their parents (p. 36). The fate of the pawnshop demonstrates this decline. The number of pawnshops reached their peak at the break of WWI when 5087 pawnshops were in operation. By 1949, only 1654 pawnshops were still in business. In 1987 Lohr reported that there were only 175 pawnshops operating in Britain.

Hire purchase shifted the focus of credit transactions from the local and personal lender to institutions. The character of financial exchange altered. Lenders once knew those who they lent to intimately, by name, by face, and vice versa. They met face to face in the home, on the street, in the pub. Yet, Taylor warns against romanticizing the lending of the past. He argues that pressure must have been increased when the borrower did not look on the transaction as a loan but as money 'borrowed from a neighbour' (Taylor, 2002, p. 50). Women may well have been unduly pressured into taking up the services exactly because it was offered in a personalized form. The personal forms of lending, according to Taylor, were not simply enchanting: 'There is often an instrumental element involved in the solidaristic relationships that existed within the working class' (Taylor, 2002, p. 35). The ability to say no was perhaps difficult when the person offering the service was a member of the community. It was perhaps within this milieu that the British working class forged their great propensity for paying debts.

Although conservatives strongly opposed the growing state-debt amassed to support social advances and homeownership, it proved politically impossible for the conservatives in the 1950s and early 1960s to extend the private household and rental market (Weiler, 2003; Gwen & Nevin, 1957). Yet, ambivalent attitudes surrounded state housing and provisions. The new towns had their critics on the left and the right. The working classes' suburbanization appeared to individualize and erode community ties. Even those who benefited from state housing and provisions complained. In a culture still haunted by the ghost of self-reliance, state support challenged traditional definitions of masculinity and bread-winner pride. 'Wages were the one thing a working class man could call his own' (Kalliney, 2001, p. 110).

Thus, even during its moment of greatest strength and expansiveness, the welfare state and mass market in Britain was never complete and was vulnerable to attack. As much as critics may have bemoaned the demise of authentic working-class communities, according to Clapson, the majority of working-class women who moved to new suburban housing estates reported contentment and a sense of pleasure in their new homes and higher standards of living. The post-1945 period instilled new expectations for the future, growing confidence in home comforts and convenience, and a modernized attitude towards luxury goods and hire purchase. Still, progressive retailers, American automobile manufacturers, financial houses, and building societies made the greatest contribution towards advertising, marketing, and provisioning personal finance. This situation changed post-1960 as the banks slowly turned their attention to the consumer marketplace; a fateful institutional reorientation that is the subject of the next chapter.

4
Gentlemanly Bankers Adopt a New Set of Manners

This chapter explores changes in bank organizational cultures, up to the 1980s. Notable by their absence, the British banks played little direct role in personal financial and credit market, until the 1960s when forces conspired to encourage their change. While American banks had made substantial inroads into the personal finance sector since the 1920s, it was not until two decades after WWII that the British banks began a massive transformation, reaching out to the country's unbanked.

To illuminate the discussion of bank culture I analyed 805 bank advertisements, sampled between 1950 and 2000 from the History of Advertising Trust archive, the central depository of British advertising agency designs. Advertising gathered from the newspaper archive expanded the sample. Weaving together histories of the institutional structures of the banks, I consider the cultural contribution of bank marketing (Stafford & King, 1983; Ackrill & Hannah, 2001). Using a combination of content and interpretive analysis, I draw attention to changing banking values, how those values connect to institutional changes, and what types of cultural problems the banks' promotional discourse sought to address. I also consider how the banks defined the financial marketplace in their advertising: What stories they told consumers, What advice they offered for how to manage personal finances, What products they promoted? How their messages changed over time? How might these be linked to broader cultural changes?

Many arguments set out to explain the banking sector's slow approach to the personal financial market in the early twentieth century; protectionist state regulation stands as one of the most recurrent. Some members of the banking community showed an interest in expanding into consumer finance. Evidence suggests a readiness on the part of bankers to embrace change and innovate. For example, bankers took advantage of the redrafting of credit laws in 1958 and 1974 and the less restrictive banking context post-Big Bang, to advance their services and increase their reach into the personal finance markets. Yet, conservatism lingered. The banks found it difficult to shed their traditional character mainly because it had served exceptionally well in the past. In the global imagination, the British bank stood as the very definition of prudence, stability, and respectability. This perception, crucial to legitimating the economy, was secured by state regulation and the legacy of the gentlemanly spirit that took root in the financial sector, where 'particularly London commercial, banking and money market interests – became allied with the aristocracy' (Brantlinger, 1996, pp. 236–7).

Gentlemanly banking

The joint-stock banks were never stable institutions, but they took every opportunity to market themselves as stable in relation to the private banking system they replaced. Between the formation of the Bank of England in 1664 and the early nineteenth century, British finance was funnelled through thousands of private bankers (Davies, 2002). With their small capital base these banks experienced frequent bankruptcy causing great misery for their clients. In 1825, five private banks (Lloyds, Barclays, Midland, National Provincial, and Westminster) incorporated. By the turn of the century, these joint-stock banks held a dominion over finance by merging or dissolving the litany of private banks and transforming the economic institutional landscape.

Two factors secured the legitimacy of the modern, joint-stock banks. First, their massive financial networks shaped a monopoly that won the favour of the state. The joint-stock banks forged their dominion by establishing an early and effective cartel that suppressed competition, focused on standardization of practices, set minimum and maximum interest rates, and fixed service charges. A high degree of concentration distinguished the British banks sector (Bali & Capie, 1982). By 1920, the Big Five banks, as they became known, controlled 80% of all deposits, up from 25% only 50 years before (Winton, 1982). Correctly reading the winds of British wealth, banks focused on land-holding classes not tradesmen, because these clients offered a steady stream of deposits from their rentals and made few withdrawals. Besides storing the precious jewellery and documents of the gentry, bankers offered business advice to clients in metropolitan areas, arranged remittance services, and organized cheque and bill conversions. They went on to specialize in circulating their massive funds through short-term credit to large-scale financial borrowers. In this process, London emerged as the central hub of finance because cheques cleared through the City (Stafford & King, 1983).

The state befriended the banks because politicians appreciated the easy influence over the economy the new banking structure permitted. It was more straightforward for the Bank of England to communicate directives via five massive, relatively standardized financial networks, rather than through thousands of private bankers. Most significantly, because the banks oversaw the lion's share of financial transactions, Parliament protected them from bankruptcy. This was a powerful seal of legitimacy: before the banks foundered, the country's tax system would have to collapse. Further, regulation provided the banks a dominion over the powerful current-account market, barring the non-banking sector (Building Societies, Trustee Savings Bank, and the Co-operative Bank) from participation. The banks also enjoyed protection from international competition. All of these factors helped the banks to market themselves as secure and respectable institutions.

Yet, state regulation was not completely in the banking sector's interest. For example, because banks were understood as the principle lever for controlling the economy, the state subjected banks to more heavy regulation. For example, the Bank of England encouraged banks to provide more favourable rates to companies in an effort to strengthen the national economy (Collins, 1988). In 1946, the state nationalized the banks to prevent a recurrence of the economic problems that had arisen after WWI: 'During the six years of conflict the government took more control of the economy than it had in 1914–1918' (Healy, 1993, p. 170). According to Collins, 'War and the attitude of authorities helped "institutionalise" the non-competitive attitude of clearers' (Collins, 1988, p. 583). Regulation also barred banks from the small mortgage market, insurance and other services that the state defined as the providence of the non-banking sector.

Therefore, embroiled in the affairs of state and industry, in the first half of the twentieth century, the banks had little concern for the public's everyday financial needs. In the immediate post-war period, for example, Lloyds decided against moving into the consumer market on the grounds that 'small credit-worthy borrowers were already catered for, that it would be inflationary' (Winton, 1982, p. 44). Although they offered loans, overdraft protection, and other financial services of interest to most Britons, banks preferred to target the business of the upper and middle classes. Remarkably, although retailers and utility providers had demonstrated the population's respectful propensity to pay back their debts, bankers believed that borrowers 'would probably be persons of poor repute or the improvident' (Winton, 1982, p. 161).

Likewise, the public did not have much need for the banks. Britain's strong cash culture, encouraged by the Truck Laws passed in 1831, did little to promote the general use of financial services. Legally workers had to be paid 'in the coin of the realm', in order to prevent 'truck', which according to Walker was a common nineteenth century practice:

> Workmen were paid in the form of orders for goods redeemable only at the 'tommy-shop' on the site, the owner of which was commonly in league with the employer and who commonly sold inferior goods at inflated prices. The Act accordingly required payment of wages to be in cash and forbade deductions save under stringent conditions.
>
> (Walker, 2001, p. 1240)

The Truck Laws embedded the practice of paying employees weekly in cash. Truck laws remained until the 1960s when that, 'it was made permissible, not withstanding, the Truck Act, [to honour] the employee's request to pay by cheque, money order, or direct credit to a bank'. Despite massive industrial growth and marketplace expansion after WWII, the public continued to use cash that circulated within local networks of family, peers, work, store, and pub (Blackwell & Seabrook, 1985). Weekly wage packets stuffed with bills remained dominant in Britain until the late 1970s (Walker, 2001, p. 1240). Further, banks offered few services of interest to the average consumer. Those who wished to save or invest their cash, or acquire a line of credit, did so from a diverse array of building societies, cooperatives, post offices, Trustees' Savings, and National Savings banks. The building societies offered some important advantages over the banks for working people: higher rates of interest on savings, more accessible accounts and branch networks, and longer hours (Ackrill, 1993, p. 158). People did not appear comfortable taking credit from the banks, even though the banks charged lower rates of interest. Instead, people turned to financial houses and manufacturers to arrange hire purchase (Collins, 1988; Boyd & Piercy, 1963). Indeed, through most of the twentieth century 'retailers themselves [held] a much larger proportion of the outstanding volume of instalment credit than in the US' (Winton, 1980, p. 170). Quite simply, the vast majority of the population did not conceive of the banks as potential financial service providers.

The second factor legitimizing the joint-stock banks' position in the economy was the professional personae they forged. Early private bankers did not possess airs, nor did the public hold private bankers in particularly high cultural esteem. In cultural terms, bankers were categorized along with other craft workers; bankers simply happened to work with coins instead of wood or iron. Yet, in the nineteenth century, as financial networks expanded and privileged individuals entered into the joint-stock banking trade, a sense of entitlement and a desire to distinguish emerged. Bankers redefined themselves as professionals, like doctors, lawyers, and professors. This early sense of professionalism, distinguished the banks from shopkeepers, because like all professionals bankers disliked overt salesmanship. While shopkeepers considered it proper to compete for punters, professionals viewed themselves as equals not adversaries, working together rather than against one another. This sense of professionalism aided the formation of the banking cartel.

The 'comparatively strong hold traditional aristocratic, gentlemanly, amateurish and anti-industrial values exerted on 20th century England' also tinted the joint-stock banks culture. Banking emerged as one of the preferred careers of the aristocracy, along with military service, politics, estate management, and writing (Ingham, 1996; Weiner & Mahoney, 1981; Lash & Urry, 1994; Cain & Hopkins, 1992). While acknowledging that many factors influenced banking culture, insight into bank culture might be gleamed by considering the values that public school and elite higher educational institutions, Oxford and Cambridge, maintained and imparted to some bankers and economists as they carried out their financial careers.

Elite schools in the early twentieth century encouraged public service, duty to nation, tradition, a well-rounded education, and excellence in diction and writing. Informed by a long lineage of theological traditions, education encouraged the development of character, as much as the development of the mind. Although novelist Beryl Bainbridge convincingly argues that gentlemanly nineteenth century character went down with the Titanic, gentlemanly spirit may well have found a refuge in the banks. Bankers saw social respect and authority as business aids. They displayed quiet dignity in their discussion of money matters, mindful of their client's privacy. According to Lynch, people considered the banker 'better than the vicar' at keeping a secret (Lynch & Lundqvist, 1996, p. 11). Bankers spoke little about the commission gathered for their services (Howcroft & Lavis, 1986). Ironically, the banker was somewhat indifferent to money, viewed it as a means to leisure and culture, but not a measure of creativity or character. Bankers practiced manners that helped make them appear, compared to others, uninfluenced by tides of fashion or fortune. They cultivated 'an image of stability, sobriety and dependability' (Ackrill, 1993, p. 151). This aloof demeanour signalled professionalism. For example, Healy's history of the Coutts Bank suggests that Mr Charles Adcock, the bank's chair up to 1951, prided himself on his refusal to meet with customers. Healy described Mr Adcock as 'fastidious about details', an 'exact man, impatient with carelessness', who 'hated idleness', and dressed very formally (Healy, 1993, p. 423). The practice of manners was a duty, performed to distinguish the public elite more than out of a bid to win the approval of others, convey intimacy, or emotional warmth. When correctly performed manners extended a sense of status.

To maximize trust, bankers conducted face-to-face meetings, often hosting others for a business lunch, or tea, lending a sense of leisure to their work. This pursuit of ease, gracefulness, and cultivated leisure that Margaret Thatcher later defined as laziness, is better understood as rather a different type of self-discipline and self-possession. For example, public schools encouraged highly disciplined competitive group exercises, particularly sports, funnelling individual effort in a team framework. Tradition and group honour were emphasized. Individuals gave themselves over to the *esprit de corps*. The point was to harmonize differences to keep order and suppress swagger, crass ego displays, and above all poor sportsmanship. Incremental adjustment was preferred to radical change. These types of values gave banking a club-like sensibility that supported the formation of a banking cartel.

Bankers' notions of thrift appealed to traditional notions of husbandry, paternalism, and religion. Bankers saw it as their duty to protect consumers from sinful appetites. We saw in Chapter 3, the reticence the Bank of England showed towards extending credit to luxury goods. Joint-stock bankers upheld this belief, distinguishing themselves as guardians of the customs of thrift. The banks distanced themselves from the practice of usury. They were of course, involved in hire purchase, because they lent short-term credit to financial houses, but because they did not play a direct role in organizing hire purchase for consumers, the banks could maintain a moral high ground (Einzig, 1956, p. 23). Retailers had offered hire purchase since at least 1850, but it took until 1955 for a bold Scottish bank to offer consumer credit. Conservative bankers across the country looked on in scorn and despite the clear promise of profit 'no other bank' followed suit for years (Fousek, 1958, p. 171).

Until the 1970s, banks operated more like monasteries or universities than businesses, structuring worker incentives upon status-based rewards. As rather closed businesses, banks trained their own and internally evaluated their employees, which enabled banks to effectively social-ize, reproduce, and prevent challenge to their cultures. Banks hired clean, well-mannered clerks. They valued literacy and neat handwriting more than customer service or salesmanship (Rae, 1886). Young bank-ers earned little money, but willingly traded immediate rewards for security. A job for life was the trophy for passing the inspection of the bank's hiring committee. Numerous 1950s bank ad messages targeted potential employees, rather than consumers. The ads promoted banking as a respectable career, for the bright young person, one, which would provide lifelong stability.

Banking staff conducted their business with an aura of authority, respect, and trust. The layout of the early banks emphasized the impor-tance of the bankers, not clients. Until the 1960s, maintaining accounts remained labour-intensive. Departments concentrated on processing accounts (i.e., receivables, payables), devoting more space to paperwork than consumers. The banks kept short bankers' hours to provide time to balance the books each day. Typical hours in 1950 ran from 11:00 a.m. to 3:30 p.m. The banks appreciated technology that reduced their labour (Davies, 2002).

Although banks focused on maintaining accounts, early twentieth century economists modelled a unique sensibility for the banks. British economics was thought to require a well-rounded education, where philosophy and argument were privileged over grand theories and number crunching (Wicke, 1994). In elite economic educational envi-ronments expanding the mind, seeking wisdom, and contributing to social betterment were valued above specific technical training (Hampden-Turner, 1984). For example, discussing Alfred Marshall, who founded Economics at Cambridge in the late nineteetnh century, Maynard Keynes, one of Marshall's brightest students, articulates the Renaissance knowledge base towards which the British economist was to aspire:

He must be mathematician, historian, statesman, philosopher – in some degree. He must understand symbols and speak in words. He must contemplate the particular in terms of the general, and touch abstract and concrete in the same flight of thought. He must study the present in light of the past for the purposes of the future. No part of man's nature or his institutions must lie entirely outside his regard. He must be purposeful and disinterested in a simultaneous mood; as aloof and incorruptible as an artist, yet sometimes as near the earth as a politician.

(Keynes, 1924, p. 322)

Alfred Marshall, product of a religious household, 'ensured that Cambridge economics was founded on the representation of character instead of empirical facts', a position distinct from American economic traditions that placed weight more exclusively on scientific principles (Trexler, 2007, p. 863). Elite British schools developed economic traditions from historical and political perspectives, and did not introduce technical training until 1899. Graduate business schools focusing on financial pragmatics did not exist until the 1960s.

These economic sentiments seeped into banking management structures in a variety of ways. For example, according to Stamp, one of the first government commissioned studies of the financial sector, the 1931 MacMillan report revealed that bankers viewed 'the management of currency and credit as an art, not a science' (Stamp, 1931, p. 430). They preferred 'a nice set of rule of thumb instruments' in economic research. Pragmatic and intimate, rules of thumb applied an approximate measure of the world, relying upon traditions, heritage, and the passing on of procedures of practice or experience (Ackrill, 1993, p. 154). Bankers made little effort to produce data or studies of their banking practices. As a result, according to Bain, the banks offered no statistical information about hire purchase and there was 'a dearth of even short articles on the subject'. The information that existed was 'fragmentary and of doubtful content and coverage' (Bain, 1966, p. 124). Those British bankers interested in larger financial trends, looked to American statistics to bolster their arguments for changes in the financial sector.

Advertising

The symbolic presence of banks in culture was also limited. Early bankers preferred to conduct business through word-of-mouth channels, instead of advertising. 'Each bank saw advertising as a low priority with a very low nominal budget for the limited and sole aim of keeping the name of the bank in the limelight, or at least out of the shade' (Stafford & King, 1983, p. 23). Some members of the banking community viewed advertising agencies as threats to the professional reputation they had worked so hard to build. The banks stressed the need to maintain a fiduciary relationship with customers, and according to Stafford, believed,

'Advertising has to be particularly sensitive to any communication, which might, in any way, be misrepresentative or exaggerated' (Stafford & King, 1983, p. 113). The banks imagined advertising to possess the power to overcome consumers' financial resolve, which they saw as their duty to protect. To maintain the cartel's *esprit de corps*, bankers forbade the use of television advertising, which they believed would ignite a promotional war between the banks. Bankers' fear of advertising interlocked with their general aversion towards the idea of selling financial services:

> For years financial groups shied away from the notion that their product could be sold like baked beans. There was the feeling that the saver might recoil in horror from a punchy commercial. 'We used to wait for consumers to walk off the street', says one bank marketing man.
> (Rothwell & Jowett, 1988, p. 13)

Suspicion towards advertising combined with the banks' meagre advertising budgets meant that financial accounts tended to be shuffled to the bottom of the agencies' lists of priorities, relegated to moderate creative talent, or used to train new agency staff (Burton, 1996).

Bank advertising that circulated in the 1950s reflected the culture outlined above. Advertisers emphasised bank honour, reputability, and trustworthiness. Because the cartel and bankers' sense of professionalism downplayed competition and distinction between banks, the ads sought to create general public respect towards the banking sector. The name of the bank typically appeared at the bottom of the message in large classical font, usually Times Roman print. As discussed in Chapter 1, a good name had long been associated with financial security. Promoting their good name signified that banks were solid and stable institutions that had a firm grip on the economy. The name of the bank, like barristers or doctors, signified a profession more than a business. Sometimes an emblem accompanied the bank's name, but because it varied in shape, these icons showed little adherence to principles of modern branding.

Reflecting banks' closed and tradition-oriented cultures, their 1950s ads conveyed a deep sense of nostalgia. In the image of the ads, the twentieth century had not even begun. Some designers went back as far as ancient times, such as a 1951 Midland campaign that revolved around fairy sprites and Greek goddesses. Victorian streetscapes were common, although the wide boulevards repeated in the advertisements were more reminiscent of Paris than London. A common motif was men in morning coats and women in dresses en route to the bank.

The sheer physical presence of the banks was stressed, with the front of the bank endlessly shown. Stone architecture was offered up as a symbol of endurance, history, and solidity.

Messages shown banks as national anchors and community builders. Many of the ads highlighted the banks' agrarian roots and common rural settings. Domestic industry and agriculture remained an important part of the banks' business during this time. The advertisements spoke to an entire community or to the public, not to an individual consumer. The ads celebrated the diversity of local communities. For example, the advertisements noted variously that the banks 'appreciate the importance of differing characteristics', and realized that 'every place has its own special personality'. They respected 'the value of local tradition to countryman and townsman', had 'strong local ties', and employed the 'intimate knowledge of the districts they serve'. Lloyds Bank likens itself in one advertisement to the intimate, private banks of the past. The philanthropy of the banks is communicated with advertisements that depicted their sponsorships of upmarket events such as agricultural fairs and horse shows. The advertisements stressed how much they respected communities and welcomed them to their establishments. The tone of the advertisements was gentile, deferential, and mannered.

The family was a popular motif, typically presented in 1950 ad sitting in the drawing room in a circle. Parents sit on chairs looking down upon their children playing on the floor. This type of visual representation bears a marked similarity to the 'family circle' Roland Marchand found employed within American material goods ads of the 1920s and 1930s (Marchand, 1986, p. 253). Marchand noted that the family circle motif was an appeal to nostalgia, which acted less as a social mirror of the family as it actually existed, than as a pictorial convention reassuring readers that all is well within family relations. Marchand claimed it represents the family as a protected sphere of intimacy, which contrasted sharply with the world of work and public life. The family was offered as a site of rejuvenation, pleasure, and social bonding, and the family circle was thought to reconcile the past and present, authority and democracy. It emphasized security rather than opportunity.

The ads also stressed the importance of prudence and safety. Ads informing readers of the need for a safe-deposit box to keep their fine jewels and important papers secure from theft, spoke unselfconsciously to privileged clients – few members of the working classes had these types of possessions. The hand and arm of the thief depicted were always black. In the 1960s, advertising disparaged Britain's cash culture by reminding readers that carrying cash in their purses and pockets was a risk. The theme of scarcity also promoted thrift. Advertisers presented the act of locking money away as a means of warding off the temptation to spend. The messages reminded readers of the principle of accumulation, how the regular squirreling away of money over time would grow into sizeable sums. Differed gratification was promoted. Readers were informed that if they could forego touching money in the present there would be future rewards for their efforts. Advertisers offered retirement and children's education as reasons for saving. Ads introduced readers to budgeting, presenting it as a new, rational, and prudent approach to financial matters. Readers were encouraged to be attentive and calculating towards their finances.

American banks and scientific management

Because US financial service techniques – mass hire purchase, credit cards, marketing – played a significant role in the later history of British personal finance, it is useful to consider some of the distinguishing features between the two banking systems. A most obvious difference is the control individual US states have over the American financial industry, leading to wide diversity in US rules and practices, compared to Britain's more uniform national control. The history of US banking also shows a more cautious attitude towards financial regulation; and no legacy of an embedded mercantile or non-banking sector. Still, as Roe suggests, until the early 1920s US banks shared more similarities with British banks than differences. US replicated the British thrift and savings movements. US banks, like the British, acquired most of their profits by cycling their massive funds into short-term credit arrangements with industries. US banks too saw themselves as stewards of the economy and valuable public servants. In the 1920s, US banks too shuddered at the thought of allowing people to go into debt to purchase luxury goods. Instead, US bankers prized themselves on their ability to make prudent investments, such as lending money for mortgages and business vehicles.

US banks' early attraction towards thrift, according to Roe, was not simply quasi spiritual but also pragmatic. Bank profits rested on consumers who deposited funds that could then be recycled as profitable loans to US corporations. Even so, early bankers, says Roe, understood themselves as 'apostles' of thrift:

> The fundamentalist of thrift viewed himself as a trustee of other people's money, and he regarded thrift deposits (the painfully accumulated savings of the industrious poor) as possessing special sanctity.

Thrift also defined an ideal lending policy – loans should be made only cautiously and for productive purposes, never to consumers for the purchase of luxuries.

(Roe, 1965, p. 621)

Yet, as wages grew rapidly in the 1920s, partially influenced by Fordism, and consumer goods became more readily available, people felt a growing confidence and a willingness to consider large ticket-item purchases, such as fridges, as an investment in their domestic enterprise. Automobiles changed from being a luxury to a necessity. As in Britain, US manufacturers, retailers, and financial houses were quicker than the banks to seize upon the public's willingness to pay regular credit bills. Banks saw themselves in competition with instalment credit providers whose 'unscrupulous advertising and financing methods' they proclaimed, wiped out the savings margins of the wage earner. Thus, because they believed their livelihood depended on it, the banks 'like a dutiful Presbyterian fighting against the sins of Hollywood' (American Bankers Association, 1933, pp. 22–3) admonished luxury goods and the false idols of the marketplace and, encouraged people to stoically resist these temptations. 'Many bankers found it impossible to overcome deeply ingrained beliefs that only the immoral would extend bank credit for the purchase of automobiles, phonographs, radios, washing machines, refrigerators and other luxuries' (Roe, 1965, p. 626).

Still, operating in a less regulated market, the banks watched, initially with interest, then envy, the massive profits automobile financiers amassed. Some banking progressives, attempting to force the sector to change, announced a 'new era' of economics in which thrift no longer made sense (appearing to have more sympathy with Keynes than the British). Still, to take the leap of faith into the credit market, the everyday banker needed proof, according to Roe, which arrived by way of the importation of scientific management techniques into the banking sector. General Motors set the example producing impressive statistics upon which managers justified their financial decisions. Following GM's lead, US banks slowly tested the waters of the credit business, gathering statistics along the way. Roe notes that poor methodologies and sporadic pooling of samples produced unreliable findings about the economy and credit, but this did not matter. Statistics provided bankers with the psychological lift necessary to breach the taboo of selling debt. As Roe notes: 'Scientific management, as plastic a notion as the idea of thrift, offered the intellectual justification for this break with the past' (Roe, 1965, p. 629).

Scientific management was hardly foreign in Britain. The military applied scientific management techniques during theWWI (Griffin, 1978). British car manufacturing was deeply influenced by Ford's manufacturing techniques. Still, according to Smith and Boyns, such scientific management was tailored to suit British culture (Smith & Boyns, 2005). Based on extensive literature, Smith and Boyns suggest that British producers made wide use of Taylor's bonus pay system, but in a 'diluted form that did not extend, like Ford the psychological and social emphasis'(Smith & Boyns, 2005, p. 210). Thus management structures developed differently to those in the US where a more hands-on corporate and human relations model emerged (Smith & Boyns, 2005).

In America, scientific management techniques, high interest (Griffiths, 2003) accounts, and use of statistics by the banks coincided with their expansion of consumer credit. In 1920, one Connecticut bank offered small loans; by 1927, when the New York National City Bank extended the service, consumer credit became an accepted part of banking. The security of statistics helped banks shift from being apostles of thrift to purveyors of lending. In 1926, the Economic Policy Commission, comprised mainly of bankers, lobbied the government to allow banks to oversee the credit sector because armed with scientific management techniques and statistics, they would be the first to detect any threat credit might pose to the economic system. Defending consumer-oriented approaches to credit, W. Espey Albig, the Commission's deputy manager asked: 'Are we satisfied in this democracy to follow simply the European countries into the shadows – old-age pensions and unemployment doles – or do we rather prefer to continue to work for our people's personal independence, achieved through a knowledge of income management?' (in Roe, 1965, p. 625).

To support people's personal independence, banks felt it necessary to socialize consumers, helping them understand their role in the new economy through budgeting. Budgeting supported a hybrid attitude towards personal finance that emphasized saving and spending. By keeping financial records, balancing credits and debts, bankers argued, consumers would assume awareness and responsibility for their finances. Advertisements of the period, says Roe, told consumers to find a balance between saving for the future and enjoying the bounty of the present. Thrift was re-framed as an aspect of Christian lifestyle: 'The thrifty man, such advertising taught, was a man who enjoyed the new consumer society to the fullest'. This new definition supported acquisition of consumer goods and 'it was but a short step to making instalment loans themselves' (Roe, 1965, p. 628).

The older discourse of thrift, paternalism, character, and self-denial became the modern ideas of self-development, individualism, and self-reliance. Scientific management helped bankers change their attitudes to suit the new historical context and rationalize two highly profitable sectors of finance: loans and securities speculation. Most significantly, the new ethos of credit, investment, and budgeting shifted the weight of responsibility from the paternal bank to the shoulders of the consumer. By the 1930s, the US boasted one of the most expansive personal credit systems in the world. By the second half of the century, the consumer economy, supported by a rich and extensive credit market, eclipsed the industrial economy of the past. According to Juster in 1966: 'consumers are now a more important determinant, both direct and indirect, of the growth and cyclical variation of the [American] nation's total fixed capital investment than are business enterprises' (Juster, 1967, p. 585).

A strong banking lobby promoted the spirit of caveat emptor in the personal financial sector. Banks worked actively to have problems in the credit market understood as the responsibility of the consumer, not seen in the wider context of macroeconomic inequalities. As Roe pointed out, this situation concealed 'the low incomes of many Americans which, no matter how scientifically managed, prevented them from enjoying consumer durables or preparing for any independent old age' (Roe, 1965, p. 633). In comparison, despite their elitism, traditionalism, and rule of thumb measures, British banking institutions embodied economic traditions rooted in moral philosophy that made it more difficult for them to ignore inequality.

Transformation of the gentlemanly bankers

In Britain after WWII, the seeds of a new type of personal financial market, planted in the interwar period, grew. 'Indeed it is usually suggested that the period of rapid income growth continued with cyclical fluctuations, but generally unabated until 1976' (Grady & Weale, 1986, p. 127). Political efforts improved the lives of returning soldiers and all citizens traumatized during the years of war. Unemployment dropped to an all-time low (3%). Wages rose steadily, and wealth was redistributed through ambitious welfare-state initiatives that included a national health service, universal pensions, and free education (Barr, 1993). State and private homeownership, so important for the dynamics of the domestic economy, expanded. There was also a period of relative calm in the international financial field, based on the Bretton Woods Agreement of 1944 (Leyshon & Thrift, 1997). People had more money.

Rising incomes relative to prices and 'the investment in consumer durables to increase (or cater for) leisure time' signalled this new period of affluence (Juster, 1967, p. 585). Acknowledging its growing importance, in 1955, a new credit act made it easier for people to obtain credit. Recognizing this new channel of wealth, the state extended its financial networks in the 1960s with the National Savings Bank and a Giro system that operated through the post office network.

So too did the banks take much greater interest in the personal finance market (Gardener et al., 1997). The banks' reorientation to the consumer market occurred at a moment when their time-honoured business practices no longer made them the same profit. British industry in the 1960s increasingly turned to the international money markets for terms that were more favourable. This international and domestic competition caused a drop in the banks' deposits. According to Ackrill, 'the share of total deposits in Britain held by the major clearers fell from 34.8 to 27.4 percent between 1961 and 1967, but that of foreign and overseas banks rose from 7.2 to 19.7 percent, and building societies from 14.8 to 19.3 percent' (Ackrill, 1993, p. 159). American banks had followed American business to Britain during the post-war rebuilding of Europe, and found a good climate for doing business, because they were not subject to the same lending restrictions as domestic banks.

By the early 1970s, the end of the Bretton Woods Agreement followed instability in international and domestic money markets. Unprecedented levels of inflation prevented the banks from continuing their business as usual. The prosperity of the 1950s and 1960s that had rested upon the Keynesian pact between big business, big government, and big labour unravelled. Floated on the international money market, the British pound had difficulty competing and had to be stabilized by the International Monetary Fund in 1976. The altered context of the global and domestic economy, according to David Harvey, encouraged many policy makers and business to now view the once prized idea of institutional stability as a liability. Institutional rigidity could no longer contain the complexity and fluidity of economies and culture:

> Behind all these specific rigidities lay a rather unwieldy and seemingly fixed configuration of political power and reciprocal relations that bound big labour, big capital, and big government into what increasingly appeared as a dysfunctional embrace of such narrowly defined vested interests as to undermine rather than secure capital accumulation.
>
> (Harvey, 1989, p. 142)

Retailers and manufacturers responded to these economic changes by introducing new technologies, intensifying the cycles of fashion, and reducing the 'turnover time' of goods – always one of the keys to capitalist profitability' (Harvey, 1990, p. 156). The laws that restricted the use and expansion of consumer credit, a known stimulator of turnover time, became subject to retail and non-banking institution scrutiny. Prime Minister Edward Heath, after non-banking institutions lobbied for the right to provide the same credit services as the banks, introduced the 1974 Competition and Credit Control Act to bring more competition to the financial sector. According to Professor Goode this act was 'probably the most advanced and certainly the most comprehensive code ever to be enacted in any country in the area of consumer credit. The point of the act was to create a more level playing field for all financial players and do away with the older division between who could and who could not provide services' (Lindgren, 1977, p. 159). Politicians also drafted the act with the hope that it might increase the democracy of credit in the British marketplace and put more credit into the hands of more consumers (Lindgren, 1977, p. 159). Several non-banking institutions were granted the right to offer full banking services. Slowly the restrictions on lending began to loosen, resulting in more credit moving towards consumers. Consumer protection was an important part of the bill. The banks were encouraged to lend to a wider number of people, avoid discrimination, and be mindful of individual rights. The age of consumer credit democratization had arrived.

Making room for the marketer

Seeking to combat greater competition, the banks began to rework their century-old management orientation, in order to protect the market share, which had previously been theirs due to regulation. According to Healy, even in the highly conservative Coutts Bank, fresh air began to flow through the traditional management structure:

> The principal officers and other senior officials were now openly expressing their opinions in a manner, which would have been unthinkable in their early days. This was to lead in the 2nd half of the decade to a complete reorganization of administration.
>
> (Healy, 1993, p. 425)

The end of their cartel in 1971, appeared to signal the banks' willingness to compete with one another, as each sought to position themselves individually in the market (Stafford & King, 1983, p. 23). All of the banks' interest was now directed towards 'meeting the needs of the personal financial sector through the development of specific marketing strategies' (Stafford & King, 1983, p. 25). The banks increasingly sought the counsel of marketers. Once closed banking boards invited marketing specialists from other sectors to enter their ranks to enable the banks to hear and benefit from their experience. Stafford points out how marketers from the fast-selling foods sector became particularly prominent as advisors to the banks, because although the banks had neither shelves, nor technically any goods, the banks believed the high turnover strategies employed in the fast-selling goods sector could bring volume sales to their organizations. The siphoning of expertise from the material goods sector to the financial service sector signalled an important shift in an industry that had traditionally sought to distinguish itself from mere shopkeepers.

The banks added marketing departments. Stafford explores the example of the Midland Bank. He notes that until 1969 Midland had a Public Relations Department, but that year it introduced a separate Marketing Department. It was not until eight years later that the bank added an Advertising Department. By the 1980s all the Big Four banks had adopted more or less the same organizational model (Stafford & King, 1983, p. 69). Showing their commitment to the marketing ethos, in 1981, NatWest implemented a set of policies intended to achieve the following: a significant shift of attitude towards management commitment to marketing; a change in culture among employees; increased skills in various areas of marketing; and a major marketing-led success within a reasonable time period.

Marketers encouraged the banks to adopt a new philosophy towards conducting business, which challenged the banks to become more culturally sensitive. Well-known market analyst Theodore Levitt summarized marketing as the incorporation of the 'consumer into the production process in order better to satisfy them and thereby increase your chances of making a profit. In the jargon of the business it is a shift from being product-led to consumers led' (quoted in Lury, 1996, p. 94). Marketing philosophy asserts that an economy based on consumer choice will create the most thoughtful and prosperous society. Competition is understood to create a vibrant economy, because it forces businesses constantly to innovate in order to meet consumers' demand, which in turn fuels economic growth.

The introduction of marketing brought conflicts, as it challenged the traditional ethos of sobriety, control, and prudence. According to Stafford, traditional bankers perceived marketers as unmannered and aggressive. Their consumer-oriented approaches seemed to run counter to the principles of financial conduct. For example, traditional bankers balked at the idea that consumers should have authority over finances, when banks assumed authority to ensure prudent accounting. Traditional bank managers, according to Stafford, believed 'that marketing managers live in the ivory towers of head offices and do not understand the role and responsibilities of managers' to the economy (Stafford & King, 1983, p. 90). Marketers required bankers to conceive of their clients in new ways, as rational individuals seeking innovations; values that did not fit into the gentlemanly structures of the traditional banks.

Clearly not all members of the banking community aligned themselves with gentlemanly values. Banking progressives viewed the traditional approach of the banks as passive, elitist, and agitated for a more modern, more market-oriented culture. Traditional bankers, in this perspective, appeared to arrogantly place their own opinions before that of consumers. Banking managers high-mindedly 'shy away from any taint of commercialisation through advertising' (Stafford & King, 1983, p. 90). Progressives pointed to the paltry lack of communication provided to the public. Until the late 1960s, bank promotion was limited to staff recruiting messages or chairmen's annual addresses 'and most press notices were simply reminders of their existence' (Ackrill, 1993, p. 152).

The voice of banking progressives won more ears in the changed economic context after 1970. Stafford documents the general acceptance of marketing and the 'positive reaction by bankers towards market developments in the promotion of the philosophy, which takes the market as given'. From the 1970s onward, the style of the banks became 'more active and aggressive' towards consumers challenging the traditionally 'passive and solicitous attitude' of the banks (Stafford & King, 1983, p. 67).

Late 1960s bank advertising shifted from an emphasis on stability and tradition to modernity, efficiency, convenience, and access to funds. The ads encouraged readers to keep up with the times, conform to new practices, or face the daunting prospect of being left behind. The ads presented finance as essential to the modern lifestyle. Juxtaposing traditional money practices to modern financial instruments, advertising rendered the latter irrelevant. For example, one advertisement presented its messages as an 'up-to-date Victorian Primer' in which readers were instructed on the etiquette of proper modern banking behaviour, implying that traditional practices were unmannered. Another advertisement, captioned 'Banking Without Tears', pedantically pointed out how non-institutional banking practices were 'inconvenient', 'lacking in wisdom', 'funny looking', and 'childish'. Opting out of modern banking was presented as childish: 'Do you still handle money like a child?'

Such ads conjured a new generation that had moved on from older money practices. Advertisers created stories that dissolved traditional community financial relations. Traditional financial networks between family and friends were rendered passé: readers should conduct their finances in direct relationship to banks. Again, we might look to the wording: 'isn't it time you had a bank account of your own?' 'So you haven't got a bank account?' 'It's time you carried a cheque book'. One advertisement advised readers on what was in and out of style. 'Old Fashioned saving is out', says a Lloyds bank advertisement depicting a couple holding a piggy bank. A 1969 Midland advertisement points out, 'Your children will have bank accounts. Are they going to wonder why you didn't?' Old ways of banks were represented as unsophisticated and childish.

Designers worked upon readers' obvious anxieties over their social standing in a time of considerable change. These advertisements conjured up a they 'out there' continually watching, judging, and demanding adherence to social convention. Readers were informed that to be without modern banking instruments is to risk social embarrassment. One advertisement, for example, pointed out: 'there are times when it might be quite embarrassing to have to admit you do not possess a cheque book'. Another claimed, 'how embarrassing if someone takes it for granted that you have a banking account'. Advertisers constructed financial services as a mark of social standing. They spoke to an audience whom they believed was deferential towards modern appeals to authority. These status-based approaches attempted to cower consumers into using banking by shaming traditional financial products.

The discovery of the unbanked fearful consumer

To manage consumers in a more modern and efficient way, advertisers and banking progressives encouraged the use of consumer research. Banks slowly became more open to dialogue, informational input, and justification (Ornstien, 1972). Research provided the means to filter information about consumers into organizational decisions. The idea of research entered the bank, but as Dawn Burton pointed out in his ethnography of a bank, the practice and use of research intelligence by the banks was cautious, complex, and conflicted (Burton, 1994).

Banks first conducted only elementary research. By referring to a census of who did and who did not have bank accounts, researchers constructed and laid before bankers a raw number indicating the size of their potential market. This map revealed that a large segment of the population was without banking accounts; the unbanked. In 1968 only 21 million people had bank accounts – roughly half the adult population. To spur the banks into change, marketers put these domestic figures up against the banking figures of other industrialized countries. Britain was deemed significantly under-banked. Marketers pointed to American banks that welcomed 99% of the population to their doors. Canada, Australia, Germany, and France were not far behind, with 95% of the population possessing bank accounts (Stafford & King, 1983).

Many factors contributed to the high number of unbanked in Britain which had little to do with the banks. Truckers' laws meant that as late as 1979, 78% of all manual workers, 35% of non-manual workers, and 54% of all workers continued to receive packets containing cash on a weekly basis. Other industrialized countries administered pay cheques and state subsidies through banking networks. In the 1970s only 1% of US workers were paid in cash. The non-banking sector also kept British people away from banks. However, the concept of the unbanked gave the arguments of marketers and banking progressives for change, more force. In classical marketing language, the banks were critiqued for under-servicing the mass market. In a period enthused by a spirit of market democracy and equalization, this finding morally tainted the banks. The banks felt immense pressure to change. The underbanked mass became the marketing agenda of most of the banks: 'The main movement of the banks during the 1970s was to reach the unbanked' (Stafford & King, 1983, p. 91).

Bank marketing in the 1970s was influenced by the idea of economies of scale and mass-marketing techniques (Tedlow & Jones, 1993). Marketers within the banks encouraged the implementation of techniques to increase the volume of financial services. These ideas seemed to work well for banks, who were saddled with very high overheads. Large-scale branch networks and the delivery of services in face-to-face interactions were highly expensive because they called for large property holdings and many staff members (Leyshon & Thrift, 1997, p. 232). Because banks were already paying to support their massive infrastructures, marketers reasoned that adding new consumers could be done at little additional cost. Profit during this period was largely generated on margin. Profit from sales and service charges became more important later.

To encourage people to enter their networks, banks offered minimal or no service charges. Universal service offerings were financed via cross-subsidizing or redirecting revenue from profitable branches and services to unprofitable areas of the banks. It was believed that even if an individual could contribute only a small deposit, taken as a whole, a large pool of capital could be amassed and reinvested to produce profit on margin. Based on the idea of economies of scale, it was believed that banks could economically justify welcoming people from across the socio-economic scale. The banks even had interest in the semi-skilled and low-incomed, as rising affluence of those in the manual trades made more attractive, these previously ignored market sectors (Tedlow & Jones, 1993).

Banks would be saddled with a systemic contradiction between their interest in providing consumer-friendly service and their need to minimize costs. The staff required to deliver services was expensive. Prudently, banks sought to maximize a high volume of business and extract the greatest value from labour by keeping staff busy, preferably on tasks that made profit. The much-maligned banking queue, despite the disruption it causes consumers, remains because it is simply not in the banks' interest to have staff wait for a surge of customers. A similar political economy discouraged banks from extending their hours of service.

Marketing thought encouraged the banks to innovate as many services as possible for the personal market. Advertisements became a battle ground between banks for the distinction of who came first, who offered the most, and who had the best interest rates. All the banks struggled to make the claim that they had the best services. Advertisers coached readers about how easy it was to switch banks, and some advertisements even stressed how holding an account at the bank was not necessary to undertake specific services. Financial services fall into one of three general categories: investments, credit, and general transactions, and all three changed in this period. General transactions became more customized and the speed with which they were carried out was increased by new computer technology. Taking advantage of looser regulations, the banks began to offer services that were once the privileged domain of the merchant banks. To encourage people to open accounts, the banks issued new guidelines that made them easier to open. (The banks would remain cautious about who received current accounts, for it is only with recent technology that they have been able to prevent consumers from going into overdraft). Gifts, other incentives, and special offers, were also used. Research showed those in low socio economic catagories were more enthusiastic towards rewards, discounts and gifts than others (Stafford & King, 1983, p. 94). Interest began to be offered on accounts during this period to encourage people to put their money in the bank (Ackrill, 1993, p. 157).

Repositioning towards the mass consumer

Freed from their cartel, banks could independently decide how best to position themselves in the market. Barclays, Midland, and NatWest, all decided to orientate towards the unbanked (Ornstien, 1972), but Lloyds, the smallest of the Big Four, and unimpressed by the rush to the mass market, departed from the trend. Lloyds targeted the more profitable socio-economic groupings (Stafford & King, 1983, p. 102). Lloyds' marketing manager called the bank's approach 'refined' and argued that it would 'entail improving our [Lloyds] share of personal bank account, particularly by selective activity in markets, which have above bearing potential' (Stafford & King, 1983, p. 103). Lloyds believed that the personal market would soon be saturated with bank account ownership. Refusing to acknowledge the propensity of everyday consumers to payback their debts, Lloyds management argued that the pains involved in recruiting the lower classes were not worthwhile, for in the long run, the bank believed, most would prove not to be profitable clients, draining the bank's resources. Small accounts with a high transaction volume did little for a bank's profits, and even with the introduction of modern computers during this period to handle the bulk of work; small accounts still caused high administrative expenses (Bickers, 1994). Lloyds was happy to let others absorb the lowend of the market, and to establish itself as a solidly middle-class enterprise. The one exception Lloyds made to its rule of refined targeting was to concede the importance of the youth market. The bank's marketing manager noted there were 'few other options for business volumes, since 65 percent of all new account holders are aged under 35 years' (Stafford & King, 1983, p. 103). Marketers argued that youth were a transient market that could not be guaranteed to remain in the same socio-economic class throughout their life. Thus, Lloyds hedged its bets in the complex matter of social mobility.

Stafford describes the innovative strategies Lloyds undertook to reach this refined market. Borrowing techniques from American banks, they cross-sold services to compete with building societies for the mortgage market. Although other banks used heavy-hitting promotion campaigns to entice people to take up home loans, Lloyds chose to distinguish its mortgage provision by packaging an ensemble of services, justified on the idea that a mortgage was just the beginning of one's financial needs, because homes required renovations, new durables, insurance, and a host of other financial services. The service was labelled 'Home Makers' and aimed at young married couples setting up a first home. Not only did Lloyds attract new clients, and forge ongoing relationships, it uniquely positioned the bank within the marketplace. Lloyds was rewarded for recognizing the importance of the domestic economy.

Although it is difficult to measure financial advertising spending with great accuracy, in 1970 the growth rate of the increase in bank advertising budgets was spectacular (although modest in absolute terms). According to Stafford, building society budgets grew 641% compared to the banks' 583% from their 1960 levels (Stafford & King, 1983, p. 13). With few other financial institutions pursuing advertising, and merchant and bond-bank commitments to advertising actually declining, banks and the building societies dominated financial promotions during this time.

Money was spent on advertising that positioned the banks as populist institutions. Advertising suggested that there was a democratic revolution taking place in the banking sector, as the copy and images of the messages made frequent reference to the sheer number of people becoming bank customers. A 1975 advertisement typified this critical mass approach with its caption: 'More and more people are banking with The Royal Bank'. The banks proudly promoted the vast size of their institutions. A massive number of clients was a sign that people trusted and liked their banks. In keeping with the spirit of populism, testimony within the advertisements began to be delivered by non-elite sources. The lack of celebrity endorsement was not, however, entirely voluntary: regulation forbade the use of celebrities in financial advertisements until the mid-1980s.

Research also brought to light crucial information about the public apprehensions of banks. King's widely read research project asked the prudent question: why do people shy away from banks? The answer: social fear about not being able to access money and being caught short of cash. People felt uncomfortable with the idea of non-cash transactions because they believed placing money in the banks made it inaccessible due to limited banking hours. Consumers also expressed anxiety about a potential loss of privacy. They did not trust the banks to keep their financial records confidential (particularly from their spouses) (King, 1981). The Central Policy Review Staff report of 1981 revealed similar findings. This review found that there existed 'deep seated social attitudes towards banks particularly among older workers' that caused them to experience banks as alien environments. Banks' clientele remained heavily weighted towards elite members of society, much to the government's dismay. A Giro system was launched directly after this period, precisely because the banks were failing to attract a broad public to their institutions. Many people still favoured building societies and TBS (Collins, 1988). Although the commission saw this as 'a real impediment to banking, they regarded it as transitional and likely to reduce over time' (Stafford & King, 1983, p. 97). Still, the committee encouraged the banks to adjust their practices and image to minimize anxiety, and to stay open longer.

Findings such as these introduced the banks to the idea that social background and psychological disposition were not trivial matters but directly informed consumers' banking behaviours and attitudes. The public negatively interpreted the dignified and respected position of authority so carefully manicured by traditional bankers. Many unbanked consumers reported that they felt a sense of inferiority in the face of bank staff who threatened their self-respect or self-image (Stafford & King, 1983, p. 97). Research such as this encouraged banks to think more therapeutically about their businesses, and as we shall see later these findings had a profound impact on how banks communicated to consumers.

To combat these accusations the banks extended their branch networks to appear inclusive instead of exclusive. Hardly a high street in the country lacked the presence of one of the four banks. Using the principles of cross-subsidy, all bank branches were outfitted with the means of providing full service to consumers. New technologies for carrying out the processing of accounts freed up floor space within branches. Burton notes a telltale reversal in the banks' layout that illustrated the growing importance of the consumer. Staff were pushed back and the consumer was given the larger part of the floor space (Burton, 1996). Banks became more self-conscious about their look, style, attitude, and emotional tenor (Mullineux, 1987). Greater attempts were made to brand by creating consistent styling and co-ordinating the use of corporate symbols to distinguish each bank from its competition, and reassure consumers that regardless of which branch they entered, they could expect the same services and treatment. Sharper window displays and more stands containing information were added to branches. Windows were enlarged to provide a greater feeling of freedom and openness and to calm shy consumers who could now peek inside and see what they could expect. Modern open-floor plans made waiting areas homlier. Consumers were offered coffee or tea and magazines to make their wait more pleasurable. Through the 1980s, colourful awnings and lights, both inside and out, turned the dowdy old bank branch into a theatrical stage. An architectural commentator noted how the shift to marketing was manifested in the very materiality of the bank: 'Recently ... architects have reacted against a naked show of strength adopting a more humanistic approach, which is sensitive to the environment and individual' (Booker, 1980, p. 49).

This attention and expense devoted to branches was very different from banking's traditional approach. Ackrill tells the story of how in 1968, when the National Provincial and Westminster banks merged, there was an assessment of the interior of bank branches. Westminster Bank head office staff were appalled by the 'threadbare carpets and creaking lifts' of some of the National Provincial offices. It seems that to 'traditional National Provincial men, this austerity was intended as a reassurance to customers and shareholders that profits were not made at their expense, but were passed on in reasonable terms and good dividends' (Ackrill, 1993, p. 158).

Banks used a populist language to break down older class-based marketing habits in the financial sector. Remaking banks required that they be dislodged from references to British heritage and nationhood. Rural landscapes and agrarian lifestyles faded as banks refocused on depicting modern consumers in urban areas. According to Stafford,

> [a]part from the individual approaches adopted by each bank ... the general purpose of all advertising ... is towards breaking down the mythology that banking is associated with marble halls, stern and remote managers and cold institutions.
>
> (Stafford & King, 1983, p. 17)

Advertisers presented an image of the old bank as frightening, unemotional, intimidating, and exclusionary, by contrasting it with warm and friendly modern banks. One advertisement in the 1970s noted, 'How different it is today', in Lloyds. The advertisement forefronted 'friendliness' and disparaged the 'stiff cuffs and standing on ceremony of yesterday'. NatWest launched its campaign, 'You'll find we're only human' with the belief that projecting a supportive image was essential to meeting the real problem of actually getting people into a bank. The objective of the campaign was to reassure consumers that they would be met with an attitude of courtesy, understanding, and down-to-earth humanity. The bank manager received a makeover in ads; his prudent, efficient, authoritative face was replaced by a friendly smile and open arms. Closing the distance between consumers and managers, a Westminster Bank advertisement put it that 'our managers are above all, good neighbours'. The 1970s ads endlessly presented banking staff as personal and interested in offering friendly advice.

To help consumers overcome their bank phobia, without belittling them, consumers were presented images of the 'reality' of banking to demystify and soothe apprehensions. Photography enabled realistic depictions of the bank, and this was welcomed, for it provided the means to help timid, unbanked consumers to see what they might expect. Readers were presented with lifelike pictures of what we assume was an actual banker. We are told his first name, place of work, accomplishments, and hobbies. Should there be any doubt that he was friendly, the copy reminded us: 'The manager is Don Mackay, a very approachable man.' Seeing an actual manager, hearing that he was ordinary, was to allow consumers to think of the banks as more emotionally open institutions. There was also a social levelling in the portrayal of the manager. The manager depicted in the ads had once sat behind a desk, but now he steps out to meet consumers. A common tableau depicted the consumer and bank manager shaking hands and smiling. Midland Bank used animation during this period to give the bank a warmer, more friendly image. A new 'structure of feeling' entered the advertisements of this period that prized intimacy, friendship, and inclusion. The conservative and patronizing voice of earlier advertising was replaced by a more conversational and respectful tone.

Representations of the family remained popular in the 1970s as the banks continued to assume that consumers were part of a larger social group. Advertisers, however, presented a much more intimate, emotionally warm family in which the traditional hierarchical roles between parents and children, husband and wife lessened. Besides sitting in the drawing room, the family was shown in the more private domains of the bedroom and the kitchen. The ads placed more stress on emotional bonds in the family. Parents clutched children close to their beasts or lay informally on their back holding their child in the air in a gesture of play. Advertisements reassured readers that the nuclear family remained intact. Feminist and counter-cultural movements at the time may have influenced advertisers' use of emotional openness and informality in their depictions of social relations. While males still dominated the advertisements and occupied the majority of positions of authority, more women appeared in advertising in the 1970s and were frequently represented as primary customers. However, no people of colour appeared within these ads.

Advertisers promoted financial services as tools for actualizing ambitions and securing achievement. However, instead of chastising readers to keep up with the fashions of modernity, advertisers at this time were more likely to offer role models for consumers to emulate. Characters in advertisements received rich back-stories. For example, in one advertisement we meet Norman Barnes who worked his way through 'unusual jobs', spent 19 years as a teacher, then undertook a BA with honours, which led to a 'lectureship'. Barnes achieved his personal ambitions to be a top career and family man. From the same campaign, we are introduced to Graham and Kathy Johns, who work together and believe 'the good life takes effort, enthusiasm and teamwork'. Another advertisement promotes an image of a 'working mother'. Advertisers here reassure readers that the good life is achievable with hard work and banks. Designers accented social mobility, merit, and the potential for change.

Advertisers stressed the practical benefits services offered to consumers, specifically, convenience and timeliness. Convenient access to funds became the banks' mantra in the 1970s and early 1980s. Promotions assured readers they did not have to be fearful that their money might become inaccessible, because special accounts offered greater flexibility in accessing money. Advertisements announced the expansion of the banks' branch network. New local branches were introduced: old branches were relaunched. Advertisements stressed the consistency of the banks by noting that urban and rural branches were equal. Consumers were reassured that no matter what branch they accessed, they would receive the same level of service. Advertisements celebrated the expanding networks of the banks. One advertisement claimed: 'London's a long way when your financial problem needs a quick answer.' Another points out that 'not all decisions are made in London'. The banks also promoted their willingness to go to extraordinary lengths to meet their consumers face to face (e.g., the banks' new mobile banking units in isolated regions). These mobile banking services stressed that the banks were convenient and accessible to consumers.

The Price Commission's report of 1978 argued, 'there should be greater flexibility with regard to opening hours so that retail bank services can be available to the public whenever there is a commercially justifiable demand' (Stafford & King, 1983, p. 80). However, bank workers resisted workdays of more than eight hours and objected to opening on Saturdays as it was simply not profitable to stay open longer. Introducing Automated Teller Machines (ATM) helped to ease this conflict. These machines, now so familiar, were at this time very radical. Although the modern bank had always used technology to make accounting more efficient, the ATM became a symbol of marketing spirit in that it put technology in the service of the consumer. Barclays was the first British bank to offer ATMs in 1966. These machines provided consumers with the ability to process general transactions and access cash 24 hours a day. Throughout the 1970s, all other banks extended their ATM networks. Consumers embraced the technology because it offered a way to subvert the banks' short hours and long queues and avoid interaction with staff.

The promotion of ATMs made a profound contribution to the over-riding emphasis on money access during this period. For example, in one advertisement the ability to access cash through a machine elicited expressions of pleasure and astonishment in the faces of the customers. The ATM was often shown at night to signify the revolution in banking hours, which were now 'around the clock'. Technology was represented as a wonder cure for customers' worldly banking frustrations such as queues and other bureaucratic bothers. In some advertisements, technology appeared to release people from the burden of the bank balance itself: 'Put in your special voucher and 10 pounds in bank notes pop out'; another, 'It's quick, easy, automatic.'

Expansion in the credit market

In the late 1960s, the banks engaged in a series of mergers. The National Provincial Bank and the Westminster Bank merged in 1968 to form NatWest, reducing the Big Five to the Big Four. In an effort to con-solidate their position in the lucrative consumer credit market, banks joined forces with financial houses.

Some members of the British public felt financially secure enough to embrace the American Express credit card offered to them in 1963, and Barclays introduced the Barclaycard in 1966, through a direct-mail mar-keting campaign. Barclays built up its cardholder base from 1m to nearly 5m, over the 1970s. Lloyds, Midland, and National Westminster jointly launched a rival card, Access, in 1972, winning more than 4m cardhold-ers. The British embrace of revolving credit would distinguish it from some European banks. In West Germany, Holland, and Belgium there was fear that card operators would erode the banks' consumer lending business, therefore cheques were defended. Eurocard, the plastic card sponsored by German and other northern European banks, offered only short-term credit and like American Express and Diners Club balances could not be carried over, but had to be paid in full each month.

Yet, just like today, there was a negative reaction towards the marketing of credit. The direct-mail campaign 'was a contentious action regarded by some as provocative and outraged recipients wrote complaining that they were somehow being forced to hold the card' (Ackrill, 1993, pp. 157–8). By 1979 surveys revealed 9% of the population had one or more credit cards, but with only 6% of this group labeled as semi or unskilled workers it was clear that credit cards began as play toys for the middle classes (Parker, 1990, p. 38). The rich and those with low-income levels are much less likely to use credit. Indeed, those in the lowest income brackets rarely use credit (NCC, 1980). According to Parker strong reservations towards credit prevailed through the 1970s as many people balked at the use of credit and store cards feeling these instruments would 'make them act as if they had money which, in reality, they had not' (Parker, 1990, p. 113).

Researchers explored what consumers were looking for in a credit card, sought to position the card to outstrip the weaknesses of competitors' cards, tried to identify sectors of the market most receptive to cards, what types of terms consumers preferred, and which consumers were most likely to use a another bank credit card. Apart from undertaking specialized commissioned research, banks used consumer data from their in-house files. This was a very novel practice for the privacy-oriented banks. By 1979, Access lending was estimated to be £750 million. The success of the card helped to sell the importance of segmentation research. 'In the financial services industry, research techniques into customer attitudes, market segmentation and development have been applied to an ever increasing extent throughout the 1970s' (Stafford & King, 1983, p. 75).

By 1979 cards provided roughly £1.5 billion in credit, one third of all non-bank consumer credit in the country (Economist, 1979, p. 52). The demise, in the 1971 Competition and Credit Control Act, of advertising restrictions for their credit services, and the loosening of other financial restrictions in the early 1980s, led banks to move more aggressively into the mass credit market. Credit was much more widely available, contributing to the consolidation of a more consumer-led economy in Britain. The banks also moved into mortgage, insurance, and investment services. 'The proportion of the population using credit cards rose from 1/5 in 1969 to half in 1979 to well over half in 1987' (Parker, 1990, p. 104). By 1980 credit had lost much of its stigma, as only '30% of the population felt using credit was never a good thing' (Parker, 1990, p. 107). As Table 4.1 demonstrates Barclaycard experienced considerable growth during the 1980s.

Table 4.1 Growth of Barclaycard

	1967	1972	1977	1982	1986
Total cardholders in millions ('000)	1100	2060	3800	6634	8600
Annual card turnover (pounds m)	10	118	585	2179	5391

Source: Barclaycard (Smith, 1987).

Personal financial market success

The banks were rewarded for their efforts. Bank deposits rose from £6.7 billion in 1956 to £38.6 billion in 1979. Only 39% of the adult population had a current account in 1970; by 1979 56% did. There was also growth lower down the social structure in the early 1970s, with those in semi skilled workers showing the highest increase in banking accounts than any other social class (see Appendix 1 for the complete list). Between 1974 and 1980, their presence in the bank market jumped 13% (Stafford & King, 1983, pp. 98–102). Part of this success in making inroads with cde socio-economic groups related to the banks' circumvention of the truckers' laws. Promotional campaigns encouraged employers to deposit employees' wages directly into bank accounts. The banks had a strong selling point, for this practice promised to make the employers' accounting procedures easier and cheaper. A 1980 industry report noted that increased credit card use and paying workers by cheque instead of cash were major incentives driving consumers to the banks: 'More people are banking because of a rise in bank-linked credit cards and an increase in the number of employers using cheques for payrolls instead of cash' (NCC, 1980). The banks' ability to insert themselves as a link between employee pay represented a crucial transformation in Britain's personal financial culture. Many in the manual classes remained faithful to the building societies and TSB, taking up bank accounts, but still maintaining building society accounts. But these institutions remained branded in the public mind as places for saving. By 1984, for example, banks had only 37% of savings deposits, compared to building societies which held 48% and the National Savings, which held 22% (Bevon, 1984). Banks struggled to make sure access, investment, and credit were the mantras of the closing decades of the twentieth century because their networks privileged these services. This increased institutionalization of economic exchange lubricated the speed of commodity circulation, aiding the consolidation of the consumer culture. So profound were these changes that Frazer and Vittas called them a revolution (Frazer & Vittas, 1982).

Cracks in the mass ideal

Success always arrives with new problems, and one of the most pressing for banks throughout the period between 1960 and 1980 was how they became associated in the public mind with the negative connotations of mass institutions. The phenomenal expansion of their financial services shaped banks into something akin to supermarkets that offered a broad range of services to mass markets. All banks appeared the same. As financial services could not be copyrighted, competitors kept careful watch on one another's service innovations and replicated or slightly improved each other's service offerings according to a 'herd mentality' (Gardener, Howcroft, & Williams, 1999, p. 21). Building societies, because they had to be careful about how extended they became, tended to carefully research the profitability of financial services before making a decision to add them to their roster. Banks on the other hand, feeling secure with their established and expansive economies of scale, deemed it cheaper simply to add the services rather than to make the investment into researching market viability. Banks' efforts to universalize their services by promoting their massive institutional scale and progressive use of technology, paradoxically created what was for some an uncomfortably uniform, alienating image of institutional power that had the potential to overwhelm and denigrate diverse interests. The very success of the banks became their new promotional nightmare. Advertisers of the period picked up on this contradiction and began to address it by creating messages that rejected the mass ideal. One advertisement reflected that far from making the bank better, computer technology had made the bank impersonal: 'Your friendly neighbourhood bank clerk?' over a picture of a computer. Ads reminded readers to notice how 'bigger' banks were less personal, acknowledging the cultural weariness and the end of the assumption that bigger was necessarily better in banks. Another advertisement reminded readers of the institutional alienation of mass banks: 'nobody remembers to call you by name any more'. And you may have begun to feel that you're being stamped, processed and churned out. Having conjured up the associative chain of an impersonal world, the advertiser then offered the antidote: banks were presented as astute enough to treat 'people like people' and 'machines like machines'. A 1975 Coutts & Co. advertisement recognizes that 'You're a person, not a cipher.' Attempting to soothe the alienation of mass society, another advertisement presented a crowd of people over which a magnifying glass was imposed to draw out a single individual. The copy read: 'You've got to have something special to stand out in a large crowd – like being a Midland Bank customer.' These advertisements suggested that designers were beginning to acknowledge the limits of the mass-market ideal. In the next chapter, I explore how banks sought to remake their massive financial networks in a more progressive and positive light.

5
Big Bang Banking

In this chapter, I trace how changing global economic circumstances, cultural sentiments, and the political climate of the late 1970s altered banking culture and practice. A different type of relationship between the banks and the personal financial market emerged. By the end of the 1970s, 76% of Britons had bank accounts. Targeting the unbanked no longer made sense after the banks' rapid expansion as marketers pointed out: 'The unbanked as a vast army of untapped banking business has become a myth that banks would do well to forget' (Smart, 1984, p. 13.). Another marketer pointed out, 'What many banks are now beginning to understand is that the notion of a homogeneous mass market is quaint and dangerous' (Mooney, 1995, p. 58). Further, the banks' extensive networks proved a liability for a new generation of consumers who grew weary of the mass model. The idea of mass-banking too easily appeared to suppress uniqueness: the friendly-smile management could appear as simply a cover for an alienating bureaucracy.

In the 1970s, the banks found themselves caught within the turbulence of difficult economic circumstances. From 1974 to 1979, when Labour was the government, with Harold Wilson and then James Callaghan in office, politicians discussed nationalizing the banks to combat inflation. The banks fought back with a collective advertising campaign that reminded the public that bankers, not government officials, were best qualified to manage the economy (Stafford & King, 1983, p. 117). The re-election of the Conservatives in 1979 ensured that all plans to nationalize the banks drew to an abrupt halt. Prime Minister Margaret Thatcher pushed the banking sector in a profoundly different direction. Prime Minister Thatcher loathed that international corporations and investors looked elsewhere to arrange their finances, and saw high taxes, protectionist regulation, and labour unrest as the cause. For her, the gentlemanly banking system was elitist and in need of a shake up. Her deregulation of the financial system in 1986 did just that. Pressured by the state and unable to turn the same profits on margins, the banks reworked their cultures once again.

Leyshon and Thrift, reviewing banking changes in the early 1980s helpfully remind us that state politics represented just part of the impetus for banking change. The global political and economic climate at the time, no doubt, forced Prime Minister Thatcher's hand in many of her decisions.

> Faced with an increasingly internationalised financial system, largely dominated by foreign institutions, there were two options open to the City. It could either have remained firmly behind a barrier of restrictive controls as business steadily migrated elsewhere, or it could attempt to introduce international 'financial best practise' into its operations. Forced by state pressure into the latter course, the viability of the City as a financial centre has been considerably enhanced.
>
> (Leyshon & Thrift, 1997, p. 135)

Still, state discourses and regulation were of prime importance and deserved attention because they helped shape a new financial structure and most importantly gave new meaning and cultural significance to the British financial sector.

Margaret Thatcher's influence on banking culture

James Thomas argues that the media's construction of what he calls the 'Winter of Discontent' myth gave Thatcherite rhetoric added force. Through his detailed comparison of how newspapers accounted for the political economic situation in the 1970s, and information drawn from other primary evidence, Thomas demonstrates how the press accounts simplified, exaggerated, and dramatized the strikes, riots, and political discord of the period. He notes the press virtually ignored the many social and political advancements of the period, particularly the empowerment of women. Journalists failed to register the public's support for social democratic policies in their notebooks. Instead, the media continually linked the labour government to corrupt unions, crippling strikes, and economic disaster. The press focused on striking funeral and rubbish collector workers to ignite the deep cultural taboos associated with burying ones' dead and the horror of disease excited by the idea of rats multiplying in garbage piles.

Detailed histories of the period and statistical evidence, however, show that 'life continued largely unaffected'. The press did not focus on how essential services continued to be carried out, nor did they mention the role management played in perpetuating the discord. Overall, Thomas found the press account exaggerated the length and severity of the strikes. Thomas provides evidence to suggest that the press was fully aware of their role in shaping the Winter of Discontent. Thomas quotes Derek Jameson, then editor of the staunchly Conservative Daily Express, who in 1999 confessed to negatively framing the events of the period: 'we pulled every dirty trick of the book; we made it look like it was general, universal and eternal when it was in reality scattered, here and there, and no great problem (Thomas, 2007, p. 271).

The Winter of Discontent myth provided fertile ground for Thatcher's neo liberal economic rhetoric, particularly for the young, born after the 1970s, who lacked the direct experience of the period to counter the image. As one cabinet member, Bill Rodgers argued, the 'dramatic' media images 'had much more impact on opinion than the public's own direct experience of the strike' (in Thomas, 2007, p. 272). Thomas feels Labour politicians contributed to their own demise because they failed to develop countervailing points to challenge the Winter of Discontent myth. Margaret Thatcher was thereby given the open ear of the public, in which she announced a powerful new ideology that suggested the country would flounder unless Britain opened its markets and dismantled state regulation and programmes (Thomas, 2007, p. 273).

One of Thatcher's first attacks on the Labour government related to their decision to turn to international bankers to bail out the pound. Although the pound had been battered by years of warfare, Thatcher argued public debt was Labour Ministers' 'high minded profligacy'. Labour politicians' adherence to Keynesian principles and their interest in maintaining welfare-state provisions, said Thatcher, was bankrupting the country. In an article to the *Daily Express*, Thatcher invoked an image of Labour politicians on their knees begging for a bail out. This 'humiliating episode', as she called it, wounded Thatcher's national pride and her belief in Britain's worldly entitlement. She high-mindedly believed that the international financial community had always, and should always come to Britain; Britain should not beg international bankers for money.

As noted in the last chapter, global financial flows increasingly bypassed Britain in the 1970s. The London Stock Exchange was merely the 13th most powerful global financial network, well below the New York Stock Exchange, which was number one. Courting international bankers in 1978, Thatcher promised to revive Britain's global standing: 'I am determined to recreate in Britain a climate in which you will want to invest, and where we, for our part, will once more be free to put our talents and our savings to the service of a wider world. It is time for us to put behind us the years of timid introspection and passive decline. Time for Britain to be up and about.' She vowed never to borrow so much from the collective as to have to turn to moneylenders. 'If ever I am head of a British Government, there is no way in which I am going to land us in such a shameful mess. Anything rather than that' (Thatcher, 7 February 1978).

Thatcher framed the public debt as a moral issue. Thatcher saw public debt through the gaze of her heightened sense of thrift. She imagined state-spending lining the pockets of corrupt union officials, and maintaining a welfare state that stripped people's sense of self-reliance, ability to own property, and innovation. She believed public debt created inflation, which prevented the housewife from getting good value for her money. Having conjured Labour as spendthrifts, she presented Conservatives as productive, hard working, and thrifty. She proclaimed her party believed 'in thinking hard about creating wealth, before getting down to the more agreeable task of spending it. To us, the only honest idealism is based on wealth we are already creating. We don't finance our ideals with dud cheques' (Thatcher, 1 May 1979).

Unlike Keynes, Thatcher was an internationalist who saw the fortunes intimately linked to global capital flows. Because she viewed the entire world as best conceived as a market, she argued against protecting state finance and industry in favour of promoting national enterprise. She high-mindedly believed Britain would not simply compete well, but secure a leading role on the world stage. It is now well established that this position borrowed from the US experience. The 'monetarist' economic path carved out by Milton Friedman guided Margaret Thatcher's policies. She studied with interest how the US was re-securing their place of dominance in a period of economic turmoil. She found more in common with Reagan, than other UK or European politicians and their state-based policies, because she unabashedly believed in open market principles: 'And to me the very bedrock of a free society, the essential condition without which it cannot long survive, is a free and open market' (Thatcher, 25 April 1979). The public elected Reagan in America and Thatcher in Britain on the promise that this monetarist doctrine would overcome the cracks emerging in the welfare-industrial state. And whatever else one can say about it, this new policy not only showed the invisible hand of shopkeepers (and bankers) in its writing, but had achieved some of its economic ambitions. What Thatcher was unable to imagine at the time was how the monetarist focus on open markets and low interest rates to fuel business investment, also fuelled financial speculative booms in finance and retail consumption purchased on personal credit.

Radical economic policies packaged as Victorian values

Reviewing her rhetorical flourishes, Ralph Samuel draws attention to the profound contradiction upon which Prime Minister Thatcher's political project rested. She secured wholly radical monetarists principles by appealing to old home-grown Victorian Values. According to Samuel, Margaret Thatcher had little idea how deeply appealing Victorian values would be when she 'stumbled on the phrase in the early days of her career' (1992, p. 10). Nostalgia proved to be a powerful source of political rhetoric. Responding to positive feedback, Prime Minister Thatcher reinforced the myth of Victorian values. Over time she fashioned herself not only as a humble shopkeeper's daughter, but the offspring of a Victorian grandmother who taught her to work jolly hard, prove yourself, display self reliance and self-respect, be clean, and help your neighbour. Summoning the spirit of nannas, Thatcher stressed the importance of living 'within your income', practicing thrift, prudence, and restraint (Samuel, 1992, p. 12).

Hall suggested that Victorian values proved supremely suited for attacking the state, for as we saw in Chapter 1, Victorian culture was deeply suspicious of the state. Margaret Thatcher positioned the state as an obstacle to freedom, social advancement, and self-expression. The state, in this trope, became a nagging mother who 'meddled, intervened, obstructed, instructed and directed'. Taking a page from a line of argument produced by de Tocqueville centuries earlier, Thatcher argued that people were on the dole not because of economic hardship, but because the state put them there. Thatcher challenged the secularist state idea of universal social welfare with Victorian sensibilities in which 'handouts' and 'charity' were villainies – signs of social shame for those who received them and undermining charity among those that could provide it. People took the money but the state provided no incentive for them to take responsibility. The welfare state, according to Thatcher, had robbed working men of their self-reliance, taken their self-respect, and made them paupers in a time of abundance. Previous politicians, she implied, had not followed the will of the British people. The state's new role was to put 'people's destinies back into their own hands'. Instead of rewarding people for their hard work, the state took people's discretionary income away through taxes and used the funds for inefficient state projects and to support a bloated state administration. State support weakened moral fibre, 'coddled' and attacked the family, creating a society of scrounges.

Most important, in relation to personal finance, was Thatcher's attack on council housing. Although Conservative politicians had long made private homeownership a central platform of their rhetoric, until Thatcher, they found little success in challenging state housing policy (Weiler, 2003). As late as 1968, most Britons did think about acquiring their own home. The wars had left a powerful legacy of state responsibility for housing. Thatcher refashioned this responsibility into a restriction on people's freedom. In 1980, Margaret Thatcher urged the working classes to buy what they had received at subsidized rental rates. Her rhetoric fashioned state politicians as lairds who 'clung to the role of landlord – they love it because it gives them so much power' (Samuel, p. 24). Under state supervision, over two million families were forced to pay rent and were subject to 'petty rules and restrictions, enforced dependence' (Samuel, 1992, p. 25). The state was a barrier preventing people from achieving self-reliance and the dream of homeownership, said Thatcher, and in so doing mobilized broad support even from the working classes for neo liberal policies. Her rhetoric invoked householder pride as a symbol of national wealth and locus of respectability. Her speeches that framed council houses as cages created by bureaucrats to oppress people's freedom, was particularly grating in a period of expanding notions of consumer sovereignty and identity politics. This combined with Thatcher's bold coaching rhetoric that praised British citizens' productive potential, calling people to arms, proved deeply seductive for large numbers of people who were traditionally not Conservative voters. In Samuel's opinion, working-class agreement with Thatcher's statements led to its allegiance to a more authoritarian state under Thatcherite rule (Hall, 1980).

Flattering women

Also of great significance was the way Thatcherite rhetoric flattered women, albeit in complex ways. By promoting the importance of self-reliance and market freedoms and defining the state as an oppressive bureaucracy, Thatcher championed the power of the individual. Before anyone could look after their neighbours, she stressed, they had to look after themselves. She applauded merit as the measure for reward. According to her 'independence, originality, genius' were the sources of all the 'richness and variety of life' (Thatcher, 13 October 1978). The striving, singular, exceptional individual had made the nation great, not the collective sympathy it had shown in the post-war period. For the many who felt that social mobility had reached a stand still, the secular script of Victorian values tantalizingly promised a new way out via hard work, thrift, and looking after one's own patch of ground. Enterprise was valued over the collective distribution of social resources through the state.

According to Samuel, by emphasizing merit, hard work, and talent as the measures of success, rather than class and gender privilege, Thatcher tipped a hat to women who knew their work was under acknowledged, and their ability to get ahead thwarted by forces of social discrimination they could do little about. For women, saddled for years with the responsibility of minding, caretaking, and provisioning for others on top of paid labour, the exceptional individual appeared to unburden them from the unequal share of the collective burden they had so long been expected to carry. Further, taking a page from Victorian housekeeping textbooks, Thatcher stressed her conviction that the managerial skills of women were supremely fit to run the state: 'The many practical skills and management qualities needed to make a home ... give women an ability to deal with a variety of problems and to do so quickly. And it's that versatility and decisiveness which is so valuable in public life' (Thatcher, 13 October 1978). Besides the blurring of the traditionally separate domains of public and private politics, statements such as these boldly suggested that women were not just equal but superior to men.

The far-reaching consequences of monetarist policies were boiled down for the public into a simple 'exercise in frugality'; applying the principles of household budgeting (living within your means) to the management of the national economy. She defended her position against great opposition, noting at a Lord Mayor's banquet in November 1982: 'Some say I preach merely the homilies of housekeeping or the parables of the parlour. But I do not repent. Those parables would have saved many a financier from failure and many a country from crisis' (Samuel, 1992, p. 17). Thrifty women had made ends meet and maintained the household. Many people were simply too used to sponging off of the state, they felt that the line of credit would never run out, they felt an endless supply of milk would flow from the nanny state. 'Good Conservatives always pay their bills. And on time. Not like the Socialists who run up other people's bills.' Her monetarist policies had to be put into practice to instil 'an old-fashioned horror of debt' – albeit public debt, not private debt (Samuel, 1992, p 13).

Other winds of change

It is important not to give Margaret Thatcher's rhetoric more power than it deserves. Thatcher and her Victorian values failed to impress many people. Her rhetoric circulated alongside and most importantly was not strongly challenged by other significant cultural discourses at the time, which also undermined notions of mass society. The many riots during the 1980s manifested the demand for change. The decade opened with a Peace Camp organized in protest over the housing of 96 cruise missiles at Greenham Commons. Throughout the decade, the IRA struggled for Irish independence from England via bombings, shootings, and fatal hunger strikes. In 1985, police involvement in the deaths of Cherry Groce and Cynthia Jarrett sparked the charge of institutional racism and led to riots in Brixton and Broadwater Farms. These struggles signified women, colonized persons, and minorities' refusal to submit their interests to dominant ideology and norms. Academics debated the arrival of postmodern society, rejecting universalistic, grand narrative versions of history and intellectual inquiry. Celebrating plurality, diversity, and difference, postmodernist researchers framed traditional notions of shared culture oppressive.

Researchers at the time also questioned the usefulness of traditional class categories, suggesting another area of cultural fragmentation. Trying to explain the changing character of British society, researchers looked to changing work patterns, consumption practices, and the reworking of gender relations. The intensification of the service sector and entrepreneurialism seemed to focus people's attention on their personal career instead of their alliance with other workers in their class (Mingione, 1981). The old antagonism between the shop-floor worker and the capitalist, an important source of class-consciousness, became muddled. Service sector workers viewed themselves as professionals and entrepreneurs, internalizing the values of capitalism, and embracing merit-based structures. According to Ralph Samuel, finer gradations of hierarchy in the 1980s workplace blurred the lines between management and worker, owner and labour to the point where class 'hardly enters into the new middle class conception of themselves' (Samuel, 1982, pp. 124–5).

While they may have lacked class-consciousness, the new middle class worked as hard if not harder than traditional middle classes, as the new merit structures called upon them to clock long hours for the reward of advancing their individual career. Individualized consumption also assumed a greater role in people's lives and sense of self. Samuel, explaining what he and other researchers recognized as the new middle class, noted how spending had bypassed saving. Governed by a different 'emotional economy' than the pre-war middle class, the new middle class also emphasized instant acquisitions over long-term deferral. Religious values failed to resonate with the secularist interests focused on the 'have now' instead of the 'here after'. Nor did the new middle-class struggle in the same way over indulging their sensual pleasures.

Samuel argued that sensual pleasures became 'the very field on which social claims are established and sexual identities confirmed'. New politics emerged as people asserted their interest in displaying what they deemed 'good taste'. The home and food 'emerged as a critical marker(s) of class' (Samuel, 1982, pp. 124–5). Gender identities wove complexly into these changes. The resurgence of a feminist movement in the 1960s and 1970s contributed by the 1980s to the breaking down of 'sexual apartheid which kept men and women in rigidly separate spheres' (Samuel, 1982, p. 124). The erosion of the traditional patriarchal household bought the flowering of a diverse set of living arrangements; gay couples, singles, prolonged roommates, and lodgers; families separated by divorce and reconstituted around step-families. New urban dreams competed with moving to the village and commuting. Particularly for two professional households, the desire to minimize commuting by being close to work grew in importance. For women, the enhanced efficiency a household enjoys close to shops, laundries, restaurants, and child-care facilities was important. Housing demands grew alongside processes of gentrification that saw those with economic means takeover selective lower income neighbourhoods and contributed to a buy-for-let phenomenon (Smith, 25 February 1987).

The reworking of traditional masculine and feminine distinctions enabled both genders to devote themselves to a food and home decoration culture. Building the appropriate lifestyle was an important part of building a family. Cooking and eating rituals changed as people expressed themselves through food-shopping patterns, restaurant visits, kitchenware, celebrity chef adulation, and body maintenance. In their homes, according to Samuel, traditional concerns for privacy and reserve loosened making way for new forms of engagement, such as hosting of parties and affairs. People 'opened up their homes to visitors, and exposed them to the public gaze by removing the net curtains from the windows, and took down the shutters from their shops'; pubs scraped the painting from their windows. The age of the open plan arrived. 'In their houses they make a fetish of light and space, replacing rooms with open-access living areas and exposing the dark corners to view' (Samuel, 1982, p. 124). These changes permitted one to showcase their good taste.

It was exaggerated to assume that the changing gender relations of this period signalled women's complete emancipation. Women continued to undertake the lion's share of housework, provisioning, and childcare, while making less than men and still being under-represented in positions of power. Further, the changes empowered women unequally, as women of higher socio-economic position and better education more easily accessed a range of previously closed occupations than did other women. Still, the ability of men to limit women's contribution to the economy, their access to jobs, property, and credit dissolved. Women could imagine their futures on a larger map with fewer insurmountable precipices. Most importantly, women became a growing target for estate agents and credit providers. This situation was historically unprecedented.

People no longer appeared to pattern themselves in the older, more predictable ways. An entire consumer culture literature began to take shape in the 1980s as authors recognized the arrival of more intensive individual consumption patterns (Lee, 1993). Retailers' use of more intensive marketing and advertising; manufacturers' employment of technology and global production arrangements, put a diverse array of more customized goods in circulation. Styles turned over more rapidly. Advertising encouraged individuals to see their commodity choice as sovereign. Consumption was recognized as a just reward for hard work. As a deeply meaningful aspect of people's identity, it became impossible any longer to argue that consumption-based interests were less fundamental than production-based (class) interests. The diverse lifestyles fashioned out of commodities, challenged simplistic attempts to link consumption to class. Those from the same profession, income, class, and educational backgrounds could diverge in their taste, but some general patterns were recognized (Bourdieu, 1984).

The Big Bang and the banks

Changes in British banking culture reacted and contributed to these ongoing cultural shifts and tensions, most importantly by way of the expansion and marketing of consumer credit and mortgages. Margaret Thatcher's 1986 regulation, drafted out of an interest in stimulating global financial capital flows through London, also stimulated the sale of mortgages and credit. The banking sector posed a particular problem for Thatcher's vision of entrepreneurial Britain. She believed regulation supported discriminatory old-boy banking network ways. The gentlemanly banking culture's traditional contempt for the marketplace irked Prime Minister Thatcher. Although banking culture had been opening up to the personal financial market since the 1960s, the banks' non-sales orientation, their cartels and status-based promotion systems that selected workers from within, signalled for Thatcher an unconscionable node of elitism. Further, her enterprise act, which provided support to the unemployed who risked starting a business, was not enough. Small businesses needed investment and loans from banks, not the government and Thatcher was suspicious the lazy-boy banking network would fail in this duty. She insisted that

> [t]he manager of every branch of every bank, and every investment manager of every pension fund must know what to do if another Barnes Wallis or another Frank Whittle walks through his door, whether it is in Cornwall or Savoy Place.
>
> (Thatcher, 25 February 1981)

In some ways she was correct. Despite their inroads into the credit markets in the 1970s, it was still difficult for those of limited means to access credit in the 1980s. In 1980, 83% of the most wealthy, held significantly more current accounts than those down the social scale.

The culture of the city and of the banks

Surveying the banking situation seven years after her election, mindful of the global economic forces conspiring against Britain's financial sector, and disappointed that banks had not embraced an entrepreneurial spirit, Thatcher introduced significant changes to government financial regulation in 1986. Her infamous 'Big Bang' deregulated the London Stock Exchange and among other things did away with specialist work distinctions, removed fixed commission rates, allowed trades to be conducted by phone and computer; rather than just on the stock room floor, and permitted foreign ownership. The lines that demarcated high from low finance blurred as commercial banks, merchant banks, stockbrokers, stockjobbers, and building societies could all undertake the same financial tasks. Almost immediately, banks responded by consolidating to secure their place within the market. The Hong Kong Shanghai Bank took over Midland; Lloyds and TSB merged. Across the non-banking sector, older mutual society arrangements were abandoned in favour of incorporation. The 11 most powerful building societies in Britain abandoned their society status and incorporated to draw in more investment.

Many changes took place in London post-Big Bang. A rapid influx of international financiers, mainly US bankers at first, then European, brought new technology, a more aggressive marketing style and competitive spirit, all of which helped to drive out the last vestiges of gentlemanly banking. Similar changes happened to the social background of those in finance. The need to undertake trades on the stock exchange floor had served a powerful gatekeeper function that prevented women and those from lower down the social scale from gaining employment. Exaggerating the changes in the financial sector was unreasonable because the city remained a masculine sphere. Still, the removal of this sanction, allowed for a more diverse set of employees to enter the industry. The use of computers vastly increased the speed of financial transactions, calling for quick decisions and creating an even higher pressure on the workforce. The changes post-Big Bang led to a skills shortage. Wages increased considerably, the city's pay structure came in line with New York and Tokyo. The new environment handsomely rewarded those with specialist skills, or who appeared adept at making money (Leyshon & Thrift, 1997, pp. 141–2). Celebrating the changes Thatcher noted:

> The City's growing confidence and drive owe a good deal to young people. Its vast new dealing rooms are run by the young. People who made it not because of who they know or what school tie they wear, but on sheer merit. That is the kind of society I want to see'.
>
> (Thatcher, 10 November 1986)

Perhaps more than any other sector, financial workers came to epitomize the cultural tendencies associated with the new middle class (Graham, 25 October 1996). What united those working in the new culture was a belief in risk taking, working, selling, frequent partying, and spending hard. The new Turks of the financial sector had a profound sense of entitlement expecting higher pay, but also low tax rates, good services, and amenities. The new financial class showed a particular taste for property and nice homes and for a time, they had the money to pay top price for real estate. Recent reviews suggested that 20 years after the Big Bang property prices in areas coveted by bankers, Chelsea, Notting Hill, and Islington, rose by 404%. With a 278% growth in the FTSE 100 index, bankers led the way in demonstrating that bricks and mortar were a sounder investment than stocks (Finfacts Ireland, 24 October 2006).

Although always international, the city became even more so. London rivalled New York in financial exchange dominance. London became a more cosmopolitan city. While much of the wealth that flowed through the LSE had been generated elsewhere, nevertheless, it became a key node for global capital circulation. London, served as a formative service centre and the new bankers used their bonuses to satisfy their interests. Although accounts of the transformation are so frequent and similar that they have become clichéd, the rise of financial sector workers heralded the arrival of trendy bars, restaurants, and gyms, replacing traditional sandwich and barbers' shops. 'Before Big Bang it was de rigeur to have a pint and a pie,' said Richard Wyatt, Chairman of Panmure Capital, who began his career as a stockbroker in 1980. 'Now it's more common to have takeaway sushi and a bottle of mineral water – both of which were unheard of 20 years ago' (BBC, 26 October 2006). Thatcher enthused: 'And we now have a new Britain, confident, optimistic, sure of its economic strength – a Britain to which foreigners come to admire, to invest, yes, and to imitate' (Thatcher, 9 October 1987). Although the money that circulated through the city was largely foreign, there oozed from the city in the 1980s a notion that Britain was back, complexly weaving into a brash new sense of confidence that enabled people to dare to take the plunge and invest in themselves by way of increasing their consumption, self maintenance regimes, and homes.

A changed tone in advertising

The bank advertising in the 1980s and early 1990s signalled both the changing culture of banks and a sense of cultural optimism. Banks invested more in promotion than at any point in their history, aggressively targeting the personal sector for profit. Technology and research allowed the banks to target their profitable financial commodities, consumer and mortgage credit, to consumers. The banks let go of their mass market and focused on market niches, encouraging people to use a wider variety of services and more frequently. They also developed more refined risk scenarios, which gave them the courage to lend to consumers who were previously excluded from loan considerations.

Responding to the interests in individual consumption and contributing to them, bank advertisers now spoke to consumers using singular pronouns instead of addressing people as members of a community or family. This was part of an alternative discourse to the mass market, which placed emphasis on discrete and autonomous clients. The consumer addressed was no longer conceived of as the fearful unbanked, but a demanding, savvy, and wily individual. A late-1980s Midland television campaign depicted this demanding consumer, in promoting a new account called Vector, customized for the young urban professional. A young male enters a financial advisor's office and rattles off a list of services he would like his new Vector account to offer. The advisor listens with a startled look that would be typical of a traditional banking employee. The advisor informs the young man that he must speak to his superiors. He returns, and, slightly surprised himself, relays that the bank will honour his demands. At the end of the advertisement the advisor asks: 'And your service charges?' To which the consumer replies: 'I'll keep them the same, thank you.' How distant this representation of the consumer is from the deferential, compliant British consumers American marketers bemoaned in the early 1920s in Chapter 3.

A new self-reflexivity also expanded in the discursive messages of the banks. For example, the Midland's 'listening bank' campaign, according to Allen, Brand & Marsh, the agency that developed the campaign, was conceived to help Midland stand out from other commercials by speaking from the point of view of the consumer, rather than from the bank's point of view. One advertisement thanked consumers for coming up with the open floor plan implemented at the bank's new Oxford Circus address. The caption reas: 'the design of our Oxford Circus branch owes more to you than it does to us.' The theme continued in the late 1990s, within a new campaign that thanked consumers for teaching Midland about the types of services they should offer. For example, one advertisement featured someone having their hair done and who tipped-off Midland consumer spies as to how she was being overcharged for her mortgage, expressed thanks: 'For the woman in Janet's Salon who was worried about paying "through the nose" for what was advertised as a "bargain mortgage"'. The ads communicated a willingness on the part of the banks to survey and adjust their practices based on customer input. Advertisers present the banks as involved, adaptable, and versatile.

Competition was a central theme of this advertising. The banks thought more intensively and invested in promotion of their brand, particularly through television advertising. The friendly banking of the 1970s simply did not suit the tenor of the new financial times. The banks' research suggested consumers were less concerned about affability and niceness than informativeness, competence, and convenience of service delivery. Consumers cared about practicality more than mollycoddling. The friendly manager became a bureaucratic obstacle slowing down consumers' uptake of financial services. Many ads did away with the manager altogether. For example, one advertisement employed the following consumer testimony: 'I didn't need to see the bank manager to get a loan'. Another advertisement noted, 'our manager usually won't ask to see plans or estimates. In fact, it's quite likely he won't even need to see you'. Credit was now assessed by credit checks not face to face.

In the 1980s banks began to make substantial investment in new technology that allowed people to access their funds without going to a bank branch. Advertising designers celebrated this technology as an important consumer benefit. Technology was presented as the means to give consumers more control over their finances. The number of positive depictions of technology rises in the advertisements of this period. The ATM came to powerfully symbolize access to money 24 hours a day. Ads reminded audiences of the importance of having access to money at all times – one ad likening the need for money as essential to survival as water. Messages no longer told consumers how to access the bank, rather how to access money. The outside or the inside of the bank, ceased to be the primary *mise-en-scène*, as action in the ads now took place either around new technological delivery systems (e.g. telephone and Internet banking) or in the private home. Advertisers presented the banks less as socially embedded community institutions, reconstituting them as points of access to the economy. In this sense, the bank itself disappeared from advertising rhetoric.

This emphasis on continual access was linked to the theme of time, which became increasingly compressed and scarce in the advertisements. Contrapuntal to traditional notions of thrift and deferred gratification, financial services were sold as solutions to the dilemmas created by time pressures. The old emphasis on watching savings grow over time was now replaced by the expectation that money must be constantly available. For example, given that consumers experience a great deal of stress over arranging mortgages, an advertisement of this period offered the bank's mortgage as a remedy: 'Just when you think it's within your grasp, will you be kept hanging around for a mortgage ... you'll be pleased to hear that we've designed our mortgage service to make at least one part of the trauma a little easier and quicker'.

Because the new financial regulation allowed them, the banks reoriented themselves as investment houses, and promoting services such as unit trusts and stock options – once the domain of high finance – to ordinary consumers. The banks offered themselves up as tax havens, as they had been for larger corporations for some time. Tax was presented in the ads as the consumer's enemy, personified as the 'taxman' a biting, grabbing, character in relentless pursuit of people's hard-earned money. The bank promoted special financial services to protect the consumer from the taxman. Some of the advertisements reminded consumers they were eligible for tax credits and shelters. Other advertisements promoted financial products specially designed to take advantage of taxation loopholes. Some of the copy read as follows:

> Is the taxman still taking the bite out of your savings? ... earn high interest and cut out tax ... it's a snip. Get tax-free interest with a little help from our friends. It works hard but it's never taxed. The tax-man won't be able to get his hands on it.

Financial experts began to appear in late 1980s' advertisements to help manage consumers' funds in a turbulent financial marketplace. Far removed from the friendly banker, this character spoke to a new financial instrumentalism and pragmatism. For example, a Lloyds advertisement presented two unsmiling financial experts and was captioned: 'Nobody tells our fund manager what to do'. The copy invokes the image of a competitive world of financial investment in which tough and independent financial experts were needed to help consumers secure large dividends. The management of funds took so much energy that the expert was not expected to expend time on gentlemanly conduct or friendliness. Another advertisement reminded consumers to get their emotional needs met at home, not at the bank, where the focus was on making money. The copy reads: 'If you're looking for sympathy go see your Mom.' These ads, while blunt, reflected an important truism, responsibility for managing money lay with consumers.

Interest rates were an important, new selling point, and rate information filled the advertising copy of this period. Competition over rates for ordinary lending, mortgages, and investments led to a proliferation of numerically based promotions in this period, particularly in print advertising. The banks competed over rates as a way to encourage consumers to switch banks. For example, some of the advertisements of this period noted: 'If your monthly payments on credit cards, store cards and personal loans add up to say £200, First National Bank could halve them to £100 or even £50 a month'. 'Barclays Bank is now giving 15% p.a. interest to regular savers with our new Bonus Saving's account. That's one per cent more than any High street clearing bank offers on normal deposit accounts'. Interest rates were such a strong selling point by themselves, and endlessly changed, that advertisers spent little effort working rates into elaborately detailed cultural formats. These advertisements offered little aesthetic interest: designers employed a stock set of metaphors. Rates were most often associated with climbing, soaring, or elevations (mountain tops, Zeppelins, rock bluffs). Consumers no longer worked, their money did. Consumers were endlessly reminded of the productive potential of money. Saving under the rhetoric of interest rates was no longer for its own sake, but to earn money to spend.

Regulation allowed the banks to fully exploit consumer credit and the banks wasted no time promoting their most lucrative of services. The banks also competed with the building societies for the mortgage market. The old Access credit card consortium broke down as each bank opted to enter the credit market on its own. The expansion of credit unfolded in tandem with an intensified market and commodity sector within Britain supported by Thatcherite policies. Bank services enabled quicker access to commodities and a steadier cash flow. Consumers readily accepted the credit that the banks offered. By the end of the 1980s, 50% of the British population possessed a credit card. One in three members of the public carried a mortgage. So successful were the banks in extending their financial services in the 1980s that Leyshon and Thrift called this decade a 'financial high summer' and noted the very high profits made by the banks (Leyshon & Thrift, 1997). Much of that profit was the result of the banks' more professional sales teams. Staff was hired now less for their accounting skills than for their sales ability.

At no time in British history had so much promotional discourse circulated about the wonders of credit. The ads directly linked credit to consumption but stepped away from instructing consumers about what they should buy. Although luxury items adorned advertising copy, designers emphasized the promise of easy and quick access to money, leaving the consumer free to decide how they would spend the money. Some of the typical advertisement captions of the 1980s include: 'Any car, any model, any colour, any questions?' Another notes: 'We'll lend you the money. Where you put it is up to you'. And: 'Head for the shops. We'll foot the bills'; 'money's always there, just waiting to meet your needs'. Still another notes: 'You see them. You like them. You buy them'. Lloyds Bank said: 'Car loans and how to accelerate them.'

'NatWest can give you a personal loan to take to the sales. (After that you're on your own).' These ads suggest how difficult it was within the burgeoning consumer culture to reflect the diverse expansion of taste. The banks, in response, acquiesced to the consumers' consumption expertise. The advertisements made more of an appeal to the sensual value of gratification in consumption, an emphasis that barely registered at other moments in bank-advertising history. The financial community's taboo against luxury goods had clearly ended.

New debt

Competition within the credit market through the 1980s led banks to chase volume with increasingly tighter margins and 'drove them to take on low quality, low margin business' (Leyshon & Thrift, 1997, p. 212). Leyshon and Thrift document how UK consumers welcomed the offer of relatively cheap credit. By the late 1980s, household indebtedness reached 105% of disposable income, greater than in many other industrialized countries (Leyshon & Thrift, 1997, p. 207). It began to dawn on Margaret Thatcher in the later 1980s that her enterprise culture was not only producing the rugged, independent, hardworking, thrifty investors, but also debt-ridden consumers. Speaking to Scottish bankers in 1988, she admitted that a trade deficit was emerging as imports of consumer goods exceeded domestic production and exports:

> Moreover too much of the buying has been financed by too much borrowing. And that, at a time when savings have fallen sharply. The Government has cut its borrowing to the bone. ... But the personal sector needs to save too. So the Chancellor has taken the necessary action. ... Higher interest rates will give a substantial incentive to savers and a disincentive to borrowers. It is in everyone's interests that we get the balance between savings and investments right.
>
> (Thatcher, 8 September 1988)

Yet, to dictate how consumers spent or to limit the amount of money they borrowed, flew in the face of Thatcher's free market principles. She was able to demonize state debt and spending, but how could she possibly demonize consumers, the key variable which made the British economy turn? Thatcher had overseen the formation of a more open market system in a changing culture in which individual consumption was a central value. The consumerist genie would not go back into the bottle.

A recession in the early 1990s demonstrated the limits of a credit-led boom. The one tool the government had for controlling the market – interest rates – proved ineffective at a time of instability in the currency markets and inflation. In 1989, the housing and mortgage-led boom faltered, resulting in a catastrophic recession. Nearly ¼ of a million people had their homes repossessed, an experience that left scars on people for years. Despite a profound collective belief in the financial viability of bricks and mortar, housing proved as prone to rupture as any other site of speculation in the market. The Big Bang did little to circumvent the historic booms, and bust cycles that had traditionally disrupted the stability of capitalist politics.

By the 1990s, all consumers recognized that access to money was essential for their happiness in a consumer society. To be denied credit therefore was to be, in some way, excluded from the basic necessities of living – of hope, possibility freedom, and self-esteem. Many found, in face of turbulent economic circumstances such as a divorce or illness in the family, more debt became the only means of financial survival. Interest and inflation rates therefore became the focal point not only of one's economic, but also psychological well-being. Amid the economic downturn of the early 1990s, economic psychologists Lunt and Livingstone found that self-esteem and social respectability were still linked to financial solvency. Yet, they found debt-ridden consumers felt not only social shame and fear of public humiliation, but also a sense of enslavement and the loss of personal liberty that their debt imposed. Their surveys also showed that deeply indebted consumers expended considerable psychological resources to manage their complex and contradictory feelings towards money which both empowered them as consumers and enslaved them as debtors (Lunt & Livingstone, 1992). The psychosocial corollary of seeming domestic affluence apparently was constant worry about money. Addressing these types of problems proved immensely difficult in an economy founded on services and consumption.

The public drew a direct link between the recession and the banks. A chilling lack of confidence in the banking sector set in. In response, banks utilized their powerful promotional arms and acquired another new language for speaking about credit. One of the best examples of how marketers and advertisers worked together to overcome a backlash against credit is found in Barclays' launch of a new credit card in the early 1990s, called Assent. According to a Barclays' spokesperson, the card's design sought to ease the anxiety consumers felt towards losing control over their use of credit:

We wanted to give a clear idea of exactly what the card has to offer ... the general climate towards credit at the moment is fairly negative – a lot of the media are getting quite hysterical about it, although the problem is mainly with store cards. We needed to assure people that the card does give you control.

(Easingwood & Storey, 1991, p. 6)

The idea behind Assent was to have consumers pay a set monthly bill, to give them a greater sense of control over finances, and guarantee the banks a minimum payment. Credit became management of debt. To convey this idea to audiences, advertisers created a television campaign that emphasized the unpleasant experience of having bills arrive unexpectedly by showing a stream of bills cascading onto a doormat marked 'Unwelcome'. A letter follows from Assent that lands on a mat labelled 'Welcome'.

Besides trying to repackage credit as a source of control, the bank advertising took on a more therapeutic voice. Banks sensed consumers' need for counsel and supportive advice about their debts, which the banks had supported in amassing. The financial advisor emerged. This financial character was not an administrator (someone who tells you what to do) but rather a more egalitarian coach or mentor (someone who guides and helps). A television advertisement from this period clearly depicted this new relationship: a man and a woman discuss fears of their accumulating debt load with a financial advisor. The scene is of a confidential therapy session. The characters' faces are censored. The discussion is in tearful and shameful tones. Like a therapist might, the advisor does not tell the couple what to do, but helps them realize that their fears are manageable. He notes, 'no one said it was going to be easy', and encourages the couple to confront their problems. Within advertisements the number of references to limits on financial services increased. Commonly presented on a sliding scale, restrictions were lighter for those with larger incomes. This refashioning of services helped the banks deal more accurately with credit risk. Thus, the banks learned from the credit scare, how to customize credit services to target profitable and less risky parts of the market. Drawing upon American experience, British banks developed better skills at adequately covering the costs of credit, in order to avoid repeating the difficulties they experienced in the early 1990s (Sacks, 1991).

However, although inflation, interest, and unemployment rates subsequently stabilized, Thatcher's dismantling of the social safety net, the deregulation of money markets, her attack on trade unions, and the absence of support for traditional industrial sectors resulted in fears of the growing divide between the wages of increasingly precarious service sector workers and of city jobs that afforded a sweepstakes bonus structure. The banks had acquired a new power within the domestic economy. Their practices now closely influenced people's lives. This presented a new public relations challenge for the banks.

New Labour lingering old conservatism

By the time New Labour took office in 1997, the down turn of the early 1990s was washed away in a new sense of optimism. New Labour's economic policy, as many noted, deviated from the Conservatives only slightly. New Labour was unwilling to tax the top 1% of the population and believed that it was important to support industry and global relations. The Conservatives made their interest in privatization clear and drew clear lines of distinction between the state and the economy. New Labour blurred public and private. Thatcherism had become tarnished as uncaring, and New Labour addressed this by adding a caring twist to the rhetoric. The reason for a strong economy, argued Tony Blair, was to make sure that Britain could afford to retain its massive welfare structures, the NHS. It was New Labour's brilliant strategy to retrieve monetarism from Thatcher's backward-looking Victorian morality, by restoring its modernizing feminist impulses of caring for the most vulnerable (the poor and children). Catherine Needham drew upon interviews and a detailed study of New Labour documents to confirm her thesis that New Labour, in a move that went beyond Thatcher's wildest dreams, extended marketplace values to the public sector. New Labour, according to Needham, consumerized public service and constructed the citizen-consumer that constituted citizens 'as customers in search of satisfaction' (Needham, 2007).

Nothing spoke more to New Labour's alignment with conservative policies than Margaret Thatcher's endorsement for some of Tony Blair's decisions. She felt he too understood the importance of Victorian values, that he was a man of integrity, and she saw him as a bold leader, particularly in his decision to support the US in the invasion of Iraq. In Thomas's analysis, New Labour enjoyed electoral reward largely because the party accepted and 'even promoted' the Conservative Party's framing of social democracy as a problem to which Britain would not return. In so doing, New Labour, according to Thomas, 'helped strengthen the mistaken perception among both political elites and the general public that historically there really was no – or only a limited – alternative to

Thatcherism. This is perhaps the most damaging legacy of the "Winter of Discontent"' (Thomas, 2007, p. 280).

A more targeted and cost-sensitive approach

Competition in the financial sector in the late 1990s grew intense. A host of new financial service providers also entered the market, from such diverse sectors as supermarkets to British Gas. What was perhaps most important about the new competition, according to Gardner, was the way it 'cherry picked' the banks' most profitable services. 'The cherry picking tactics of the new competitors have meant that the ability of the clearing banks to cross-subsidise other products and even provide some banking services free of charge is increasingly coming under threat' (Gardener, Howcroft & Williams, 1999, p. 23). As the financial market became more competitive and flooded with financial products, margins remained important but the banks also increasingly recouped costs and expanded revenue streams via service charges and sales. The banks reached out to as many consumers as possible. The proportion of low-income households without a bank account fell to 10% by 2004/05, down from well above 20% in the late 1990s (Palmer et al., 2006).

Free services and incentives continued to be offered particularly to clients that promised profit. In 1999, no major financial institutions offered 0% interest rate credit, yet by 2004 close to 45% did. A study of credit suggested that 7% of all unsecured debt was interest-free. Employed people who owned homes reported higher levels of 0% interest rates. The report concluded, 'So interest-free credit seems to be targeted at – or more accessible to – households who are likely to represent better credit risks' (May, Tudela & Young, 2004, p. 422). Research revealed that 85% of bank profits came from just 35% of their clients, and in the saturation period business increasingly reoriented around this coveted group (MAPS, 1995). Bank marketers found they could make just as much money, if not more, and with less risk from the more wealthy sectors of society. Marketers today are most interested in the top 30% of households because they hold more than one half of all income.

The cherry picking of their services made it difficult for the banks to cross-subsidize general transactions (their least profitable, but most in-demand service) as they had traditionally. Thus, the banks increasingly sought to recoup the cost of general transactions by imposing service charges or a minimum account balance. Research revealed that an account required a balance of at least £1000 to cover costs. In working out equations such as these, the banks created benchmarks for driving low deposit holders out of the network or imposing service charges. The amount of interest offered on standard current and savings accounts also dropped. Other cost-cutting measures included a serious re-evaluation of the idea of universal service distribution and massive branch networks. Branches began to be closed, although Leyshon and Thrift expressed surprise that the banks were able to hold out so long before doing so. They speculated that the retention of costly branches related to the history of protectionist regulation in Britain that encouraged banks to conceive of themselves as oligopolies that did not think competitively or cost-efficiently about service delivery (Leyshon & Thrift, 1997). In the saturated period, this was increasingly not an option available to the banks.

Banks became more serious about delivering their services through technological means. It cost banks about 30 pence for each ATM transaction; one pound for a branch transaction (Cruickshank, 2000). In the climate of cost cutting, technology seemed to be the better option. Banks increasingly saw the value of their ATM networks, and extended them beyond their branches to include them in stores or other convenient areas. Consumers had come to rely on the machines, which now could carry out a variety of services including bill paying. The sheer size of a bank's ATM network was an important competitive advantage. Consumers chose banks based on the availability of banking machines. Banks became protective of their ATMs, and began to issue service charges for access. Up to £1.50 per transaction was levied on non-member consumers. A spokesperson for the *Bankers Magazine* applauded the new service charges believing they illustrated that the banks were learning to operate more cost-effectively in a competitive market: 'The fact is selectively charging for ATM use simply makes good business sense. It just signifies that banks are getting better at tracking consumer profitability at the account level' (Faust & Mooney, 1995, p. 3).

Banks also invested in new modes of service delivery to increase sales of financial products and to cut costs. First Direct's highly successful telephone banking service was emulated throughout the industry; Prudential launched a new phone and Internet bank called Egg, and Barclays launched B2 and an Internet banking service. B2 offered special accounts that enabled clients to play the stock market through their computer. All these initiatives were launched in the context of consumer intelligence. Telephone and Internet banking changed the traditional conception of face-to-face banking.

By the late 1990s, banks were undertaking lavish campaigns to target the upscale credit market. Moving from sober reporting to daily entertainment meant moving into a world dominated by video clips, the rush and clash of symbols, and the need to entertain minute after minute, day after day (Clark, Thrift & Tickell, 2004, p. 303). Barclays attempted to present Barclaycard credit as central to both luxury and everyday use (Archer, 1997). Rich cinematic pictures of inviting vacation spots such as Goa were captioned with: 'Don't put it off. ... Put it on'. A 1990s NatWest campaign captured a similar sentiment. The ads focused on memorials in various locations such pubs or on park benches: the memorial message noted that the person died not having taken the vacation they wanted, or repaired their home as hoped. The messages reminded readers that life was finite and that they should live it to the fullest and in the moment. The advertisements link pity towards those who neglected to use credit to live their lives to the fullest.

Conclusion

The financial industry in Britain achieved fantastic power by the twenty-first century; supported not by protectionist state regulation, but two successive governments who invited international bankers to Britain, provided them with maximum freedom, and minimum taxation. A most dramatic rise in housing prices began in 1997, and the decision to keep interest rates low to increase investment contributed to high levels of speculation and retail spending. The banks supported those changes by selling mortgages and credit instruments. They were very well rewarded for their efforts. The assets of the UK banking sector increased from 762 billion in 1987 to 5526 billion in 2005 (Larsen, 25 October 2006). All told, financial services contributed £165 billion to the UK economy. Nearly half of that came from the City of London and Canary Wharf. A staggering £2.15 trillion of capital flowed into the UK in 2007 – some £295bn more than the US (Mathiason, 11 January 2009). Financial industries enjoyed an unprecedented level of autonomy. Britain celebrated its ability to attract the supposed smartest minds in the world, with the promise of quick fortunes and low taxes.

Margaret Thatcher's vision was achieved. The banks were not simply attentive to consumers needs, they actively marketed financial investments to them daily. But, Thatcher failed to imagine the direction low finance and consumer credit might take over time. Her identification with the spirit of the shopkeeper made it difficult for her to imagine potential contradictions associated with consumerism and an open market of credit instruments. Her construction of the British public as thrifty made it difficult for her to imagine that people might employ personal credit, which she encouraged the banks to extensively market, for anything but enterprise and prudent utilitarian consumption. New Labour had no such difficulties in imagining the British consumer and invited them to keep the high street going by delivering successive waves of low interest.

Consumers took up financial services offered by the banks to achieve their collective dreams of homeownership, lifestyle advancement, and economic security. Because of their dependence on banks, consumers now had much more to say about bank practices, and much of it was negative. In the state's retreat from domestic banking regulation, consumer organizations and the media became a more formidable force in voicing concern over bank self-regulation practices. The next chapter looks at discourses the broadsheet press circulated about the personal financial market.

6
The Press Takes on Personal Debt

This chapter explores how journalists constituted the personal debt crisis in the British Broadsheets in the twenty-first century. Since their earliest inception in the seventeenth century, the *Times*, the *Packet*, and the *Post*, served as conveyers of shipping news about the colonies; vital channels of communication about business, social welfare, and the world events. Finance stories have long been part of the news. The consumer economy and the role of personal finance within it became a regular beat of journalists in the 1980s. Journalists handled homeownership as a social contract, worthy of political debate. They reconfigured discussions of taxes upon concerns about interest rates. Meanwhile their attention to personal debt waxed and waned; making headlines in the early 1990s recession with record numbers of home reposition and bankruptcies reported, but dissipating as the economy began to recover through the later 1990s. In what follows, I focus on the re-emergence of concern towards personal debt in the twenty-first century.

In the 1990s, broadsheet papers repackaged money sections, once a few brief pages crammed between sports and lifestyle, as an independent supplement. This shift coincided with financial service providers' increased marketing efforts post-Big Bang. The *Times*, *Independent*, and *Guardian* created dedicated money sections, while the *Telegraph*, distinguished itself with a personal finance section. The money section's *raison d'etre* was to assemble a specialized audience towards which financial advertisers and public relations material could be directed. However, readers were ostensibly drawn to the sections for sound advice about how to manage their finances which did not always correspond with marketers' interests. Thus, bringing these two interests together created a profound contradiction. Articles focusing on financial products revealed the heavy hand of financial public relations staff on the shoulder of financial journalists. To attract readers, the papers focused on human interest of personal financial stress and success. Consumers were invited to pose questions about finance and were given tips about prudent money management. The sections focused on individual concerns and assumed that readers were responsible for their personal finance choices. Broader cultural, social, and economic constraints placed on consumers' decisions burden of the production of this type of copy. So, for example, the copy asked people to address economic recession by tightening their individual belts.

The business section had long been an important source of political news. Reporting on the daily dealings in labour, corporate mergers, commodity stock, and consumer markets, journalists sought to make visible the complexities of national and interconnected global economies. The cultural importance of personal finance led journalists to many sources. Central among them were politicians. Government and business sectors communicated their interests to the public in the press. Each read the papers and the information constituted a platform for debate. Journalists provided political spokes for people with a platform to articulate their interpretation of the economy; yet, also questioned government rhetoric, for to do otherwise threatened their credibility and their ability to maintain the public interest necessary to sell newspapers. Journalists questioned political parties about how they would address soaring house prices preventing first-time buyers from getting on the property ladder; what the government planned to do about collapsing pension schemes; and reported on how 'easy credit is helping push debt and personal bankruptcies to new highs' (Warwick-Ching, 30 April 2005, p. 22). Journalists turned to economists, accountancy firms, retailers, academics, debt counselling organizations, and people on the street to shape their diverse tales of personal finance.

While it was impossible for the media to close down the multiple interpretations the audience made of stories, media and journalists could draw people's attention to particular topics and not others by way of a process McCombs and Shaw called agenda setting (McCombs and Shaw, 1972). These authors suggested that salience was created by the sheer repetition of a topic, its placement on the front page, discussing the topic at length, and spinning the topic into a variety of different subjects (McCombs & Shaw, 1972). To keep audiences focused on the topic, the media framed their messages through provocative word choice, compelling tone, and hooks to maintain the ongoing focus of the reader.

Placing personal debt on the agenda

Between 2000 and 2007 broadsheet journalists forcefully put the consumer debt on the public agenda. They reported thousands of stories about personal finance and consumer credit. If we took the agenda set by the media seriously, considering the sheer number of column inches devoted to a topic as an indication of its significance, we would have had to conclude that the threat posed by consumer debt outweighs environmental degradation by far.

Journalists repeated the gross personal debt figures, making it virtually impossible to miss the blunt tale: the nation of shopkeepers had become a kingdom of debtors. A favourite form of presentation highlighted how personal debt had surpassed 'the country's annual economic output, three times the level it was in 1990' when the economy had entered a recession (Cave, 30 March 2005, p. 3). Journalists presented personal debt as a ticking time bomb, growing one million pounds every four minutes since 2004, reaching £1.43 trillion in 2008 (Redmond, 19 June 2004). Coverage of the debt crisis circled around several different areas: inequalities in the property market and home repossessions; growing reliance on unsecured debt; bank writing off debts; rising personal bankruptcies; growth of collection agencies; increased numbers of Individual Voluntary Arrangements; and expanded use of debt counselling services.

Home: Dream or nightmare?

Journalists' accounts recognized the economic and cultural importance of the home property market. Money was cheap because interest rates were low, contributing to a historic property boom that took flight in 1997 with the election of New Labour. Worth £551 billion in 1948, by 2007 the property market's estimated worth was £6.5 trillion, representing 60% of the country's wealth. Sub-prime or 'credit impaired' mortgages became the pragmatic solution to addressing the widespread demand for houses. Some economists interviewed by journalists explained how the sub-prime market met the realities of twenty-first century finances where it was no longer uncommon for an individual to loose their credit record because of job-loss, relationship break down, or illness. Institutions that had never extended mortgages to those with adverse credit records, rewrote the rules. Instead of deciding between righteous debtors who lose their credit ratings due to hardship and those who simply spend 'too much or lose track of their bill payments'

(Kassam, 13 April 2005, p. 20), lenders applied the rational logic of the marketplace by increasing the amount of interest charged on mortgages to cover the risk. Credit flowed to 'a new group of homeowners, who may have one or two blemishes on their credit histories but whose debts were not so serious that they should be treated as high-risk' (O'Connor, 23 January 2006, p. 4). By 2005, sub-prime mortgages made up over 20% of the mortgages in Britain. The increased numbers of individuals signing mortgages created powerful new sources of capital. The papers quoted bankers who celebrated the expansions in the property market arguing that mortgage choice and competition were 'good for everyone' (Farrell, 22 January 2006, p. 4).

Yet, other journalists pointed to property market inequalities, blaming a number of different parties for the situation. Some journalists pointed to the rich foreigners. Always attractive to the wealthy, in the late 1990s global millionaires entered Britain in large numbers, attracted by the 'honest government' and good tax rates – New Labour refused to tax the top 1% of earners. Journalists suggested these fantastically wealthy foreigners colonized the property market, making London, next to Moscow, the most expensive property market in the world. Journalists also blamed financial workers (many of whom were foreigners) for seeding their massive bonuses into the property market and driving up house prices to a level ordinary people could not hope to reach. The financiers' desire to purchase part of the pastoral to escape at the weekend, said journalists, had contributed to a 20% rise in farmland prices. Others blamed a greedy middle class who leveraged their superior credit lines to purchase second homes in London (often council houses), because they saw property, quite rightly, as a more attractive investment than stock.

When *Times* journalist Rosie Millard wrote an article admitting that acquiring a second home left her fraught with money troubles, she set off a brief debate about the class inequality of the property market. Critics argued that without governmental support or caps on the principle amounts extended and usury charged to lower income groups, economic problems like those currently taking place in the mortgage market were inevitable. Simply, the more wealth you hold the cheaper you can acquire money. The middle classes purchased second homes as an investment strategy, creating another layer of speculation within the market.

Millard's confession aired the cultural forces that conspired to encourage debt. Following the advice of her peers, themselves heavily invested in property, Millard had climbed up on the property ladder.

With the double income her marriage brought, friends stressed: 'Extend yourselves as much as you can'. Following the logic that states you 'actually spend money to make it', Millard and her partner promptly purchased a home, followed by a 'famously chic flat in Paris'. Although the flat was meant to save them money otherwise spent on vacations, it was difficult to rent. The properties also required appropriate life-styles accoutrements. As the commodities flowed into the households, a £40,000 debt load rose. The Millards complained that French bank managers were less forgiving than British and Millard moaned that the debt cramped her desired lifestyle. She spent one frantic day each month shifting debt from one interest free credit card to the next. Bank managers became part of the family providing essential guidance on financial management. While Millard frugally cut back on her use of black cabs, she found it impossible to forego 'a decent haircut every eight weeks, vaguely designer-style suits, Stila makeup and The New Yorker' because, as she said, 'to keep working you have to look the part' (Shaw, 29 January 2006, p. 18).

Some read Millard's confession as middle-class smugness. One rebuttal came in the form of a website fashioned as an appeal for African debt relief, but, with tongue in cheek, asked the public to give generously to help poor Rosie Millard. The website's text listed the extensive equity of Millard's property holdings and a recorded voice stressed that debt was preventing Mrs Millard from acquiring ball gowns, expensive makeup, and limiting her trips to West End theatre productions. Millard's financial strife, when placed in the context of low-income families and pensioners, was indeed laughable (Murray-West, 10 January 2006). By way of contrast, Kempson, Mackay, and Willitts's in-depth random sample study of debt found single parent families raising children in rental properties on incomes of less than £15,000 a year. No matter how much additional work they took on, these families were unable to get out of debt (Kempson et al., 2004). By contrast, the sale of one property holding would solve the Millard's debt. Focusing the debate on class inequalities is a helpful inclusion in the public discourse about finance, yet, Rosie Millard's confession raises another less widely discussed point: even for the privileged mid-dle class, chasing the dream of property ownership delivered anxiety, not contentment.

Guardian journalists in particular, emphasized that Thatcher's right to buy legislation, had not provided those with low incomes with a home, but had taken their homes away. London, long prized for its mix of housing for those of different incomes, was declared a property ghetto because social housing once available for those of modest means had been privatized. According to George Monbiot, in 1981 there were 6,305,000 properties rented from local authorities; by 2005, the figure had dropped to 2,803,000. Owner occupation rose by 50% – from 12,442,000 to 18,405,000. Monbiot argued, 'new Labour has been as Thatcherite as Thatcher' for under their reign the number of social houses built each year diminished from an average of 46,600 during Margaret Thatcher's term of office, to 17,300. Close to 50% of council houses were sold off (Mobiot, 27 November 2007). By 2002, 69% of homes were privately held, the same rate as America. Only 14% of all households were rented from the council, compared to 31% in 1971. Housing stock was transferred to housing associations that increased to 7% of all rentals up from 1% in 1971 (National Centre for Social Research, 2004). Another journalist underlined, 'Sixty-nine per cent of the country is owned by only .06 per cent of the population. Of the 7500 new homes built in Islington South between 2000–5 1581 were affordable. There are 13,120 families on the waiting list and 4500 who have enough points to bid for re-housing' (Elliot, 24 November 2006). As Chancellor in 2005, Gordon Brown upped the nil-rate stamp duty band to £120,000 from £60,000, extended existing interest-free and shared homeownership schemes for first-time buyers, and as Prime Minister he promised to build new houses. Some journalists, however, dismissed these proposals as cosmetic. Forceful housing policy was not attractive to the government that supported a more free property market. Thus, said some journalists, the largest of the banks remained the most viable option.

The press sent clear warnings about the precariousness of the situation prior to the economic crisis that hit in the summer of 2007 (Seabrook, 2004). They stressed that borrowers were offered as much as four or even five times their income (Farrell, 22 January 2006). Journalists reported in 2006 that mortgage repossessions rose by two-thirds, growing from 6000 in the previous year to 10,000. Auctioneers reported a rising number of repossession of the assets of buy-to-let second homes (Croft, 22 February 2005). Other articles warned, with reference to the US situation, of the normalization of people using their homes like an ATM machine, withdrawing cash by refinancing in order to supplement their wages. The spectre of rising interest rates haunted coverage as reports noted that a rise in financing charges would place the indebted homeowner in a particularly precarious position (Swann, 20 January 2006). Journalists presented compelling personal accounts of how the homeownership dream was lost to young people, who even with parental support, were unable to get onto the property market (Bromley, & Humphrey, 2005). 'James Seccombe, 22, an accountant, although tired of "throwing away money on rent" found it impossible to "afford the costs of purchasing an appropriate property in his area of Manchester" (Monks, 15 May 2005, p. 17).

In this line of argument, journalists spoke to the rights of the public, 82% of whom were reported as preferring owner occupation to any other form of tenancy. In so doing, they reinforced the long-standing efforts to position private homeownership as the golden standard of economic, social, and psychological goodness. There was good reason why the home was culturally understood to be an instrument of social mobility, a nest egg for one's offspring, and a shield from the harsher aspects of capitalism. The extension of mortgages to neglected groups, women and the poor, promised to create greater economic equality. Nothing speaks more forcefully for the growing empowerment of women than that their names increasingly appeared on title deeds. Yet, few questioned the fundamental limitations inherent in an open property market, until the recent crash.

The press did not mask the problems of the property market, but they did ring fence homeownership as worth striving towards, carrying forwards the long-standing celebration of mortgages as prudent investments. Their discourse separated productive from unproductive debt, stressing good consumption from bad, and positive money management from imprudent money management. The faith in the property market was bolstered by the overwhelmingly negative picture journalists drew of unsecured credit. Collectively, press coverage suggested that the real problem of personal finance was the credit card. As one reporter put it, 'it hasn't been the mortgage which has dragged them [over-extended consumers] under but other spending on store and credit cards'.

Insecurity about unsecured debt

Journalists documented the rise of plastic finance, which by 2005 overtook cash as the most popular form of payment (Morgan, 17 May 2005). In a country where up until the 1980s people were still paid in cash, the change was flagged as salient. In 1989 there were 26 million credit cards in circulation and by 2006 that number jumped to 71 million. Adding together debit and cheque cards, the total number of plastic cards reached 160 million (Thornton & Brown, 3 July 2004). Credit cards were the fastest growing area of consumer debt. In 2006, mortgage debt had increased threefold to £967 billion and unsecured borrowing had risen fourfold to £135 billion, but journalists underlined that credit card debt had increased seven times to £58 billion (Seager, 16 March 2006). Britain's hunger for unsecured credit was stressed by placing it in the context of other countries' debt. All the EU countries combined used less than half the amount of unsecured credit as Britain (Hickman, 3 January 2006). Britons were reportedly spending £1 billion more via debit and credit cards than cash, prompting the Bank of England to consider reducing the amount of currency in circulation (Evans & Morgan, 8 July 2004). Credit cards surpassed debt on store cards. In 2004, for example, £2.6 billion was owed to store card companies compared to the £53.5 billion owed to credit cards (Times, 27 October 2004). The average credit card balance was £2097 and total credit card borrowing, worth £54.3 billion, accounted for approximately 6% of the £1 trillion debt. By 2006, credit cards accounted for £2.32 of every £10 spent on the high street (Guardian, 7 January 2006; Millard, 3 April 2005). Over one-third of the money spent by consumers at Christmas was borrowed. Most of the consumers using credit were said to be still carrying debt from the previous Christmas (Daily Telegraph, 12 December 2005). By 2006, the average household debt was said to be £7650.

Journalists indicated that credit card debt assumed an increasing proportion of the bad debts written off by the banks each year, a practice so normalized that it was considered a cost of doing business. In 2004, credit cards accounted for '30 per cent of banks' write-offs, three times what they were in 1998'. In 2006, when Barclays wrote off £1.57 billion in bad debts, mostly related to its 11 million Barclaycard consumers, management worried that the 44% increase from 2005 was too steep. In 2007, the number of people unable to repay their debts hit a record high, as over 100,000 people went bust (BBC News online, 16 February 2007). Readers were reminded that debt levels were rising faster than incomes. The average income increase between 1994 and 2004 was 41%, while, during the same period, average debt loads soared by 91% (Hardy, 10 January 2004). So too, did journalists point to the rising number of collection agencies, which jumped from 270 in 2003 to over 500 in 2005, as another sign of an overly stretched consumer debt situation (Pilston, 14 August 2005). Some doorstep lenders, most notably London Scottish Bank, reported that profits made from their debt collection arm had risen 45%, to £8.9 million (Independent, 3 July 2004). The number of complaints about the practices of debt collectors also increased (Croft, 21 January 2006).

Blooming bankruptcies

Journalists presaged that bankruptcies were reaching dangerous proportions. Although records did not exist until the 1960s, journalists highlighted the sharp upward trend in bankruptcies since the 1980s (Hall & Watts, 30 October 2005). Bankruptcies peaked in 1992, during the recession, when a total of 36,000 people were declared insolvent. About 30,000 bankruptcies were declared each year throughout the rest of the decade (Brown, 27 March 2004), yet the numbers spiked in the twenty-first century. The numbers of people declaring insolvency, said journalists, doubled in three years from 54,000 in 2003 to 110,000 in 2005 (Hurlston, 3 January 2006). The amount of disposable income devoted to debt repayment and interest reached 20%, 'the highest since 1990'(Warwick-Ching, 13 May 2005, p. 28). Part of this upward swing was blamed on new laws that removed some of the difficulty associated with declaring bankruptcy. Bankruptcy was once a difficult task, taking several years to resolve. Until the late 1980s, only 4000 cases of bankruptcy occurred each year, an amazing testimony to the public's vigilance towards making their debt payments. But, in the post-Thatcherite push to encourage greater entrepreneurialism, inter- est grew in changing the laws to stimulate the economy by instilling a risk-taking culture into business. The model for the proposed laws came from the US.

Up until 2005, US bankruptcy laws were the most lenient in the world and they attracted the interest of British policy-makers (Roberts, 16 June 2005). Originally written to ease the burden of farmers whose crops failed due to natural disasters, modern US bank- ruptcy became a means of preserving jobs and sustaining businesses through economic disaster. These laws were thought to support the acclaimed culture of risk-taking, said to be central to US growth. Bankruptcy was explained as 'the most efficient system you can imagine for reconciling conflicting interests' (Cumbo, 21 October 2005, p. 17). While originally designed for businesses, by the twenty- first century, individuals made extensive use of bankruptcy laws to handle their burden of debt. In 2005, 2.04 million individuals declared themselves unable to pay their debts, representing one in every 50 US households (Croft, 12 February 2004; Daily Telegraph,

12 January 2006). Privileging business over personal consumption, in 2005, George Bush Jr deemed the number of personal bankruptcy cases unacceptable, and thus instated new laws that made it more difficult for people to wipe out their debts. Writing off credit card debts became almost impossible. These changes spoke to the growing role consumer debt was playing in the economy and sent a clear signal that the state drew a line between credit card bills and business expense accounts.

In 2002, New Labour introduced the Enterprise Act, designed to amend the 1986 Insolvency Act and to bring UK bankruptcy in line with US laws. One of the most important changes was the speed with which one could write off debts – in as little as one year. Ministers celebrated the new laws in the press arguing that they removed the stigma that surrounded debt, thus promoting a risk-taking culture (Nisse, 19 September 2004). As in the US, it was increasingly individuals – not businesses – declaring bankruptcy. In the 1990s, 60% of bankruptcies were related to business failures but, by the twenty-first century, 80% of bankruptcy cases were private individuals (Croft, 30 December 2005; Derbyshire, 17 August 2005). Although traditionally creditors had forced individuals to declare bankruptcy, the press publicized a new pattern emerging for individuals to self-declare. In 2004, more than three-quarters of all bankruptcies were personal. In the first three months of 2005, 9418 people declared bankruptcy, which represented a rise of one-third over the same period the previous year (Dunn, 6 November 2005). Commentators showed little mercy for those declaring bankruptcy. One journalist suggested that people 'ran up their debts out of sheer greed'. Another underlined that the new laws, allowing consumers 'more or less straight back on to the high street with fresh credit cards is rather like the badly-drafted law in New York State that gave newly released sex offenders entitlement to free Viagra' (Clark, 30 May 2005, p. 20). The amended laws were said to make bankruptcy too easy. People could now 'apply for administration by fax, rather than having to argue the case in open court', making 'the procedure significantly less painful' (Brown, 27 March 2004, p. 27). But, other journalists sought to counteract the idea that the new laws were a free ride. The press provided a platform for those overseeing bankruptcy cases to stress the efforts they engaged to distinguish legitimate cases from those where individuals sought an easy means to escape financial obligations. Those who declared bankruptcy without legitimate reason faced punishment (Mawson, 2005). Bankruptcy, journalists warned, severely impacted credit ratings while some debts, including student loans and credit cards, were exempt from bankruptcy. The laws signalled an unwillingness to excuse debt acquired through what they deemed lifestyle choices.

The business of individual voluntary arrangements

Individual Voluntary Arrangements (IVAs), another measure used to address debt, were also widely commented upon in the press, which signalled their rising numbers as a concern. Invented in the 1980s when most bankruptcies involved businesses, IVAs emerged out of the 1986 Insolvency Act and offered an alternative to the courts (Thomson, 19 December 2004). Special practitioners working with indebted clients were required to get 75% of the creditors to agree to an arrangement in which typically close to half of the debts could be written off, and interest rate limits extended for five years. Bankruptcies were overseen by the courts: IVAs are a business. Specialist brokers received up to a third of the money collected (BBC News online, 23 February 2007). Stock-listed companies such as Debt Free Direct, one of the largest firms handling IVAs, turned their attention from the business community to personal finance, understanding it as an area of growth and profit. Those working in the area told reporters personal bankruptcy growth was a good sign and indicated consumer debt 'could outpace rising demand for its business insolvency operations' (Jopson, 5 July 2005, p. 23). Journalists underlined the way IVAs were marketed to consumers, drawing attention to one company's website that contained publicity about a couple who easily addressed their £22,000 debt load with a IVA. The couple boasted about the service in publicity: 'They reduced our monthly payments from £900 to under £300, arranged for nearly £10,000 of our debt to be written off, stopped all interest charges and, best of all, it didn't cost us a penny. The service was free'. The website of Freeman Jones, a Manchester firm, boasts: 'Clear your debts with up to 75 per cent written off – as seen on TV' (Hall, 3 June 2005, p. 26). In the six-month period up to 31 October 2005, journalists reported the value of this company reaching £1.85 million, a significant increase from 2004 when it was worth £148,000. Freeman Jones' shares doubled in value. By 2005, Debt Free Direct began to pay dividends after doubling its revenues to £8.4 million (Blackwell, 29 June 2005, p. 23).

From a consumer's point of view, the agreements cost them little and, by minimizing the negative impact on credit ratings, bestowed less social stigma. Unlike bankruptcy law which typically required the sale of all valuable assets to pay off creditors, IVAs allowed individuals to maintain some assets, most importantly their homes (Downes & Levene, 7 January 2006). Between 2003 and 2005, the number of IVAs rose 70% to 10,752, a higher growth rate than that of personal bankruptcies which grew by 48% to 35,898. But the papers warned that IVAs were allowing people to wipe off their consumer credits (Hall, 3 June 2005). Creditors, initially positive towards IVAs because of the likelihood to recover more of their debt – 40 to 50% compared with 10% by more traditional means (Hall, 3 June 2005) – lost interest over time. The banks became less willing to enter into the agreements because they felt they were not receiving their fair share. Creditors complained IVAs too easily excused middle-aged males with around £40,000, making savvy use of the agreements, when they could have paid off their debts.

Extending helplines the indebted

Journalists also pointed to the growing line-ups at debt counselling organizations as an indication of the personal financial crisis. Consumers could turn to a host of organizations, including a national debt line co-funded by the government and the credit industry, a consumer credit counselling service funded by the credit industry, and the charity Citizens Advice (Moore & Watts, 15 January 2006). These organizations became spokespeople for the indebted public. Their published research reports documented a doubling in the number of individuals seeking help between 1998 and 2006. The average amount of debt held by those seeking help in 2006 was reported as £13,153 (BBC News online, 24 May 2006). Debt Free Direct estimated 18.3 million people owed an average of £5993 each on credit cards, loans, and overdrafts. Consumer Credit Counselling Service reported that the average client seeking help owed '£27,000 to 11 different creditors, compared with less than £22,000 to nine creditors four years ago' (Barrow, 15 February 2005, 4).

The debt organizations stressed how many were living on the edge of financial catastrophe, where a small change in income or interest rates could tip them over into financial difficulties. Citizens Advice estimated, '1.1m people who asked for advice on handling debts last year did so as a result of a cut of only 10% in their annual income'. Christmas presented a particularly difficult time. Calls to the debt counselling services surged in January (Times. 21 January 2006). Most of the debt organizations agreed that the aggressive marketing of the banks and poorly informed consumers contributed to the debt crisis.

Journalists did not mask the growth of personal debt in the twenty-first century, but rather took it as the subject of hundreds of their stories, and in so doing contributed to its popular construction. Journalists called upon a large cast of characters from government officials to debt counselling services, and from accountants to ordinary people to tell the tale of personal debt. They presented reams of statistics to highlight the personal debt trend, placing those numbers in a variety of different contexts to show the severity of the problem. They underlined how personal debt surpassed productive output and how Britain's debt loads surpassed other European countries. They drew attention to the growth of bankruptcies, IVAs, collection agencies, and the number of banks writing off debt. Journalists highlighted the inequalities that took shape within the booming property market, yet, never lost faith in the home. Rather, they offered unsecured credit card debt as the personal debt villain, reminding the public that the common wealth was not to be drained to bankroll those who could not manage to pay for their individual lifestyle choices. In 2006, the year before the economic down turn, a journalist chastised then Chancellor Gordon Brown, captain of the good ship Britannia, for driving the country into an 'economic iceberg', and the public for blithely shuffling their deck chairs 'in a mist of myopia' (Daily Telegraph, 14 February 2006, p. 2). Journalists had placed personal debt on the agenda. The next chapter explores the discourses that emerged to explain the causes of the debt.

7
Three Personal Finance Discourses

Apart from pointing personal debt on the news agenda, as I suggest in this chapter, journalistic accounts of personal finance can be understood as streaming into three broad discourses. One discourse, voiced mainly by government spokespeople, economists, and retailers, celebrated consumer's rising debt load as a positive sign of affluence. The democratization of credit encouraged greater numbers, than at any other point in history, to invest in their futures. Reports reminded readers that debt levels were lower than those of the recessionary period in the 1990s and wholly manageable by the vast majority. Retailers celebrated the willingness of the consumer to find and purchase their pleasures on the high street. The second discourse was contrapuntal, focusing on the banks' role in shaping the mountain of consumer debt. Financial institutions, according to this argument, abused their privileged position by selling credit to consumers who could not afford it, reaping vast profits along the way. Journalists exposed the manipulative marketing techniques of the banks and financial employees' fat bonuses to shock the public into concern. The credit counselling organizations said the banks played a major role in subjecting the public to financial strain. The third discourse looked to the consumer to explain the expansion of personal debt. People's disregard for thrift and embrace of consumerism was the cause of personal debt, according to this perspective. The press suggested that women, young people, and especially young women exemplified the new spirit of hedonism and anti-thrift attitudes. Banks and the credit card companies simply did their jobs, the problem lie with young people and women's quest for 'champagne lifestyles' on budgets that could barely afford the purchase of a beer.

Discourse I: Don't panic, personal debt signals affluence

Intertwined within the ominous press reports of debt disaster, a discourse that stressed the productive gains achieved in Britain emerged. A thriving free market kept interest rates low, fuelling consumer confidence and retail spending, allowing new businesses to grow and prosper. Newspaper coverage celebrated the homeowner and the spending consumer who were investing wisely and successfully managing their credit to fulfil their pleasures. New Labour built upon the myth that everyone who applied themselves, worked hard, and minded their finances could not only get ahead but deserved consumer rewards. Those who failed to take advantage of the potential offered by the expanded marketplace, the tax breaks, and new programs of the government, or who could not succeed in spite of them, had no one to blame but themselves.

The press promoted homeownership as the best means of securing financial stability. Economists stressed that there was 'probably no business anywhere in the world that is a better hedge against a vicious tax system than being a home-owner in Britain'. Reinforcing mortgage populism, journalists reminded their readers 'that most people consider mortgages a good deal'. Economists stressed that rising levels of personal debt were simply a signal that UK consumers were taking prudent advantage of the low unemployment and interest rates. People quite rightly took on more debt to acquire homes and advance their standards of living. A report from Credit Suisse First Boston celebrated the growing purchase power of the public: 'Emboldened by a strong economy and the rising value of their homes, people have spent an extra £10,000 each' (Schneiders, 24 July 2005, p. 6). Building Societies suggested that consumers were reaping the benefits accrued in their houses. The number of people taking out equity from their homes rose to 44% in 2002 (Hunter, 13 June 2004).

Using the statistics of the 1990 recession as a baseline, twenty-first century debt loads were viewed as fully manageable. Financial managers like Chris Rhodes of Alliance & Leicester reported that data from a poll of 2700 individuals conducted every three months showed that debt loads were 'comfortable compared to historic levels'. Interest rates were a third as high as they were in the 1990s (4.5% compared to 14.6%). People were in a better position to manage their debts because their household incomes had doubled, suggested journalists. Debt servicing was 13.8% of income compared to 26% in the 1990s. The public was enthusiastically assured that the country's housing market, shattered in the early 1990s, had 'roared back to life'. Debt loads appeared inflated because house prices had tripled since the 1990s. This was a positive situation, according to the banks, because mortgages as a percentage of home value fell from 58% a decade ago to 41% today. Mr Rhodes concluded: 'Overall, households with mortgages are comfortable – in sharp contrast to 1990. People are spending a smaller proportion of their incomes on their mortgages. Arrears and repossessions remain at historically low levels' (Hall, 8 January 2006).

The UK personal financial sector was also compared to the US and deemed to be well within the limits of reason (Coggan, 6 December 2003). Following the collapse of a number of employer-run pension schemes, the main political parties in 2003 developed policies to once again stimulate people's faith in pensions and savings (Warwick-Ching, 30 April 2005, p. 22). While consumers were saving less, they were characterized as much more thrifty than US consumers. The savings ratio fell to a historically low 5.6% in 2004, but journalists stressed this figure was still 'well above that of the US, which is about 1 per cent' (Cave, 30 March 2005, p. 3).

The papers stressed that those with debt problems 'tend not to be homeowners'. Unsecured borrowing as a percentage of household income was said to be the highest among those living in private rented accommodation, whose average debts totalled over £8000, an amount equivalent to 41% of their income, double the national average (Seager, 16 March 2006). Many renters were under the age of 30. But, here too, the papers suggested there was little cause for concern because most of their debt was student loans, not credit card borrowing (Seager, 16 March 2006). Next to the home, investing in tuition was highlighted as a secure investment. Over time these young students would parlay their education into high-paying jobs that would provide the income to take on mortgage debt and get on the virtuous property ladder. The papers reported that the value of Britain's home equity was close to £2 trillion, or 60 percent of British wealth. A quarter of the property market was owned outright (Elliot, 24 July 2006).

Credit democracy and consumer common sense

Although unsecured credit card debt was, unlike mortgage debt, approached equivocally for the most part, most agreed the 'democratisation of credit' was wholly preferable to the days of 'heavy-handed regulation'. Journalists warned readers: 'It is easy to forget at a time when we are besieged with adverts offering us 0% credit and buy-now-pay-later deals that women once needed to produce a letter from their husband if they wished to take out a bank loan. The fact that everyone now has equal access to credit is to be welcomed' (Independent, 3 January 2006, p. 28).

Financial consumers' common sense was also stressed. Consumer minister Gerry Sutcliffe argued that most people used credit wisely to increase the material pleasures in their lives: 'For the vast majority of people, debt and credit is not a problem. Credit is an integral part of our daily lives, allowing flexibility and driving the economy' (Inman, 20 July 2004, p. 14). A credit card CEO went on record to give his support for rising debt levels: 'Debt is healthy in a thriving economy like the UK. It is the backbone of a strong economy. People should be able to borrow and buy things they want, but we have all got to be cautious on both sides that people do not overextend themselves' (Ryle, 15 May 2005, p. 5). The Bank of England revealed figures that demonstrated the 'vast majority of people are comfortable with the debts they are holding and are able to service them'. Sir Andrew Large, Deputy Governor of the Bank of England, noted that since debt-servicing costs are low and stable – at about 10% of disposable income – 'servicing high levels of debt seems quite realistic' (Hardy, 10 January 2004, p. 2). Stewart Dickey of the British Bankers' Association stressed that, even with slightly easier bankruptcy laws, only a 'tiny minority' saw it as a 'lifestyle' choice (Mawson, 2005). According to a 2004 study by the Association of Payment Clearing Services, the trade body governing electronic payments, most credit card holders were reining in their spending and using their plastic sensibly. The report noted that 73% of cardholders paid off their balance in full each month, meaning no interest payments for the card issuers, while just 6% of people paid the minimum. 'The overwhelming majority of consumers borrow responsibly and deals with debt responsibly', said Paul Rodford, head of card payments at APACS.

Other stories stressed that only a small minority of individuals had difficulty managing their finance. A 2003 report noted that almost half the population (43%) did not have any debts. The article suggested that concern lay with the minority of individuals (57% of the population) who were responsible for pushing 'the overall household debt-to-income ratio to a record 129 per cent' (Elliot, 12 December 2003, p. 22). Journalists reported research by pollsters MORI, which examined credit card data from 48,000 consumers and concluded, 'only one person in every hundred with a credit card is in any danger of getting into unmanageable debt'. The vast majority of users (68%) fell into the group known as 'convenient controllers', older people who use credit but pay it off every month. Despite this rosy picture, three years later, the banks, under pressure, tightened their provision of credit turning down '50 per cent of all its new credit card applicants' (BBC News online, 16 February 2007).

Just as hard work and self reliance was culturally praised, so too, did the press remark upon the great integrity the public showed in shouldering their debts. This was not a generation of spendthrifts according to this line of argument, rather, consumers 'did their utmost to pay off their loans' (Hardy, 10 January 2004, p. 2). This heroic spender who faithfully paid their mortgage and credit card bills was propelling Britain's unprecedented economic growth. Journalists celebrated the public's positive attitudes that allowed them to ignore the debt doomsayers:

> The public were right to increase their borrowings, to invest in property and to keep their nerve as consumers, workers or employers, through the period of financial turbulence, which started, with the bursting of the dot.com bubble. And they will be right not to worry too much about a modest increase in interest rates, either today or in the months ahead. Economic conditions in Britain remain very healthy and even the housing market, while it is certainly pricey, is not yet as overheated, as many people believe.
>
> (Kaletsky, 6 May 2004, p. 20)

A *Times*'s economics reporter argued that while the 1970s recession was weathered by strong export growth, and the early 1980s recession held at bay by increased capital spending, the consumer's willingness to purchase goods and utilize their credit cards had lifted the country out of the devastating 1990s recession. Since 'early 1992 consumer spending has risen by an average of 2.7 percent a year'. Consumer spending, not government or corporate investment, was promoted as the primary factor transforming the economic situation; thus spokespeople celebrated and encouraged consumerism (Rozenberg, 5 January 2006, p. 48). Gordon Brown confirmed that consumer spending had underwritten much of the 50 quarters of continuous economic growth the country had enjoyed. New Labour celebrated this economic success that represented 'the longest period of continuous growth since 1701' (Kassam, 13 April 2005). A Guardian journalist noted how politicians' attitudes towards consumers: What Chancellors have loved about them [British consumers] is their predictability. They are good-hearted, trusting people, inclined to look on the bright side. Give them an interest rate cut and they'll buy a new car. Give them another interest rate cut and they'll start looking for a new house (Observer, 18 December 1994, p. 18). As long as interest rates remained low was there any reason to worry about personal debt? (Thornton, 9 January 2006).

Retailers worship the indebted consumer

The retail sector fawned over the 'Shoppers' enthusiasm to spend in spite of debts' (Chisholm, 21 January 2006, p. 4). Retailers panicked as the slightest drops in their retail sector were seen as catastrophes instead of common fluctuations in economic cycles (Daneshkhu, 30 December 2005, p. 3). Journalists used highly colourful, vivid, and dramatic language to project a terror towards economic downturns. For example, 'shock' was said to befall the retail sector in 2006 as it experienced the 'worst performance since Second World War'. The 'shopping boom' was said to be running 'out of steam' (Seager, 17 February 2006, p. 27). Because Christmas is the retail high season, extraordinary concern accompanied winter downturns. Lack of consumer spending in November created a 'wrist-slashing time for retailers' as 'Britain's high-street traders are heading for a Christmas Armageddon' (Jamieson, 13 November 2005). Another headline chastised consumers for being tight wads: 'Britain has become a nation of Scrooges this Christmas. Haunted by the twin spectres of unemployment and falling house prices, consumers are spending less and saving more' (Bush, 24 December 1992; Thornton, 5 January 2006, p. 52). Consumers were thought to have developed a negative 'discount mentality' that had made them a 'wary, suspicious creature, shuffling along the high streets, counting the pennies – a veritable Scrooge right down to the soles of his discounted shoes (Observer, 18 December 2004, p. 18). Journalists in these stories present consumers' decision to not circulate their earned income and credit through the consumer marketplace as the equivalent of a moral indiscretion.

Retailers threatened that, should the Bank of England dare raise interest rates, bankers would wear the blood of financial disaster on their hands. Indebted consumers were defined as 'far more interest-rate sensitive' than the Bank of England allowed, and a rise in interest rates would quash the expectation that 'the consumer will maintain the stoicism displayed in recent years' (Chisholm, 5 January 2006, p. 3). Were the government to 'stoke' the interest rate, journalists warned 'previously disposable income that would have found its way into the shops would be eaten up and the growth of the economy would cease (Wheatcroft, 6 May 2005).

Economists who dared to recommend interest-rate hikes faced the wrath of retailers who were promoting credit as passionately as their products. Low interest rates and easy credit were considered essential to keeping consumers active on the high street and preventing people from tipping over into bankruptcy. Retailers and debt counsellors united, insisting the government keep interest rates low to prevent both a slowdown in the economy and undue hardship for indebted public. What is important about this first discourse is that it celebrated personal debt. At the same time, and often in the same paper, other articles vilified public debt and blamed the banks for its expansion.

Discourse II: Modern day loan sharks

Journalists, like the public, had a pragmatic expectation that the state, with some goading, would address at least the most egregious aspects of consumers' financial situations. There is some evidence that the elected politicians bowed to journalistic pressure. In 2005, new legislation limited the amount of service charges the banks could charge. Banks were required to stop hiding the risks of credit in the small print in their advertising. These important victories for the public were supported by the press. Still, a more harsh and full-scale attack on the moneylenders was difficult. The city put the UK back on the international map, by supplying the credit consumers used to spend and fostered economic recovery in the late twentieth century. There was much at stake in biting the financial hand that fed UK-prosperity. Further, although many people thought that banks' practices were problematic, they were weary of government intervention in limiting access to credit. Politicians had to strike a fine balance between appearing to do something about banking malpractices and their broader belief in free market principles for the health of the economy. This left journalists and consumer organizations to investigate 'the bankers, the list-brokers, the lifestyle analysts' who made Britain 'the most credit-addicted country in the world' (Ronson, 16 July 2005, p. 19). Headlines suggested that lenders were 'encouraging a binge debt culture'.

To highlight the inequality, several stories focused on the massive bonuses those in banking made by peddling consumer debt. By 2006, journalists reported that UK banking industry had achieved record-breaking profits of about £34 billion, equivalent to the gross domestic product of Croatia (Croft, 18 February 2006, p. 19). In 2007, analysis by the *Guardian*, of preliminary data from the Office for National Statistics (ONS), revealed a 24% rise in bonuses to £26.4 billion. Journalists highlight the relatively small numbers of people who shared this windfall, reporting that more 'than half, £14.1bn, was earned by the 1 million people in the financial services sector'. A small number of hedge-fund managers received bonuses in one year upward of £200 million each, while the average wage of workers in Britain was said to have grown by only 3.6%. Some journalists rooted out the inconspicuous ways in which bonus-rich financiers spent their money acquiring lavish properties and luxury goods. Journalists found it immoral that there was a five-year waiting list for a new Rolls Royce, and that yachts of more than 80ft were becoming increasingly common.

Journalists noted with disapproval that bankers' yachts were kept afloat by the expanding consumer debt. The banks, they said, bombarded people with promotions that contained the myth that credit was an easy means of instantly accessing one's desires. Critics argued the promotions needed 'to be balanced with equally uncompromising warnings of what lies in store for a buy now, pay later culture' (Warwick-Ching, 14 May 2005, p. 28). Banking staff, no longer simply tellers or advisors but sales people attempting to meet quotas for loan and insurance sales, were said to bully consumers into accepting more debt than they might have otherwise (Croft, 2 June 2004). Offers of interest-free periods enticed consumers to take on a credit card or switch providers. After the initial interest-free love affair was over, consumers were left stranded with large bills and high interest rates. Critics chastised financial providers for increasing credit card limits without asking consumers. The distribution of high interest credit card cheques in the mail was deemed a money grab (BBC News online, 16 February 2007). Critics argued that including credit card cheques in marketing material during the holiday period encouraged people to spend more (Shaw, 11 December 2005). The Financial Services Authority, the principle watchdog of the city, rang the alarm in a 2006 report, which stated that the 'banks, building societies and finance houses' could severely damage their reputations because 'they have given credit to large numbers of consumers who are unable to afford their debt repayments'. The watchdog noted that consumers were also making financial decisions based on an 'inadequate understanding of the potential risks' (Miller, 26 January 2006, p. 3).

Journalists also tracked rising bank service charges. Banks and building societies refused to report the amount of money they made from unauthorized overdraft fees, deeming it competitor-sensitive information. This led BBC reporters to go undercover and find £20 to £35 charges common on unauthorized overdrafts. Customers who went over as little as 37 p reported receiving fines. Credit card users claimed they had not been fully informed about the charges, learning about them the hard way, after they had forgotten to make a payment. Spokespeople from the British Bankers' Association claimed the fees merely covered the cost of recovering debt. But, journalists suggested unauthorized overdraft fees hit one in four UK bank-customers during 2004, for a total cost of £3 billion.

The banks' interest-rate charges also raised concerns for journalists. While the Bank of England base rate ran around 5%, credit card providers were charging three or four times that amount. Immune to competitive pressures, retailers and lenders had little incentive to 'reduce annual percentage rates (APRs) on store cards, which currently averaged about 30 per cent' (Elliot, 27 January 2006, p. 18). A commission exploring personal finance argued that interest rates higher than 25% 'should have a "wealth warning"'. Estimates suggested borrowers were 'being overcharged £100m a year due to inflated interest rates' (BBC News online, 21 December 2005). 'Mr Barrett, who earns £1.7m year as chief executive of Barclays bank, parent company of Barclaycard, stunned the Treasury select committee by saying he did not use plastic to borrow "because it's too expensive"' (Treanor, 2 January 2004, p. 20). Mr Barrett said that he discouraged his son from acquiring a Barclaycard.

The Office of Fair Trade took the criticisms seriously and capped late payment charges at £12, an amount deemed sufficient to cover the administrative costs associated with late payments. The Consumer Credit Bill in 2005 required card companies to print warnings in normal size, instead of small print, inform consumers how much it would cost them to settle bills by paying only the minimum amount each month, and make their interest charges more visible to consumers (Nicolson, 18 January 2006).

The press highlighted some of the perils associated with the expansion of credit in the twenty-first century. With an eye on expanding its market, in 2006, MasterCard targeted teens with a credit card (Farrow, 29 January 2006; Morgan, 26 January 2006; Daley, 11 February 2006). Unlike the banks, critics refused to view teenagers as independent economic subjects, thus expressed outrage that financial bodies marketed to the vulnerability of children. The democratization of credit took on a sinister hue. Doorstep lender, Provident Financial, provided Vanquish, a credit card for the poor, a potentially progressive act, but they charged 64.9% interest. Consumer advocates concluded this was loan sharking. A survey in Liverpool, cited by the government's Social Exclusion Unit, showed that annual percentage rates charged to clients in pawnshops and by door-to-door debt collection agencies ranged from 69% to 365% (Daily Telegraph, 23 January 2006). Families with household incomes of less than £11,500 a year reported spending an inordinate amount of their income to service their debts. In 1995, the debt ratio represented 16.3% of their income. By the twenty-first century this had risen to 36%. Those making £50,000 or more also devoted more of their income to debt payments, but during the same time period their debt ratio rose from 3.4% to 12.6% (Berwick, 5 June 2004). One in six borrowers did not qualify for the headline rate advertised in financial advertising (Dunn, 4 December 2005). The democratization of credit, from this perspective, added another layer of economic inequality upon those that suffered the most.

Although the Banking Code, the voluntary set of good practice standards, expected bankers to undertake credit checks and refuse to extend additional credit to heavily indebted consumers, researchers found several instances where bankers failed to live up to their code (Warwick-Ching, 10 May 2005). The banks explained that the credit referral agencies used to supply credit checks gathered information through different sources, thus contributing to an underestimation of debt levels. As a newspaper article pointed out, 'a bank may be unaware that a potential customer could have 10 existing credit cards with £20,000 of debt outstanding, if the applicant is simply paying the minimum payments. It could easily accept an application for an 11th card'.

A BBC Real Story documentary exposed Lloyds TSB for its failure to make adequate credit checks. An internal Lloyds TSB document detailing a review of 185 loans showed that, in more than half the cases, the bank did not have files required to show that proper financial checks had been made. It found staff, pressured to meet targets to boost salaries, manipulated paperwork, selling loans to people unable to afford them. On average, nine in ten credit card holders were not asked to show they could afford repayments or prove their income before being issued with plastic (Daily Telegraph, 23 January 2006). David and Wendy Dickerson were offered £100,000 by the bank. Mr Dickerson was on health benefits and Mrs Dickerson was earning just £5000 a year. Embarrassed by the negative press, the bank wiped clean the family's debts (Ashworth, 14 May 2005). Others reported that Lloyds TSB was not an isolated case. The banking industry's practice of lending to borrowers who clearly could not afford to make the repayments was 'endemic' and resulted in 'derailing careers, retirements and stress-free lives'.

The National Consumer Council said: 'The culture is currently one of hard sell, with too little effort to protect the customer'. NCC spokesperson Mike Taylor noted: 'Time and again we get calls from people with huge debts, which they cannot afford to pay and which are given without the borrower undergoing a full credit check or fully understanding the risks involved in borrowing such large amounts of money'. One article noted how a 'vulnerable' man earning £150 a week managed to rack up debts of more than £100,000 across nine personal loans (Ashworth, 28 January 2006). Another report told the story of a 50-year-old warehouseman with a poor understanding of financial matters who amassed a level of debt that he had no hope of ever repaying (Jones, 28 January 2006). Reporters admonished the banks for putting the achievement of sales targets above a prudent assessment of the creditworthiness of loan applicants. Reports also warned the banks that their poor financial decisions made shareholders nervous and ready to remove money from the banks at any hint of loss (Kollewe, 28 August 2007). Fearing regulation, some banks responded to the criticism by agreeing to share more data with all of UK's three main credit reference agencies, Experian, Equifax, and Callcredit (Davies, 15 April 2005).

A Christmas tale

None of the press stories captured the struggle over the moral boundaries of personal financial more vividly than the bankruptcy of Farepak, a Christmas savings group. The centuries old practice of collectively saving for the Christmas season, by the twenty-first century, had become a business. In 1969, a butcher in Peckham sought to ensure the sale of his turkeys by selling coupons to help poor families afford all the Christmas trimmings. Highly popular, the practice was corporatized and called Farepak. By 2006, it employed 25,000 low-income earners to sell the coupons within their communities. By selling the Christmas saving scheme to their friends and neighbours, agents received vouchers and hampers to extend their own Christmas bounty. The saving schemes were conveniently brought to people's homes, sparing them the cost of long journeys to impersonal banks or lending institutions. Agents were known and provided regular reminders about the need to save. While large-scale retailers, banks, and even store cards offered better rates, Farepak provided financial services with little red tape to those who lacked means. Retailers agreed to accept Farepak vouchers and provide goods for its hampers at a reduced rate because it assured them customers.

While these practices echoed the self-help financial movements of the nineteenth century, Farepak was a modern publicly traded company and subject to downturns in the market. In the fall of 2006, the Halifax Bank of Scotland (HBOS), which held the account of Farepak's parent company, European Home Retail, decided, based on EHR's poor history of payments, to prudently pull in its chips and cut losses. EHR, and consequently Farepak, went into administration. The 300,000 individuals who had put aside weekly savings totalling on average £500, some upwards of £1500, were lucky to receive a small fraction of their savings back.

The closure of a minor business like Farepack was a common marketplace event. However, because Farepack's business was predicated on the cultural ritual of social caring, the closure of Farepak came to symbolize banker's greed. Affected constituent complaints alerted MPs who investigated Farepak and EHR on 13 October 2006. Business and political journalists brought the story to national attention. Who were the scrooges that had spoiled people's Christmas? Fingers quickly pointed to the financiers. Why had EHR not protected savers' income? Was it true that EHR (continentalists) had used the savings of desperately poor (British) people to pay-off their own financial mismanagement? Could those wealthy bankers at HBOS with their huge profits not have shown the decency to wait until after Christmas to close the business?

The consumer affairs minister declared the collapse of Farepak a national emergency, demanding stronger financial laws to protect consumers. MPs and reporters labelled the bankers involved in the case, Dickensian Scrooges. Misery, a favourite Victorian term used to describe the immense unhappiness associated with massive debt, was constantly invoked in the coverage. The same people who, in other contexts had been labelled welfare scrounges, were reclassified as thrifty, honest folk struggling to provide their families with a nice Christmas by a respectable means, not handout or debt. Mary Riddell summed up the moral indignation projected at the financial managers of Farepak who became 'the objects of such odium that few would mourn if they were boiled with their own puddings, in accordance with the old Scrooge recipe, and buried with a stake of holly through their hearts' (Riddell, 12 November 2006).

In true Victorian fashion, a charity movement was instantly organized. The consumer affairs MP invited fellow MPs to donate a day's wages to prevent the affected parties from being thrown into the jaws of loan sharks and allow them to enjoy their Christmas. Major retailers put up £250,000. Bowing to the pressure of consumer groups' call for a boycott, HBOS provided £2 million compensation. Individual donations also were put forward. One Farepak agent appeared on television telling how she had taken £2500 of her own money to payback people who had through her agreed to become part of the scheme. She was compelled to give because she had met with savers every week, some members of her family. Audience's tears no doubt fell when the people refused to take her money claiming that she should enjoy her Christmas.

While the aura of condemnation of evil moneylenders was voiced most strongly in the *Guardian*, most of the public reported little surprise, expecting businesses to do anything within their power to create profit. The Cruickshank report (2000) on competition in the banking sector made it clear that British consumers had been reluctant to employ the most powerful protest available to them: to withdraw their deposits and search out more cost-effective and thoughtful service providers (59% of bank clients held the same account they opened at the start of their financial life). The report spelled out the banks' formidable hold on the important current account market, the gateway to other electronic banking procedures (80% in 1998). The 2005 Consumer Credit Bill sought to provide consumers more protection against lenders. Statutory protection from lenders was available since 1974, but prosecution was difficult. Licenses were required for lending. The effectiveness of the new bill was highlighted in the widely reported case of a Birmingham 'loan shark' who was sentenced to four years imprisonment for undertaking financial trade without a licence (Davies, 15 April 2005). To bring charges up against the main-street banks, however, was incomprehensible.

Bankers' rebuttal

Richard Lambert, the director general of the Confederation of British Industry, stressed the stellar contribution to the growth of the British economy. The city had accounted for more than half of all growth in the national economy in 2007 and paid one-fifth of all corporate tax revenues the previous year (Seager, 28 August 2007). The financial sector created a large number of spin-off service sector jobs (Leyshon & Thrift, 1997). Regulation, Lambert warned, hindered economic growth by costing 'the industry £400m in lost revenue' and put 'the companies' revenue at risk' (Treanor, 20 February 2006, p. 27).

Gary Hoffman, the chief executive of Barclaycard, deflected the blame for rising levels of personal debt back onto the government and the Bank of England. Low interest rates, set by others, fuelled expansion in consumer spending, said Hoffman. Hoffman also attacked critics for questioning the banks' professional integrity saying that he found it 'a real insult to the banks that we would be prepared to lend to people who would not pay us back' (Paterson, 22 May 2004, p. 1). Evidence report-edly showed that, in the context of the consumer debt backlash, the banks were becoming more prudent. For example, HBOS and Egg began tightening their lending criteria in credit cards and loans in the middle of 2003. Nationwide, in 2005, turned down half the consumers who applied for a mortgage (Croft, 30 November 2005). Barclays introduced a more rigorous check system for loans and credit cards, increased its inter-est rates, and turned down 55% of all credit card applications. The bank also raised interest rates for its existing 11.2 million credit card custom-ers because of the concerns about a higher proportion of bad debts.

British Bankers' Association, Stewart Dickey, claimed that the Banking Code mandated sympathetic treatment of people. He said that the banks 'bend over backwards to help customers renegotiate' their debts. Moved by criticism of the Commons Treasury committee, Dickey also noted that banks had stopped automatic increases in credit limits (Mawson, 2005, p. 24). The banks argued that they did not force consumers into debt, rather simply provided the financial tools for them to do so. Spokespeople for the banks said there was no reason to feel sorry for consumers, indeed, consumers were putting the banks at risk because they cleverly used their cards to get financial advances on funds each month without having to pay any interest (Griffiths, 2003). The banking community wrung its hands over a new breed of compulsive credit card users they called 'rate tarts', who moved their credit from card to card to take advantage of the 0% financing deals. It was estimated that as many at 10% of credit customers switched credit providers each year (Davies, 15 April 2005). These practices, said the banks, required new rates to be instated to lessen their costs. The HSBC, the world's third largest bank, saw the UK as its 'most difficult' credit market. Britons, according to the bank, were becoming increasingly comfortable with life on the 'never never' and felt little need to pay back their loans. In short, the banks suggested that the rising personal debt loads were not the result of their practices but the consequence of the British consumer's greed, over-inflated sense of entitlement, and diminished sense of thrift.

Discourse III: Unthrifty consumers and champagne lifestyles

The third discourse focused on consumers' role in debt and consumption cycles. The press provided a forum for accountants, government spokes-people, and those in the therapeutic industries to reflect upon and pass judgement on consumers' behaviour. The media constructed financial characters, circulated economic norms, and moralized. Consumers spoke about their financial anxieties and confessed their credit card sins.

Journalists identified a new cultural trend in which consumers were throwing economic caution to the wind. Citizens Advice Bureau debt specialist Sue Edwards noted a new 'socio-cultural attitude to borrowing and lending' (Blackwell, 29 June 2005, p. 23). Accountants reported that people turned 'themselves in' to the bankruptcy courts expecting forgiveness for debts acquired 'out of sheer greed' (Wheatcroft, 7 May 2005, p. 93). People were dreaming above their station and making overly optimistic evaluations about their economy and prospects (Clark, 30 May 2005). Geeta Varna, a counsellor with the Consumer Credit Counselling Service, said: 'nowadays there isn't a stigma any longer to being indebted. Borrowing is OK now. More clients are coming simply because they are over-committed and over-optimistic about their ability to repay' (Cave, 7 May 2005, p. 14). Journalists suggested the public's exaggerated sense of entitlement was founded upon the belief that their property equity would cover the bills; as the cultural norm insisted: 'you can't lose on property' (Riley, 27 January 2006).

Accountant Mike Gerrard argued: 'the [size of the] UK's mountain of personal debt ... rests squarely on excessive credit and store card use, personal loans and often unsustainable champagne lifestyles' (Prosser, 6 August 2005, p. 44). Following the motto: 'live now, pay later' (Warwick-Ching, 14 May 2005, p. 28), people appeared to focus on the present and push future problems out of their minds. For example, one article warned that the 'current lack of financial preparation' and 'live for today' attitude would leave people unable to meet 'additional costs in later life', and require them to 'sell their homes' (Farrow, 4 September 2005, p. 1). Charles Turner, a director in PricewaterhouseCoopers' business recovery operations saw consumers ill-prepared to handle the consequences of their debt: 'Many consumers have been on a spending binge over the last few years and, while the party may be coming to an end, for some the hangover is likely to be drawn out and painful'. The Bank of England warned people that they 'might be taking a too rosy view of their ability to pay back what they owe' (Francis, 14 December 2003, p. 6). With an estimated '2.5 m people regularly spend[ing] more than they earn' (Hall, 12 January 2005, p. 23), journalists conjured up for their readers images of people paying for rent on cash drawn from credit cards and avoiding credit card bills out of fear of their contents (Budden, 12 February 2005; Stevenson, 5 February 2005).

The press concluded, 'Britain has become a nation of unashamed big spenders' with a fantastical 'thirst for the high life and luxury goods and services' (Smithers, 2006, p. 3). To make their trope of champagne lifestyle palpable, journalists pointed to the rising numbers of people who no longer cooked at home, but rather accrued debt by eating out five plus days a week, or purchased trendy ready-made meals at extraodinary cost. Mintel researchers reported in 2006 that the restaurant sector grew by 18% from 2002 to reach £17.7 billion. The press also associated excessive drinking with debt. Alcoholic beverages accounted for 19% of household expenditure, costing £38.5 billion. Champagne, expensive spirits, and cocktails challenged the traditional beer market. Out in gastro-pubs, the spendthrift public was said to display an appetite for 'cheap chic' fashion, worn one evening, thrown away the next. For journalists, cheap-chic garments offered less of an environmental problem than a credit card risk. With £1 billion spent on celebrity, gossip-based magazines in 2006, the press argued the union between celebrity culture and fashion retailers fuelled a constant turnover of styles, whet consumptive appetites, and resulted in high credit card bills. Instead of promoting thrift bargains, buying vintage ignited excessive shopping habits. For example, one young woman confessed her powerlessness towards fashion, claiming it was all too easy to go shopping and pick up a few cheap tops, some fake jewellery, and trousers on sale, than face a £100 bill. Journalists suggested that 'armies' of consumers, carrying out 'shopping sprees down Bond Street' and then declaring bankruptcy, besieged the country.

So too were modern parents caught under the spell of fashionability, using credit cards to acquire designer baby clothing, celebrity strollers, art décor bedrooms, and to finance lavish birthday parties complete with elephant rides (Stanley, 29 January 2006). The rising numbers of vacations and trips to luxury spas and entertainment palaces all appeared to signal an indulgent, indebted consumer culture (Lutyens, 12 February 2006). Journalists balked that cosmetic surgeries, facelifts, nose jobs, and tummy tucks, had grown 'by over a third to 22,041 in 2006'. Clinics offered 0% financing and Barclaycard's Beautysure credit card made financing as easy as a 'nip and tuck' (Dunn, 22 January 2006, p. 32). Suggesting that greed and narcissism had surpassed traditional community values of the caring society, journalists noted: 'Britons owe a total of £56bn on their credit cards, almost equivalent to the entire spending of the NHS each year.'

Youthful vanguards of debt

The press identified youth as vanguards of the new spendthrift attitudes. A Mintel report stated, 'two-thirds of 16- to 25-year-olds are in debt, and nearly a quarter of those aged between 20 and 24 owe at least £3000'. The report concluded a 'live for today' attitude ran high among youth. Youth bought up 'anything new that comes on the market, and ... funding their purchases through credit'. The Student Living Index reported that young people spent three times as much money on alcohol as they did on books. Young people confessed that alcohol and parties were central in their lives, with 84% of 18- to 30-year-olds agreeing they belonged to a generation of binge drinkers. The young reported higher interest in fashion and novelty (Davis Burns & Park, 2005), and held more liberal attitudes towards credit cards than the general public (Johnson & Yurchisin, 2004; Davis Burns and Park, 2005). Youth reported they felt more out of control of their consumption habits than older Britons. Kempton found that 46% of 14- to 18-year-olds could be labelled as 'addictive shoppers'. Close to 50% of 18- to 24-year-olds agreed they frequently purchased things on impulse. The picture of youth in the press was despairing: a generation of cocktail-swigging, hedonistic dandies.

The press also highlighted young people's unrealistic sense of entitlement (Chisholm, 5 January 2006). In 2006, financial service provider ING and Professor Paul Webley of Exeter University explored 2300 young Britons' attitudes towards paying back the money. The study found that 21- to 35-year-olds expected unrealistic and extravagant lifestyles in the future that vastly exceeded their incomes. These attitudes were compared to the modest hopes of their parents' generation. Those aged 51–65 reported they had expected little when they first started out and 80% achieved their expectations (Scott, 22 January 2006). Accountants warned that youths' exaggerated financial prospects would end in pain: 'It's almost as though younger debtors think that in time, maybe with a new job or pay rise, the problem will go away. ... But at the levels of debt we are seeing, this is unlikely' (Shaw, 22 May 2005, p. 23). ING concluded, 'today's young adults are heading for a rude awakening'. Deeming young people as lacking in common sense, the press felt the right to address them in a patronizing tone: 'When you first get a credit card, there is a sense of power in handing over your plastic. But when the credit runs out, the creditors circle and your financial future is irretrievably blighted by bankruptcy before the age of 30. How powerful would you feel then?' (Senior, 19 February 2005, p. 3).

Some journalists felt youth were rejecting the social contract of finance and refusing to pay their debts. OMD Insight research group in 2005 suggested: 'Britain's young people are increasingly flippant about their levels of debt and the way in which they borrow money'. A decade ago, 78% of 15–24-year-olds disagreed with the statement: 'I don't mind being in debt'. In 2005, that figure had fallen to 69% (Warwick-Ching, 14 May 2005). 'Many under-30s borrow more money to cover repayments of loans, and that can lead to a debt trap'. An accountancy firm suggested that those under 30 accounted for 60% of all insolvency cases (Watts, 1 May 2005). Youth did not view bankruptcy as an act of social benevolence, but rather an easy way to write-off their extravagant lifestyle debts (Barrow, 15 February 2005). The press blamed bankruptcy laws for encouraging young people to ignore their financial responsibilities. Taking this accusation seriously, in 2003, the government amended the Enterprise Act to prevent the write-off of student loans. Still, in 2005, almost 15% of all bankruptcies were on behalf of those 30 or younger, nearly double two years earlier (Moules, 10 June 2005). The press offered stories, such as young Alex Vaughn, a freelance writer, who used credit during lean times optimistically believing that another job would emerge to pay the bills. Accepting the banks' seductive credit offers, his overdraft reached excessive levels and the banks cut off his credit. Finding the mental stress of his situation unbearable, Mr Vaughn declared bankruptcy (Vaughan, 17 January 2006). Mr Vaughn expressed a sense of great relief towards a social system that allowed him to extinguish his debts.

But journalists pondered whether allowing young people to get out of their debt commitments was working the way bankruptcy was intended. Instead of embracing the entrepreneurial spirit, work ethic, and stiff-upper-lipism of previous generations, some journalists proclaimed youth were 'whingers' who lacked the survival instinct required to live in a capitalist society. They expected opportunities to fall into their laps. Journalists noted that the young 'moan' and complain that they 'just don't get paid enough'. Despite high employment levels, the envy of other European countries, young Britons felt hard done by and under-employed. They found their jobs 'unfulfilling'. They seemed to expect to secure jobs in the glamorous legal, financial, or media industries and refused to dirty their hands as plumbers.

Challenging the media construction of debtors

Still another picture of contemporary youth complicated their construction as the folk devils of the consumer economy. The most heavily indebted individuals in society were older and richer. Indeed, 25- to 34-year-olds made up a major proportion of those holding debt, but they were also most likely to be starting up their first homes and raising families, both major financial commitments. Yet, with few assets to fall back on, youth faced greater financial risk. The events most likely to lead to financial difficulties included having children, experiencing divorce, or becoming unemployed, all of which were created by relationships not individual lifestyle choice. Further, National Savings and Investments, a government-backed agency, undertook a telephone interview study of 6000 people and found little evidence of a spendthrift generation. Young, single individuals in full-time work were the most likely to save. 'Over the past three months, the under-25 age group saved 10.11 per cent of monthly income – the highest average proportion of income; followed by those aged 25 to 34, saving 7.17 per cent' (Knight, 10 September 2005).

The young had difficulty resisting the easy credit options. Francis Walker of the CCCS said: 'Young people are now offered credit wherever they turn'. Young people agreed that credit was too easy to obtain. As we saw in Chapter 5, the banks heavily targeted young people because in the saturated financial sector they represented the last bastion of growth. Higher education became an instrumental part of building the so-called knowledge economy, heavily promoted by New Labour. Contemporary youth, who lack privilege, had no option but to turn to student loans and credit cards. Student loans added to debt burdens with one in five students reporting they owed at least £15,000 in 2006 (Independent, 3 January 2006). Newspapers reported that debt helplines heard from an increased number of young people, just out of university, reporting financial stress. While some professors complained about the new generation of students who viewed their education as nothing more than a meal ticket, they ignored that websites, advertising, and information pamphlets emanating from their universities promoted the ease with which a degree could be translated into a high-paying job in a fascinating industry (Kassam, 13 November 2005). As in retail, the student loan programme helped expand and smooth out bottlenecks in the consumption of higher education. Therefore, there is evidence of wider cultural messages encouraging a view of investment in higher education as an investment that would pay-off in increased earning potential.

Young people who reported student debt 'makes it really hard to realise your dreams' were not simply whinging. Higher debt loads are known to make people more cautious. Instead of taking risks, indebted students seeking to unburden themselves of debt may seek well-paying safe jobs with pensions. They may feel pressured to take the first job they find instead of building new sectors of the economy. Further, particularly in the large urban centres, lack of money and constant invitation to spend likely fuels the work ethic as much as it diminishes it. Most students are not lazy slackers, but rather work while going to university. One of the most common strategies used by the young to pay-off their debts was to take on two jobs.

The Kempton Report, a rigorous random sample study, found little evidence of a generation ignoring their debts. Many took on second jobs or stayed in secure jobs they hated to pay their debts. Vast numbers of youth moved back to their parental home to help manage their debt. The longer tenure of young people in the family home and the extended financial dependence of children on their parents represented an important demographic shift. Moving home appeared to be a good strategy; those who did so reported fewer financial difficulties than the rest of the population (Atkinson, 2007; Ramachadran, 2005; Giuliano, 2007). The investment in one's child extended well beyond university, and supporting young adults helped circulate money back into the consumer economy.

While, like the general public, youth did not want the government to cut off their access to overdrafts, studies indicated they did want the banks to be more like nannies than hardened salespeople. Young people felt they could handle their finances better if the banks communicated to them through the technology they used daily, instead of the post. More than half of a polled group of 18- to 24-year-olds reported to journalists that they would like 'text alerts about balances or cash credits'. Close to 40% said they would appreciate warnings about their overdrafts and 25% wanted 'reminders for credit-card payments'. A third of the respondents reported that they preferred to text their inquiries to the bank instead of speaking with someone on the phone (Rowland, 24 January 2006). It was not in the banks' interest to divert some of their advertising funds towards fulfilling these requests.

Far from ignoring prevailing social norms, studies suggested young people conformed to them. Young people reported higher levels of concern about their social status, were more achievement-oriented, and valued materialism more than the general public. Based on its survey of 18- to 34-year-olds, the think tank, Reform, coined twenty-first century youth as an Ipod generation: 'Insecure, Pressurised, Over-taxed and Debt-ridden'. Answering the call of consumerism, youth reported they felt pressure to spend beyond their means and worried about their ability to fulfil their dreams. Despite contributing significantly to the state taxes, the young no longer felt that the welfare state provided benefits in return (Hattersley, 28 August 2005). They felt they would never get on the property ladder. They looked for jobs in the cultural and financial sectors because these were the growing areas of the economy. Youth sympathized with Rosie Millard. While those who value utility may not like it, jobs in these competitive fields called for networking skills and good appearances. A good haircut and stylish clothing were the costly tool belts of the age, but with no state subsidies or friendly societies to turn to, contemporary youth used their credit cards and overdrafts to prepare themselves for work. Youth also responded to the cultural message that economic survival depended upon higher education credentials – and thus accumulated debt to pay tuition fees.

Madame Bovary Syndrome

In the nineteenth century, women remained economically dependant on their family and husbands. In 1910, fewer than 10% of married women worked. Their presence in higher education and professions was negligible. By the twenty-first century approximately 67% of women worked full-time. Although the gender gap between men and women's wages continued to average around 18%, the figure has been dropping since the late 1990s. Between 1996 and 2006 young women outperformed young men on their school examinations. According to the Higher Education Statistics Agency, women earned 58% of the 353,035 higher education degrees in 2005/6. Women's presence in professions including medicine, law, and finance vastly increased. Society depended upon women's contribution to the economy, thus it would seem logical for them to be held in equal regard to men within financial discourses. This study found that this was not the case.

In the twenty-first century the old fear of women as vengeful spendthrifts hell bent on bringing the economy of the nation into ill repute continued to circulate. The papers sometimes viewed women as particularly vulnerable economic subjects, suggesting they were more easily seduced by financial marketing and less rational in their financial decisions than men. Journalists said women took on more financial risk than men and showed difficulty 'moderating their spending in the short term'. Journalists worried about women's increasing presence in bankruptcy figures. An accountancy firm suggested that women accounted for 42% of the 800 bankruptcy cases they reviewed. Another report suggested that between 2003 and 2004 women accounted for 45% of all bankruptcies. The director of Credit Action, a money education charity, reported big increases 'in the number of women going through the bankruptcy process with credit-card debt, and [a] higher proportion of these are young single women'. Increased debt accompanied women's growing economic prowess: 'Traditionally, debt was a male thing, but the gap between men and women is narrowing very quickly. We now see both men and women very regularly with debts of £40,000 to £50,000' (Johnson, 16 May 2005, p. 4).

Halifax research suggested the number of single women taking out new home loans had more than doubled between 1985 and 2005 and accounted for 23% of all mortgages. Yet, instead of celebrating women's entrance into the domain of virtuous debt, concerns arose about women's ability to payback their loans. The press suggested that women had overstretched themselves to get on the property ladder borrowing 'at very high multiples of their income'. Young women were reported as 'among the worst savers, with one in eight single women holding no savings at all' (Knight, 10 September 2005, p. 25). According to a National Savings survey, women's lack of investments in comparison to men placed them in a difficult situation because they 'have less to fall back on when debts begin to spiral, and their emergency cash reserves can be depleted much quicker' (Nugent, 16 May 2005, p. 25).

Attention focused on women's use of credit and store cards for shopping. A spokesman for the Citizens' Advice Bureau noted: 'Young women, especially, are more likely to have store card debts, which often have some of the highest rates of interest. We suspect that as more and more young people get into higher education, they get accustomed to being in debt. Another factor is that lenders aggressively target young people' (Reich, 2 July 2004, p. 23). Laurence Baxter, senior policy adviser at CAB, said: 'Women are particularly susceptible to companies' tactics of teasing customers into certain spending patterns. They want people to spend money today and pay it off another time' (Nugent, 16 May 2005, p. 25). The banks claimed that women were 'more likely to transfer debt from existing cards to plastic offering short-term zero per cent interest rates' (Nugent, 16 May 2005, p. 25). The sexist term 'rate tarts' describes the promiscuous female consumer who cheated the industry of their rightful interest payments.

A BBC *Women's Hour* programme pointed to the different purchasing patterns of women and how this had a negative effect on their ability to manage finances. Men tended to purchase big-ticket items like cars, computers, and sound systems, and consolidated debt on one or two cards. Women made more purchases for smaller amounts, and accepted a greater number of credit and store cards. Women reported they used some of their money on bills, but spent most 'on clothes and nights out'. The implications were that women frittered their money away on trivial items, and were unable to control all the cards in their wallet. Men on the other hand purchased seemingly more useful items.

The press also presented women as secretive schemers. Reports suggested 40% of female debtors kept their debts secret from their partners. The press regaled the public with stories about women's need for 'retail therapy'. For example, a 47-year-old woman ran up debts of £24,000 and did not tell her husband. Diagnosed with multiple sclerosis, Mrs Dixon opened a Lloyds TSB account to receive a monthly allowance of £1200 from her county council to pay her carer, and, despite her meagre benefit income of £600 per month, was invited to take out a credit card. Stuck at home with few employment prospects, the card represented financial independence. 'I wanted to feel that I am not totally dependent on other people,' she said. 'If you can't even get dressed by yourself, you feel like a child. Shopping was a way to assert myself. I bought fine wines, booked tickets to see Rod Stewart and Elton John and took my carer on a day trip to France'. Mrs Dixon bought clothes for herself and her daughters on her credit card and 'enjoyed the compliments and got my hair highlighted'. After four years it became impossible for Mrs Dixon to pay even the minimum monthly payments (Gibson & O'Connor, 28 January 2006). While Mrs Dixon clearly bore responsibility for her debts, the story was framed with a subplot that suggested she would not have experienced such financial problems if she had discussed her situation with her financially astute husband.

In 2001, *Independent* reported a new consumer culture malaise dubbed 'Madame Bovary Syndrome'. Drawing on the accounts from consumer help organizations, bankruptcy offices, and accountancy firms, journalists constructed a female debtor unable to control either her consumption or finances. The National Debt Line reported 40% of their calls were from women between the ages of 25–35. Of these, close to half were in full-time employment, but were unable to support their spending habits. A new generation of Madame Bovarys indulged in overly extravagant lifestyles and accumulated massive debt. Drawing upon fashion magazine surveys, the media drew up a picture of a woman in her early 20s who had given up all consciousness of thrift. Instead of taking on a mortgage and saving for the future, these young women were ringing up their credit cards on average £3850 (Guest, 23 July 2006). Like Madame Bovary in the nineteenth century, young women were said to be using debt to finance extravagant shopping experiences to satisfy their romantic fantasies, advance their social position, and feel better about themselves. Reporting the opinions of psychology lecturers, the media suggested that unlike their stoical and thrifty mothers' generation, young women wanted to have things instantly and thought little of their future. Dr Joan Harvey, a senior psychology lecturer at Newcastle University, suggested women had difficulty finding contentment within consumer culture and used shopping for mental uplift.

The press quoted a young woman who said her inability to afford a dress 'affected my confidence'. Other women spoke of how easy it was to go into debt: 'Once I knew how easy it was, I went to other department stores, and did the same. It's so addictive and you feel you've been welcomed into some sort of club. Because you don't have to pay the balance off all at once, it feels like you don't have to pay at all. It never occurred to me that I couldn't have something – be it a watch, a Louis Vuitton bag, or a brooch – because I couldn't afford it. I started doing better at work, I was happier, I was going out more, being asked out more. All these things had given me confidence, so why was I going to stop?'

For women, in particular, shopping was connected with feeling good. A member of Debtors Anonymous for ten years found an association between debt and low self-esteem because when you are 'without material "things"' you tend to feel as if you aren't good enough. 'I grew up with very mixed messages about money as a child; that material things made you happy and that you had to run after them. So my wish was, as soon as I was an adult, that I would chase these things at any cost because I wanted to be happy. Magazines, television programmes – I don't think they are to blame, but in my head, I had an idea that women who dressed in a certain way or had a certain bag always looked happy' (Reich, 2 July 2004, p. 23). Women reported that because they worked hard they deserved nice things. Nice wardrobes were touted as signs of womanhood and success. Partaking in social gatherings and buying cocktails were important to women, and although they did not like the ensuing debt, they found that it was difficult to sacrifice their lifestyles to control their bills (Qureshi, 28 February 2007).

Women's consumption was flagged as non-utilitarian and unproductive. They were read as going into debt to fuel drunken binges and ape celebrity lifestyles. Women were understood to be the 'least resistant to the lure and ready availability of easy money', lured into high levels of shopping by 'role models such as Carrie Bradshaw, Bridget Jones and Rachel from the television show *Friends* all live by the motto: "If in doubt, buy shoes"'. One young woman taken as an exemplary of her generation agreed: 'I grew up watching *Friends*. They had great jobs and spent lots of time hanging out drinking coffee and I thought that's what grown-ups did' (Hattersley, 28 August 2005, p. 5). The BBC deemed Madame Bovary Syndrome to be of such national importance that it addressed the subject in a cautionary tale drama entitled *Shiny Shiny Bright New Hole in My Heart*. The drama told the moral tale of a personal shopper who became deeply indebted because she felt entitled to the wealthy lifestyle of her rich clients. Still financial advisors bemoaned the trend. Despite pointed drama programmes, financial warnings as harsh as those printed on cigarette packets, press stories about 'lives being devastated to debt-induced suicide', the public appeared to remain ignorant of the dangers of borrowing, and the most ignorant of all were young women.

Rereading Madame Bovary Syndrome

Journalists used questionable statistics to strengthen their construction of Madame Bovary Syndrome. For example, one report claimed 'nine out of 10 women aged between 20 and 30 are in debt', but neglected to say how much debt or how long it was held. Women may possess more credit instruments overall, but this did not mean that they used them. Kempton found that four out of ten households had credit facilities that were not used. Her research showed, 'for every 100 credit sources that were being used at the time of the survey, there were another 72 that were not in use'. One report stated that six out of ten individuals did not know the interest charged on their cards, but this general figure included men and women. Within the context of a story about female debt, such a statement makes it too easy to assume women alone were ignorant about interest rates. A report about women's rising levels of personal debt noted 'personal bankruptcies are at their highest level for a decade' leaving the reader to assume that women were declaring bankruptcy *en masse*. Yet, men accounted for 63% of all bankruptcies in 2007 (BBC News online, 16 February 2007). It was logical that as women took on more debt and invested more in property their presence in bankruptcy figures had also risen, just as men's had.

National statistics actually show that women assume less debt than men in relation to their income. The research also revealed that men were more in debt than women, owing an average of £6089 compared with women's £5027 (O'Hara, 20 January 2004). A 2007 Consumer Credit Counselling Service (CCCS) study reported an increased number of mature male clients who, on average, held debt worth £36,940 compared to women who tended to report to credit agencies when they reached around £25,000 typically spread over a number of credit cards (BBC News online, 16 February 2007). Older men had a debt to monthly income ratio of 36:1 while women in debt troubles tended to be younger. Still, regardless of gender, those in most debt were 40–59. However, males held the most debt and were more likely to claim default on their bills, claim bankruptcy, or undertake an IVP order (O'Hara, 20 January 2004). Women were overrepresented in the financially troubled categories because they were more apt to act upon financial strife than men.

The press also failed to place women's debt in a broader social or cultural context leading to a distortion of the picture. As in the nineteenth century, consumer credit utilized by women for everyday consumption was subject to considerable moral criticism, while the masculinized sphere of home property received less attention. The media construction of Madame Bovary Syndrome focused on cheap-chic fashion, take away food, baby carriages, and cosmetic surgery – all feminine products – while the purchase of large ticket items like automobiles or computers, subject to fashion trends and upgrading, passed with less attention. We saw in Chapter 2 how women were constructed as the gender that would handle consumption. Castigated to the sphere of consumption, women took what pleasures and liberty they could find there, even if they were paradoxical. Women in Britain today, still make 80% of all consumer purchases, however up to 40% of those purchases are made on behalf of others (Cunningham & Roberts, 2007). They are the central provision of commodities for the table, they buy clothing for children, as well as their husbands' trousers, and in so doing they have been forced to bear the brunt of the critique of consumerism.

Three competing discourses emerged in the twenty-first century press accounts of personal finance. One explained personal debt as a positive sign of affluence being converted into pleasure. The growing levels of debt were deemed manageable and signalled populous making wise investments in their future. Their practices, according to some, were to be celebrated for they propelled economic growth and rising standards of living. The second discourse set out to document the role of the banks in the rising levels of personal debt. Journalists reported the larger bonuses and profits the banks acquired through their marketing and sale of credit to consumers who then floundered in debt. The banks in turn, blamed both governments for low interest rates that kept the price of money low and fuelled credit cycles and consumers who failed to act rationally and balance their budgets. The third press discourse delved into the financial psychology of consumers and suggested that British culture no longer adhered to its financial contracts. Young people and women were constructed as the worst offenders of the new champagne lifestyles and debt practices that were driving the country into the brink of economic disaster. Although it went against statistical facts, many stories in the press promoted homeownership as a rock solid investment and assumed that older men possessed a financial rationality superior to the young and women.

8
Personal Financial Identities in Psychology and Popular Literature

Despite the growing economic power associated with consumerism, the newspapers continued to cleave to financial moralities developed in the nineteenth century: prudent investment in private property and education assumed as good; unsecured consumer debt, non-utilitarian consumption, and superfluous lifestyles, deviant. Journalists worried that young people and women's attitudes and behaviours towards consumption and financial management diverged from notions of prudence. In this chapter, I explore how the construction of the debt-ridden shopaholic who emerged in the press accounts, also circulated in post-1980s psychological literature and a series of highly popular novels by Sophie Kinsella. This figure crystallizes many of the most deeply held cultural anxieties that surround late modern consumer culture and personal finance.

Drawing the limits of finance and consumption

We saw in the last chapter, how journalists attempted to draw distinctions between acceptable and unacceptable consumption. Their activities would have amused Emil Kraepelin, the pioneer of consumer pathology, who was one of the first to set the moment when consumption became illness. In so doing, Kraepelin established a powerful distinction between acceptable and unacceptable consumption. Kraepelin's awesome powers to pour over thousands of case studies; detail, classify, and label human thought processes and behaviour, won him the respect of his nineteenth century medical peers. Although a scientist, Kraepelin's work was interpretive and creative. Schizophrenia, manic-depression, and Alzheimer's disease did not exist until Kraepelin brought them forth in discourse; nor did, oniomania, or shopping addiction. Kraepelin argued, like other addictive substances, shopping released brain chemicals producing a euphoric sensation during and immediately following the act. Yet, the effect soon wore off, leaving the shopper with feelings of disgust. Self-loathing drove individuals back to the market, creating a cycle of despair. The dosage of shopping increased over time to achieve the initial levels of stimulation. Believing the roots of oniomania lay in body chemistry and genetics, Kraepelin legitimated the biological foundation of shopping compulsion, classifying it as a serious medical illness requiring medication (Kraepelin, 1915).

Freudian therapeutics also influenced understandings of consumer pathology. Although compulsive shopping was not the focus of Freud's work, he influenced how shopaholics were treated. A Freudian perspective viewed oniomania as a mode of escape. People engaged in compulsive activities to sooth inner anxiety and escape reality. Shopping relieved anxiety to the extent that it provided a means for avoiding negative feelings, momentarily unleashing repression and inner libidinal impulses. Yet, shopping evaded the core problem of the individual's anxiety thus endlessly frustrating the compulsive buyer. Compulsive activities stoked intense feelings of personal torment and self-loathing, in a society where compulsive behaviour was a sign of failure. Social relations played a role in shaping the compulsive shopper, thus instead of medicine Freud advocated the talking cure where a psychoanalyst supported the compulsive buyer to acquire greater self-understanding of the unconscious roots of their desire and anxieties.

Psychologists showed little interest in oniomania for the majority of the twentieth century. Interest in the subject re-emerged coinciding with the 1980s' expansion of the consumer economy. First identified in the US in 1986 (Faber & O'Guinn, 1989; Hanley & Wilhelm, 1992), later studies in Canada (Valence, D'Astous & Fortier, 1988), Germany (Scherhorn, Reisch & Raab, 1990), the UK (Elliott, 1994), Spain, and Asia documented the presence of the pathology. Oniomania was renamed impulse buying, compulsive buying, or shopping addiction because researchers could not agree if it was an addiction, a compulsion, or a mood disorder. Most researchers agreed however that the disorder was characterized by the consumers' inability to exercise control in the marketplace and resulted in debilitating social, psychological, and financial problems.

Researchers documented the prevalence of buying compulsion. The pathology appeared particular to mature consumer cultures. For example, a study in Germany, after reunification, documented a significant rise of compulsive buying in both East and West Germany between

1991and 2001 (Neuner et al., 2005). In the US, compulsive buying was thought to afflict between 2–8% of the population (Black et al., 1998). Hanley and Wilhelm (1992) argued that 10% was a more accurate figure. UK studies confirmed that 10% of the population suffered from compulsive shopping. The pathology was thought to be on the rise (Neuner et al., 2005).

Compulsive buying was correlated with irrational credit card use (D'Astrous, 1990; Davis Burns & Park, 2005). Compulsive buyers bloomed in cultures where credit was widely available (Dittmar & Drury, 2000; Feber, 1992; McElroy et al., 1994; Roberts & Jones, 2001). While compulsive shopping inflicted all income groups, a typical victim tended to make less than $50,000 per year and was more likely than others to pay-off only the minimum balance of their credit cards. Dittmar explained how credit facilities contributed to the problem, 'credit dissolves the financial constraints that once limited the ability to achieve immediate gratification'. Compulsive buyers were more likely to believe that money had a symbolic ability to enhance self-esteem (Hanley & Wilhelm, 1992). Koran et al. argued that by virtue of its uncontrollable nature, compulsive shopping almost always leads to financial difficulties (Aboujaoude et al., 2006).

Researchers developed a series of assessment tools distinguishing compulsive consumers from non-compulsive consumers. Compulsive buyers had richer fantasy lives than others. They used their imagination to stimulate acts of purchase and employed creative thinking to forget its harsh consequences. Compulsive buyers reported high levels of impulsivity. They felt powerless to control their powerful urges to shop. Psychologists deemed compulsive buyers' reasons for purchase as irrational because the pleasure they craved had little to do with possessing objects. Thus compulsive buying did not adhere to the principle of utility. Many compulsive buyers returned the goods they purchased, thus showed more interested in stores' return policies than other consumers (Hassay & Smith, 1998). Frequently left unopened, never worn, or used, compulsive buyers often hid their purchases from family and friends.

If compulsive buyers did not use goods for utility, or even status, what did they use them for? Psychologists argued compulsive buyers worked through a wide variety of emotions including anger, anxiety, boredom, and self-critical thoughts in their consumption practices (Beattie et al., 1995). Those afflicted described their experience in relation to three stages: an irresistible impulse to buy; a sense of loss of control; and a continuation of the activity regardless of social, personal, or financial consequence (Lejoyeux et al., 2005). Compulsive buyers developed a rich and complex vocabulary about shopping – they were shopping experts. Many described shopping as a great release, finding shopping more intensely exciting than other consumers (Benson, 2000). During a shopping spree many described feelings of heightened focus. Binge buying stimulated the senses; brought colour and texture into sharp relief. The experience was euphoric. Some likened shopping to a drug trip, others found it sexually stimulating. Yet, the highs of shopping quickly dissipated, returning individuals to a state of anxiety, driving them to shop again, and again (Hirschman, 1992). Binge buying contributed to higher levels of social, psychological, and financial stress. Those afflicted reported high levels of depression and self-loathing.

Hollander and Allen argued that it was essential to list the disorder in the Diagnostic and Statistical Manual of Mental Disorders IV (DSM) to provide researchers with a benchmark for their studies. They saw the problem of 'over diagnosis' and 'misuse of diagnostic labels' as less important than developing 'new treatments or prevention strategies for serious human problems' (Allen & Hollander, 2006). Until a definitive entry in the DSM was made, psychologists used as their guide 'Impulse-Control Disorders Not Elsewhere Classified'. This classification falls in a section that includes Intermittent Explosive Disorder, Kleptomania, Pyromania, Pathological Gambling, and Trichotillomania. Some researchers argued that shopping addiction runs in families, suggesting the pathology has a genealogical basis (Koran et al., 2006). Viewing compulsive buying as a biological illness psychotropic medications or anti-depressants have been administered to those with the affliction in open clinical trials. While some people reported a sense of relief from their symptoms, their numbers were not high enough to conclude anything beyond placebo effect (Muller & De Zwaan, 2004).

Constructing the addict in consumer culture

While medical professionals debated the biological roots of compulsive buying and how to treat the affliction with medication, others highlighted the growth of a consumer pathology industry. These approaches drew attention to the cottage industry that emerged to identify, construct, and treat aberrant consumers. Critics asked: what purpose these factories producing addicts served? To reproduce themselves and grow, didn't the 'pys' disciplines have to constantly reproduce aberrance? The therapeutic industries blossoming around compulsive and indebted consumers, said critics, were not innocent, but a means of social control.

Until the latter half of the nineteenth century, states directly intervened through sumptuary and usury laws. Subverted and weakly enforced, these laws nevertheless made the limits of finance and consumption clear. Until 1868, the state physically retained debtors in prison. Rightly or wrongly, financial institutions also regulated consumption and finance by limiting credit. The Bank of England, in the first half of the twentieth century, as we have seen in Chapter 3, prohibited the extension of funds for pleasure items. Foucault would recognize these forms of discipline as typical traditional governance regimes that favoured the state's physical control of bodies through the law. Yet, as we saw in Chapter 1, the idea of a liberal marketplace was founded upon an argument that sought to limit absolute power and state control over marketplace activity. In Britain this view waxed and waned throughout the twentieth century, but achieved ascendance in the post-1980s (Harvey, 2005; Slater & Tonkiss, 2001). Democratic subjects had human rights and ideally governed themselves, free from direct state interventions in their lives and consumption choices. The sway of these liberal ideals, according to Foucault, led to a different type of governance. Liberated from absolute power, people still had to realize their life chances and their freedoms within wider institutional practices and social norms.

Max Weber, as we saw in Chapter 1, drew attention to the contribution of religious discourses in constituting moral norms related to consumption, such as thrift and prudent debt. Foucault suggested that in secular liberal societies, medical, and scientific discourses became the new arbiters of social norms. Taking up the subject of the compulsive buyer through a Foucaultian frame, Reith (2004) drew attention to how notions of physical and mental wellness represent a powerful new ethical norm against which people fashion their identities. Ian Hacking's suggestion that contemporary discourses quite literally 'make-up' people, provided names and labels of subject typologies of 'new types of people' situated along a continuum that stretches from pathological to healthy. What is most disturbing for Reith is the way individuals have taken up the language of addiction to describe their experience.

Since the World Health Organization recognized addiction as the means to describe pathological subjects in 1964, the number of addicts has reached epidemic proportions, says Reith. People internalize circulating identities in a bid to achieve wellness or diagnose their sense of deviance. Individuals actively participate in their own pathologization. Whereas nineteenth century addicts had 'a deviant identity stamped upon them, today's consumer pathologies are constructed within interviews or surveys that measure consumers' subjective reflections against a norm (Reith, 2004, p. 294). Because the individual's ability to control their own behaviour and discipline their will is paramount in a consumer culture, once identified, the addict is required to confess, for, according to psychological logic, the cure can only begin when with the individual's acknowledgement that they are ill. The emphasis, according to Reith, is less on how people feel about their behaviour and more 'how they feel about their ability to control it' (Reith, 2004, p. 291).

These processes also appear in the personal finance field. Troubled consumers are encouraged to turn to debt counselling organizations. The press invites readers to reflect upon and modify their financial behaviour. Journalists documented consumers' confessions about their financial anxieties. Women and the young, those members of society with fewer financial resources, were most likely to self-identify as aberrant consumers. While 10% of the general public was thought to be compulsive buyers, Kasser (2002) estimated 15% of young people were addicted to consumption (Kasser, 2002). D'Astous also found that more young people fell into the compulsive buyer category, while older individuals were less likely to suffer from the disorder. (Hira, 1997; Garcia, 2007).

Therapeutic industries seek to reshape sufferers' subjectivity and build up their self-control and agency. Their intent is to 'fabricate subjects capable of bearing the burdens of liberty' (Reith, 2004, p. 297). In this act, Reith argues, therapeutic discourses become a form of governance; a technology of citizenship for acting upon ourselves 'so that the police, the guards and the doctors do not have to do so' (Reith, 2004, p. 297). In lieu of debtors' prison, a language of addiction and therapeutic treatment emerged. Yet, the pathologization of consumption, according to Reith, presents a profound paradox in a market society because it lies at the opposite end of the spectrum from the sovereign consumer. Shopaholics are not free to choose, rather enslaved by their excessive consumption. The addict's 'frenzied craving, repetition and loss of control' leads them to suffer instead of take pleasure from their consumption habits (Reith, 2004, p. 289).

Besides governing individuals, Lee and Mysyk argue that the pathologization of consumption is profitable, because it has deflected attention away from the devastating social and economic consequences of the consumer-driven economies of the 1980s and 1990s, and current fiscal crises. The focus on atrophied wills and aberrant identities individualizes problems that call for collective politics and wide scale social change (Lee & Mysyk, 2004, p. 1714). Lee and Mysyk find it no coincidence that the medicalization of compulsive buyers bloomed during the expansion of neoliberal regimes, leaving individuals to shoulder responsibility for the anxiety that increased productivity and expansion of commodity consumption through credit wrought. Referencing the last published work of Bourdieu, Lee and Mysyk argue that modern economies are propelled by creating high levels of insecurity in the public. Medicalization is part of the process of fear inducement. The economy, according to Bourdieu, 'gives rise to a generalized subjective insecurity which is now affecting all workers in our highly developed economy' (Bourdieu, 1998, p. 83). Insecurity 'pervades both the conscious and unconscious mind' of all people. Living in a constant state of anxiety destabilizes people's ability to rationally plan their future (Bourdieu, 1998, p. 82). According to Bourdieu, maximizing the pleasures of the moment and trying to forget about the future makes sense within a social system where insecurity about the future is constantly whipped up (Lee & Mysyk, 2004, p. 1716). This theory goes some way to explain why people might engage in excessive consumption and why rationally managing prudent debt is a challenge in the twenty-first century.

Treating shopping disorders with psychotropic medications, for Lee and Mysyk, is akin to taking a page out of Orwell's *Brave New World*, drugging the public to adjust them to a social system that abuses them. Neoliberalism oversaw the withdrawal of the traditional state buffers and the expansion of market mechanisms into previously public domains. In this new context, addicts, according to Reith, serve 'as a repository for widespread fears of unrest'. Reith suggests those who adopt 'addictive identities' reveal the failure of the social system to deliver on its promises of freedom. With no other avenues available to address the demands of late modern living, people declare mental deficiency and seek cure. 'The spread of addictions can be seen as a counter to the global proliferation of consumption: a refusal of choice that has become overwhelming; a denial of freedom that is illusory' (Reith, 2004, p. 296).

The suspect values of women

Chapter 2 explored the discourses that associated femininity to particular acts of consumption and finance. To be a woman is not simply signalled by appearance, but as Susie Orbach (1993) summarizes, is also attached to a particular mode of consumption:

> The market place, consuming, is *the* public sphere in which the woman has been allowed to act and in which she is encouraged to exert agency. Excluded as a gender from other public arenas, the market is *par excellence* the civic and secular temple of contemporary

feminine creativity. Although often hidden as a labour process, the reproduction of daily life requires time spent in consuming. Along with time one develops the skills of consuming. Being able to consume well, tastefully, economically, efficiently is an acceptable and approved of female attribute.

Consumption and finance practices hold implications for women's identity politics, a point raised by research findings that suggest women are more likely to confess to consumer pathology than men (Black, 2007; D'Astrous, 1990). Dittmar's research reported that women were over two and a half times as likely to be identified as compulsive shoppers as men (p. 117). Koran argued that shopaholism was a woman's disease while men's psyches drew towards other impulse control disorders such gambling and pyromania because their identities were bound with consumption; so too were their psychic malaise. Quite simply, women shopped more, thus had more opportunities to overbuy than men (Black, 2007; Vohs & Faber, 2004). Women were more likely to list symbolic, expressive, and fashionable goods as likely impulse purchases. These types of items, said Dittmar, support the 'appearance and emotional aspects of self' (Dittmar, 2005, p. 468). When men engaged in impulsive shopping their desire was fixed on 'instrumental and leisure items', which Dittmar argues projected 'independence and activity'. Distinct from men, women reported they used shopping to bolster their sense of self: 'shopping takes me into a sort of magical kind of journey in my mind in a way, totally lifting me. It nurtures me in a way, something that I need' (Dittmar, 2005, p. 129). Controlling shopping during gifting rituals such as Christmas and birthdays was more challenging for women than men. The desire to please others by way of presentation of gifts and presenting a fashionable emotionally aware self, conform to the broader cultural discourses that have historically constructed the good woman. Further, because of the importance of appearing beautiful and respectful before others, women may scrutinize more vigilantly how they are perceived by others.

As credit cards gave access to the goods women used to construct their sense of self, they recoiled at the thought of losing credit privileges: 'I could not cut that card up. It was like cutting my wrist. It's like losing, it's like cutting my toe off really. It's a lifeline. It is just like losing a part of me' (Dittmar, 2005, p. 135). Women reported that the use of credit cards to make purchases erased the sense that they were actually spending money (Dittmar, 2005, p. 131). Some saw bankruptcy as a useful tool for addressing financial problems and used it as men had done for years (Preston, 2005).

Fashion cycles that constantly turned over goods, made it difficult for women to relieve status anxieties and feel securely respectable. To secure prestige through goods, marketers called upon women to show constant vigilance towards following fashion. At best, the act of consumption provided momentary euphoria, but soon led to increased levels of indebtedness, anxiety, and frustration (Faber & O'Guinn, 1989; Dittmar, 2005). Other studies suggested that women's compulsive buying was a passive-aggressive strategy. A UK study found that women used excessive consumption and debt to enact revenge on, and encourage significant others to take them seriously and comfort their needs. Thus, the authors conclude that women's excessive consumption was an existential choice related to their desire to secure power and control (Eccles, et al., 1996). A complex set of reasons have been forwarded by researchers to explain women's overrepresentation in the compulsive buyer literature: from a quest to fulfill the cultural norm of their gender by giving to others and keeping up appearances to a strategy to resolve a diminished sense of self by endlessly returning to the marketplace; from a belief in materialist values that bring them nothing but unhappiness to using consumption and spending to assert power and control to simply being more willing than men to admit that something is wrong.

Shopaholic pleasures

The problem with consumption and spending, unlike some other addictive substances such as alcohol and drugs, is that it is impossible to go cold turkey. Daily, women must engage with the marketplace, against the backdrop of consumptive and financial norms of their gender. A media system advertises the wonders of commodities at the same time that it stigmatizes excessive consumption and spending. A culture that trivializes and deems pathological the consumption practices in which women find themselves. In this context I believe it is possible to understand the immense popularity of Sophie Kinsella's, 2001 book, *Confessions of a Shopaholic*. Bloomwood's life was rolled out in a series of sequel novels, *Shopaholic Abroad*, 2002; *Shopaholic Ties the Knot*, 2003; *Shopaholic and Sister*, 2005; and the most recent, *Shopaholic & Baby*, 2007. The story of Becky became a screenplay for a major motion picture.

The books followed the antics of the central character, Becky Bloomwood, who bore all the marks of someone afflicted with Madame Bovary Syndrome. In a vivid first person voice, the novel took the reader into Becky's head, followed her on fantastical shopping trips, exposed her numerous justifications for her mounting consumer debt. The novel spent weeks on the bestseller list, sparked fan websites around the world, and was released as a major film production.

Kinsella's literary renderings invoke palpable dreams for her mostly female readers. According to Scanlon, Becky provided a powerful form of identification for fans – over 90% of polled fans recognized some of Becky's traits in themselves (Scanlon, 2005). Critics locate the popularity of the novels in the escapism they offer readers. In the same vein as the equally popular *Sex and the City* television programme, the novels dared to take seriously the pleasures and fantasies that surround women's shopping and fashion interests. By recasting shopping as an arena of pleasure, social adoration, self-transformation, creative expression, productivity, and power, the novels drained the shopaholic of its pathological connotations and recast it in a respectable humanist glow.

So too did the novels tackle the subject of personal finance. Becky is in constant debt. Indeed, the catalyst propelling the narrative is the credit card chase where Becky contorts herself into various comical shapes to stay one step ahead of the debt collectors. The great pleasure as Van Slooten (2006) points out, is found in the way Becky always manages to outrun her debt, aided by divine intervention, rich friends and lovers, and kindly bankers. By presenting debt as a gentle and avoidable worry, critics have argued the books make no critical intervention into the dynamics of consumer culture, reinforcing its norms more than subverting them.

Scanlon argues that by transferring 'her emotional dependency from men to goods' Becky speaks of a new post-patriarchal order. Becky and her readers are thus interpreted as post-feminist because their pleasures have shifted from romanticism for male lovers towards capitalism via shopping. Women's consumption was once to be dedicated to the welfare of others. Becky's blatant gifts to the self, in contrast, appear liberating (Scanlon, 2005). However, claims Scanlon, while Becky appears liberated from the old constraints of patriarchy, she is re-constrained by the norms of the 'contemporary media-driven expectations of womanhood or contemporary heterosexual relationships'. A detailed examination of some of Becky's actions, I believe, provides a key to understanding many of the deeper anxieties that circulate around women, consumer culture, and personal finance.

Becky is hopeless at the traditional domestic duties of her gender. She fails miserably at craft. The cleanliness of her home does not define her. Daily food preparation holds no interest to her. She prefers to eat out or order in. She feels no pressure to play hostess in the domestic realm to highlight the social prowess of her husband. Her efforts to show her gender's sacrifice to husband and family are complicated by her equally strong impulse to sacrifice herself to acquire a 'fabulous pair of shoes'. Becky is aware of the importance of family ties and values, but they weigh down her lofty consumerist fantasies, thus she must find a way to subvert them. For example, Becky becomes annoyed at her mother for expecting her to wear the wedding dress she wore to marry her father: '*How* could she [Becky's mother] want me to wear her frilly monstrosity, instead of one of these gorgeous, amazing, Oscar-winner creations?' (Kinsella, 2003, p. 135).

Instead of mom and tradition, Becky finds self-help books, the media, and celebrities more useful guides for confirming her consumption choices. Objects associated with media coverage take on a special aura for Becky. For example, her selection of a wooden bowl is suddenly validated when the retailer tells her that it was featured on the pages of *Elle* magazine. When she finds an ink-blue Vera Wang dress, she confirms its correctness because she believes it is something Gwyneth Paltrow might wear:

> But oh God. Oh *God*. That Vera Wang dress. Inky purple, with a low back and glittering straps. It just looked so completely movie-star perfect. Everyone crowded round to see me in it – and when I drew back the curtain, they all gasped. I just stared at myself, mesmerized. Entranced by what I could look like; by the person I could be. There was no question. I had to have it. I *had* to. As I signed the credit card slip. ... I wasn't me any more. I was Grace Kelly. I was Gwyneth Paltrow. I was a glittering somebody else who can casually sign a credit card slip for thousands of dollars while smiling and laughing at the assistant, as though this were a nothing-purchase.
>
> (Kinsella, 2002, p. 235)

In the twenty-first century, celebrities appear to have replaced or added to traditional artists, as the central figures breathing life into commodities. It is, however, incorrect to recognize Becky's interest in celebrity goods as emulation. Becky wants to remain herself, but sees celebrity designer fashion, as an access code to the glittery worlds of pleasure and social admiration. Like a commodity, Becky longs to circulate herself before a wide audience. While her immediate friends and family provide her warmth, affection, and rescue, she craves adoration from a much wider pool of people thus embracing the public sphere. Perpetually restless, she longs for excitement and social interaction, not respite.

The novels are set in London and New York, global economic centres, shopping Mecca, and experiential grounds for post-traditional living arrangements. Kinsella plays with the historical rivalry and mutual admiration between these two urban centres. Having honed her fashion skills in London, Becky still feels the spotlights burn wider, brighter, and newer in New York. New York supports brash levels of consumption unburdened by Britain's history of rationing and moral condemnation for rising above one's station. Britain is a nation of shopkeepers; New York is home to elite fashion brands and opulent retail chains. New York sets the bar of style high. Becky identifies American shoppers as 'her people', who appreciate the importance of look. The anonymity of the urban streets of London and New York brings one into proximity with strangers. Fashion is a central currency of belonging and identification in these post-traditional landscapes. So too, particularly in these urban centres, have traditional gender relations and the economic control men once held over women been liberated.

Becky rejects the call to of the thrifty consumer and prudent investor. She is the spendthrift Samuel Smiles warned his nineteenth century male readers to avoid. An extensive service economy unburdens her of domestic routine. Service workers make her morning coffee, provide her with facials, check out her shopping bags, ferry her from one place to another in taxis, and even arranges her wedding. Maintaining this non-domestic lifestyle is costly requiring a rich husband and a credit card. Becky is a modern-day lady of the manor called upon to choose and enact taste. Owning a home or saving for the years to come fail to occupy her attention. Her mind is overburdened with consumer fantasies and preoccupied with repressing all traces of her debt loads. She leaves long-term investment matters to her wealthy husband.

While she does not want to buy the matrimonial home, she is very interested in furnishing it. Making a home equates to an opportunity to shop and acquire beautiful objects. The apartment becomes a stage-set filled with props of her fantasy. For example, Becky believes a 1930s antique cocktail bar will catapult her and her husband into a scene from Casablanca, thus sacrifices damaging her back to drag it home. Nor is she interested in fashioning her home as a sanctuary for relaxation. Dressing up and spending an evening out in a fine restaurant is her strategy for relaxing with her workaholic husband. She describes her skill in providing for her husband by way of an evening out on the town:

It turns into the most magical, glamorous, glossy evening of my life. I put on my Vera Wang dress and Luke puts on his smartest suit, and we go to a fabulous restaurant where people are eating lobster and there's an old-fashioned jazz band, just like in the movies. Luke orders Bellinis, and we toast each other, and as he relaxes, he tells me more about his deal. In fact, he confides in me more than he ever has before.

(Kinsella, 2002, p. 235)

In public, Becky puts her man and herself on display. The passage above implies that correct consumption brings intimacy between men and women. Part of the delight of Becky is that she enjoys consumption. She is fearless towards the norms that define consumption as sinful. Becky is a sensation-seeker who extracts great pleasure from indulgences. She delights in sweet milk products – brownies, cakes, lattes – child-type food which are used to make her appear playful and girly. She drinks champagne, often to excess. Pleasantly, she shows no anxiety about the impact empty calories will have on her figure. Her drinking brings hang-overs, but no moral regret. In these senses, Becky appears liberated from the cage of body obsession and moral panic over the drunken woman.

Becky, however, is contained in other ways. She understands that she is measured, indeed, she wilfully offers herself up for objectification. The disciplinary gaze of men trouble her less than the 'Manhattan Once-over', a quick and skilled inspection of another woman's outfit and grooming habits used as the basis to accept or reject her right to be seen. The right brand and the correct cut of dress shield Becky from rejection and protect her ego. Years of retail therapy and magazine-reading have left her fluent in the language of designer brands. She is confident in her ability to create a look and praised for her style. Yet, she knows that she must be vigilant to remain 'fashionable' as the markers of fashion constantly change. To subvert the idea that Becky is a slave to fashion, the novels show fashion as an expression of self, a source of aesthetic pleasure, and a gift to the eye of others. The novels boldly subvert the Protestant Work Ethic's horror at the worship of idols, by demonstrating the power style has in the world: new objects transform thoughts, make the drab and boring new, glittery, and pleasurable.

New goods hold potential aspects of self, moments for admiration, and psychological stimulation. This partly explains Becky's restlessness, desire for instant gratification, and novelty. Therefore, Becky is frustrated that she can pick just one dress for her wedding, for she resents the thought of being defined by one gown. Becky's consumption is partially motivated out of interest in social mobility. She seeks to escape her humble background. Traditionally marrying well provided a means for social mobility, but Becky needs more than a man. Her fantasy life is immense. Objects are appreciated not because of their usefulness, but their ability to teleport Becky in and out of her rich fantasy life. Her dreams circulate around the epicentres of female success and maximum exposure of appearance, the Oscar red carpet, and old time Hollywood. Becky is also fond of princess narratives: her tangerine sandals catapult her into Cinderella; fine cakes and the deferential treatment of retail staff make her feel like a royalty. She desires a wedding set in an enchanted forest where her prince will whisk her away on a white stallion and throngs of people will ogle at her with envy.

Her consumptive dreams also imagine her success in fields traditionally occupied by men, yet, she refuses to follow masculinized rules of play, expecting to gain entry and approval in these domains based on her special feminine talents. Thus, her shopping talents are put forward in her imaginary application to the House of Lords; she imagines that her self-help book on personal finance will win a Nobel Prize. She seeks to feminize the public sphere and have shopping talents acknowledged as respectable, creative, and intelligent practices.

Becky challenges the idea that shopping is a passive activity, as the novels richly detail the emotional, physical, and sacrificial efforts she expends to acquire the objects of her attraction. Her powerful imagination transforms shopping into a highly charged event. She looks 'around the store with a fizz of anticipation'. Still, in retail environments, she is in complete control; she relaxes and focuses because these spaces feel to her like her 'natural habitat'. She emits unremitting adoration towards a shawl, is willing to loose her job to acquire a coveted pair of trousers, and risks putting out her back to drag home a piece of furniture. The novels demand that shopping be seen as an active and meaningful pursuit.

Her right to consume and take on debt is legitimated because Becky earns her own money. She is resourceful, holding a number of different jobs. Unlike the career-oriented women of the 1980s, Becky's character suggests that consumption is more important for her definition of self than her job. Her first job as a financial journalist bores her at times, but is not demanding. She makes her job fun by ceasing every opportunity to go to financial conferences, enjoy their free lunches, drink the champagne on offer, and gather free samples and trinkets. Gathering financial pamphlets at these financial seminars, she takes notes of speeches then repurposes this information into her columns. Superfluous, recycled, and produced by a woman who has no control over her finances, the novels suggest that financial information is promotional and meaningless.

People phone in to a television programme to acquire financial advice from Becky. She uses the language of financial therapeutics, soothing people but providing few concrete tips for improving their financial situation. Kinsella began her writing career as a financial journalist. The novels ask us to consider whether in a world in which financial information is governed by a commercial logic, it can ever be judged as truthful or useful?

Although Becky loses her job as a financial advisor, it leads her to her dream job: a personal shopper at Barney's Department store in New York. The job erases the line between work and consumption and confirms shopping as a productive activity. Becky is perfectly suited for the position given her impeccable CV in consumption. She pleases others by sharing her shopping talents. She is able to earn money and receives a sizeable discount off the clothing in the store. In contrast to her husband's work, Becky's work appears non-taxing because her labour flows 'naturally' from her social and aesthetic skills. Yet, like women's work in the past, her jobs are not serious, and her paycheque is 'mad money', which signals a surplus to be spent on pleasure. Becky devotes her income to immediate gratification.

Kinsella scripts a wicked stepmother who is wealthy, well connected, emitting impeccable taste, yet, completely sacrifices her relationship with family and friends for appearances. Becky's character is redeemed in juxtaposition. Becky is capable of positive relationships, with her mother, her best friend, and strangers, thus spared being viewed as wizened, embittered, unloving, and vengeful. The novels depict a tender relationship between Becky and her best friend Suzy. Becky shares her clothing with other women and provides them with fashion advice. She is also a powerful defender attacking an investment firm that swindled her parents' kind neighbours out of their money. Just when Becky reaches her most shallow, conniving, and childish, Kinsella has her extend a noble gesture to take the edge off her narcissism and delusions. The author notes that the roundness of the character is a large part of her appeal: 'She is in some ways shallow and silly, but she is also incredibly warm, loving and feisty – and always resourceful' (Kinsella, 2003).

Many people try to draw Becky's attention to the importance of her finances. They fail. Becky veils her financial picture from her parents to protect them from worry; hence her family can exert no influence over her budget. Becky's best friend Suzy is permitted to watch Becky's spending, and she does keep a valiant eye: 'Bex. ...You're not just going to bury your head in the sand and pretend it isn't happening'. Yet, Suzy is a soft gatekeeper, who indulges Becky's consumerist fantasies as much as she admonishes them: admiring Becky's style and squealing with excitement upon seeing her new objects. Because shopping is so bound to who Becky thinks she is, she prefers the company of women, or her gay designer neighbour, who are interested in the sphere of fashion and consumption. Suze understands and supports Becky's essence as no man can. Becky notes, in the ideal world, she would love to marry Suze.

But Suze has another attraction. She is exceptionally wealthy, and bails Becky out in times of trouble. This relationship, along with Becky's billionaire husband allows Becky to face the world with less anxiety. As representatives of the privileged class, Suze and Luke (Becky's husband) are presented as far more resourceful, possessing superior money strategies, the ability to consume based on reason, and the right to pass judgement on Becky. Suze, for example, has a small, quiet, elegant wedding; Becky wants to marry in an enchanted forest populated by hundreds of adoring fans. The banks too fail to contain Becky's spending. Van Slooten points out that for every letter from the bank in the novel, reminding Becky of the seriousness of her debt, there is another letter inviting her to take on more credit. A kindly banker favours Becky and willingly extends her credit limits. Neither family nor institution imposes punitive limits on Becky's credit because to do so would limit her liberty and limit a political economic system that requires people's self-reflexive participation. An image of an endlessly giving marketplace is depicted. New jobs magically appear or painless ways for dealing with debt emerge. Becky exists in a marshmallow world that endlessly cushions her financial fall and bounces her back onto her feet.

Becky knows financial solvency is culturally valued, and for the brief moment she is able to achieve this state she basks in a feeling of goodness. But paying off her bills once strikes Becky as enough. She cannot countenance why her bills keep rising and why she has to keep trying to pay them. She opts to evade the social context of financing, engaging avoidance techniques, rationalizations, self-delusions, and lies. She refuses to open her bills and answer her phone. She shuts down in the face of a problem, actively blocking worries out of her mind. She can enjoy shopping as a mode of escape only when it is filtered through an elaborate system of justifications and half-truths.

At the same time, the novels might be read as a recasting of shopping and consumer debt as respectable activities. Much of the humour of the book hinges on attempts to justify Becky's lifestyle in relation to the norms of prudence and utility consumption. She tries to write down everything she purchases to force herself to acknowledge her purchases, but she simply creates a long list. She attempts to purchase only what she needs, but discovers her needs are endless. She turns honoured financial wisdom on its head: the need to buy quality justifies the acquisition of many expensive items. She feels thrifty because she buys more than one thing and takes advantage of samples and free gifts. All efforts to control her spending become reasons to spend more. Becky demonstrates that the cultural divide between needs and wants is porous and shows the bankruptcy of the thrift ethos in a consumer culture. Some of Becky's justifications for spending boldly challenge her parents generations' compulsion to scrimp and save as life-denying. Her acts to squander wealth in a celebratory potlatch are also valued in a consumer culture.

For example, in the first novel, Becky attempts to get her budget under control by cooking curry. Because cooking is a novel experience for Becky, she filters it through what she knows: shopping and media culture. Cooking becomes an opportunity to purchase new ingredients, bake ware, and plastic containers. The taste of the food was less important than its look. Becky marvels at her ability to make something that resembles the image in a celebrity chef cookbook. In the end, Becky demonstrates that her control of the culinary realm is best expressed through her choice of appropriate restaurants and cafes. Becky's seemingly irrational behaviour is the by-product of her fixation to constantly rationalize all of her decisions.

There are two critical moments in the novels where Becky is forced to take stock of her finances and consumption behaviour. One is an existential crisis that occurs after Becky has engaged in an excessive shopping trip:

> One Monday morning I wake early, feeling rather hollow inside. My gaze flits to the pile of unopened carrier bags in the corner of my room and then quickly flits away again. I know I spent too much money on Saturday. [...] In all, I spent. ... Actually, I don't want to think about how much I spent. Think about something else, quick, I instruct myself.
>
> (Kinsella, 2002, p. 137)

She vigilantly re-enacts hedonistic behaviours to maintain her psychic unity. Becky's self-instruction is more than avoidance; it is a regime of denial. Profound inner discipline is required for her to sustain her pleasures.

The second radical insight offered in the novels occurs when Becky's credit is cut off. Having gathered over three hundred pounds worth of goods she has no interest in, the successive credit cards that she hands over to the sales clerk are all rejected. Becky's failure to meet the contract of market exchange transforms the pleasant, welcoming, deferential clerk into a rejecting and rude individual who scorns Becky. The underbelly of the consumer culture is exposed. Becky must acknowledge that her princess-like sovereignty is predicated upon her ability to pay. Becky cannot believe what is happening, she experiences a 'nasty chill feeling' that creeps over her. She remembers all the unopened letters in her dressing-table drawer: 'No. Don't say they've cancelled my card. They can't have done. ... I *need* it. They can't just cancel it, just like that'. Like a wastrel daughter, she cannot believe her chances have run out. As she processes the shock, the clerk reminds her that other people are waiting to purchase their goods. Becky's inability to pay holds up not only the queue, but the growth of the consumer economy. Blocking the commonwealth is a transgression of high order, filling Becky with social shame: her cheeks turn red and her hands tremble with embarrassment (Kinsella, 2002, p. 20). The sense of alienation is great as she is disconnected from the lifestyle-giving force of credit. Studies reveal the confessions of bankrupts who declare life without credit privileges is hard to enjoy (Jackson, 2006). Credit is a necessity for life as it is deeply embedded within consumer culture.

Dreams of consumerism and debt

Van Slooten has argued that Becky's behaviour conforms to Colin Campbell's model of the 'modern autonomous hedonism'. Campbell would see Becky's fantasies as modern daydreams. Unlike unconscious fantasies, daydreams are not surreal or condensed but linked to the everyday, tangible – if fantastical realities. Daydreams, according to Campbell, invoke a longing to actualize mental images in the material world. The modern daydream arose as a strategy to sustain pleasure in the context of growing affluence. While traditional hedonists repeated known bodily pleasures, modern hedonists are dream artists who play with aesthetics in their mind. Perpetual novelty emerged as a new and superior form of pleasure-seeking. Campbell argues that this form of pleasure pursuit explains the contemporary interest in fashion and novelty:

> [Modern consumers'] basic motivation is the desire to experience in reality the pleasurable dramas, which they have already enjoyed in imagination, and each 'new' product is seen as offering a possibility

of realizing this ambition. However, since reality can never provide the perfected pleasures encountered in day-dreams (or, if at all, only in part, and very occasionally), each purchase leads to literal disillusionment, something which explains how wanting is extinguished so quickly, and why people disacquire goods as rapidly as they acquire them.

(Campbell, 1987, pp. 189–90)

Campbell would not define Becky as a materialist, or even irrational. She merely displays a heightened sense of fantasy, typical of many contemporary consumers:

The central insight required is the realization that individuals do not so much as satisfaction from products, as pleasure from self-illusory experiences which they construct their associated meanings. The essential activity of consumption is thus not the actual selection, purchase or use of products, but the imaginative pleasure-seeking to which the product image leads itself.

(in Van Slooten, pp. 221–2)

While explanatory, Campbell's analysis neglects the role credit plays in the circular dynamics of daydreaming, consumption, and pleasure-seeking. Credit calls forth a different type of dreaming that requires individuals to optimistically project their ability to cover their debts in the future. Financial fantasies are the bedrock of the late modern economy. To enjoy current consumptive privileges for many requires an optimistic projection that assumes house and stock values will continue to rise, employment will be steady, and wages will increase. But, as I shall outline in the conclusion, there are limits and consequences to these individual and collective financial fantasies.

Conclusion

This book set out to examine the cultural dynamics of personal finance. Unlike psychological or economic approaches, a cultural perspective highlights how meaning, customs, morality, collective sentiments, and institutions mediate individual financial fantasies and practices. Debt is hardly new to Britain. People have long lived out of one another's pockets (Finn, 2003; Muldrew, 1998). The impulse to enter into and payback debt contracts is as deeply rooted and morally charged as the enduring outrage that has followed those who charge undue interest or deceive the vulnerable (Atwood, 2008). Yet, the conditions of personal finance have profoundly changed. In the twentieth century, financial institutions turned their ear from the old religious condemnation of debt towards a secular emphasis on investment and economic growth. Debtors no longer wallowed in prisons. Instead, a psychiatric profession attempted to help them reclaim their willpower and take control of their spending. A modern emphasis on democracy, financial freedoms, and rights replaced traditional class ground and exclusionary credit systems. Many celebrated these changes, with good reason: banks became responsive to consumer interests; wealth expanded, much of it generated by the financial sector; women achieved more financial equality; a greater percentage of the population bought homes than at any other time.

Yet, the economic recession of 2007 turned attention to the problematic elements of the expanding personal finance, neglected in the celebration of wealth creation. It is to this debate that I add my conclusion. In Chapter 8, I took Becky Bloomwood as the point of access to a cultural history that refocuses attention towards the dynamics of wealth distribution and gender relations. Becky illustrates the contradictions surrounding contemporary upward mobility, while exposing the gender tensions that continue to underpin the domestic economy.

Acknowledging the many benefits of expanding consumer credit, in what follows I argue that women and those with low income have paid an unfair toll for entry into the relations of modern personal finance.

Chapters 1 and 2 traced an emerging cult of domesticity that became the fulcrum of contemporary consumer culture and personal finance. Inside the home Victorian attitudes towards middle-class domesticity reworked thrift as a moral and aesthetic ethos. With 60% of the country's wealth now circulating in the property market and billions more in spin-off consumer goods and services, few imagined that homeownership was anything but rock solid, until recently. Journalists reported housing inequality and the troubles young people experienced trying to climb on the property ladder, but few questioned the overwhelming collective faith in the property market. British economist Andrew Oswald was unique in this regard.

Oswald dared to poke at the quasi-religious faith vested in homeownership and economic security. Oswald acknowledged that owning property was one of the most important means of accruing wealth in Britain; however, the property market deterred growth in other areas of the economy. Holding a mortgage for a home in an area where jobs had taken flight, posed an acute dilemma for people. Oswald's study of several major developed economies between 1960–96 found a relationship between increases in homeownership and increases in the unemployment rate; a 10% increase in homeownership correlated with a 2% increase in unemployment (Oswald, 1999). People locked into long-term debt could stop taking risks. Driven 'to make the mortgage payments and handle ones credit card bills does more than make people risk averse towards starting new businesses, it prevents people from taking risks in their own lives to secure more contentment. It becomes particularly difficult for those with major credit commitments to risk their cash flow' (Searjeant, 17 February 2006).

This conservatism surrounding indebtedness would not surprise Lendol Calder (2001) who argued that the reigning definition of credit that constitutes it as a handmaiden of hedonism and freedom is obfuscating. In his ground-breaking cultural history, Calder draws attention to how the rapid expansion of instalment credit in America during the 1920s marked a turning point in the mental disciplines demanded of American consumerism. Because the American dream was bought on 'time', not on impulse, people did not experience a life of freedom and unbridled pleasure, rather credit trapped people in an iron cage of getting and spending in their quest for the 'standard package' of mass suburban home and car ownership. The modern cult of domesticity saddled the American consumer with a life-long debt that conditioned the ways they could think and act in the future. For Calder what was so remarkable was that the vast majority of people adhered to their credit contracts. They would go to great lengths moon-lighting and endure considerable anxiety throughout their lifetime in order to pay for a new house or their consumer lifestyles. Credit is a disciplining force within culture, as Calder rightly argues, not freedom.

To explain this process, Calder extended Weber's notion of the iron cage of debt. Consumers, he argued, are driven by a deep cultural impulse, which, as we have seen, emerged long ago within religious discourses that equated debt payment with a state of grace. Just as working hard was forged as an appeasement to god, so too was the payment of debt and thrift constructed as divine. According to Calder, the drive of people today to do all they can to pay-off their debts, is not simply materialist greed, but adherence to a social norm that equates debt payment with what it means to be a good human, and a productive member of the society. He rejects the views that Americans are shopaholics with no sense of thrift, redefining them as good people following a troubling social value system.

> If my analysis means anything it means that modern consumers run the risk of being both deceived by consumerism and dragged along by consumer credit. To say there have been worse ways of living is not to say this is a good way to live.
>
> (Calder, 2001, p. 33)

What Calder found ludicrous was a social system that equated expanding indebtedness with democratization, freedom, and social advancement.

Chapters 3 and 5 traced the British embrace of American hire purchase, credit cards, and corporate banking marketing practices. Adoption of these financial institutions and instruments gave the British domestic economy form, legitimacy, scope, and velocity. Thatcher granted corporate banking an unprecedented level of autonomy, believing competition would discipline the elitist gentlemanly banker. Her assumption was fanciful. When the British government commissioned the Cruikshank committee to look into the problem of personal finance in 2000 (Cruikshank, 2000), the committee's report concluded that the banking sector was rife with monopolies that did not always work in the consumers' interest. Cruikshank found unfair service charges and non-transparent marketing practices common among British banks. The Big Bang reduced the traditional diversity of financial institutions to the corporate model without increasing socially beneficial competition.

While it is convenient to blame America for Britain's current economic woes, Britons democratically elected a government bent on unravelling state controls and made it politically untenable for subsequent governments to deviate from this course. The welcoming of 'free market' was not foreign. As Frank Trentman notes: 'Britain gave Free Trade to the world' (Trentman, 2008, p. 2). The worship of private property, particularly the home as a source of economic value, was a British dream transplanted to America, not the other way round. Further, it took much more than American marketing techniques, slick bank advertising, and the circulation of glitzy American lifestyles on television to propel Britons into cataclysmic levels of debt. Credit use, I suggest, hinges upon a deeper British common sense rooted in a healthy secular belief in enjoying the pleasures of the material world in the here and now – but paying for them later. The disciplining of payments rested on the indigenous fantasy that ever-increasing property and stock prices, higher wages, and stable jobs would cover debts.

The modern credit networks emerging from hire purchase in the late nineteenth century bloomed from affluence, not poverty. Historians noted how rising levels of affluence troubled traditional categories of class, especially after the WWII. As outlined in the introduction, by 1980, some analysts of the consumer culture found the categories of class so ill-suited, they dropped an economic focus from their research. Yet, this study insists that the distribution of wealth, whether achieved through wages or credit access, remains a crucial issue for the analysis of the consumer economy. Free markets in credit can reinforce inequality, as much as erode it.

Mandated by successive governments, bankers sought to achieve the noble goal of democratizing credit throughout the social system, and did so according to rational economic calculus of lending. Subprime mortgages provided those with poor credit histories access to funds, thus spreading homeownership. The subprime sector was highly successful, growing 9.1% more than double that of mainstream mortgage lending growth in 2006. The banks covered associated risks by increasing the interest rates on the principle sum. In 2007, the International Monetary Fund reported that the British property market was overvalued by 40% more than property markets in the US. UK house prices were nine times yearly earnings, compared to five times in 2001 (International Monetary Fund, 2008). And when the meltdown happened, the wrath of the market was not equally distributed, visiting at the doorstep of the poor more than the rich. Subprime mortgages accounted for 8% of the mortgage market, but 23% of mortgage default (Chapman, 14 March 2007). Blame was not hard to find. The Financial Services Authority, reviewing the role played by 11 subprime lenders accounting for more than half the market, concluded they had failed to execute their responsibilities as lenders, making 'inadequate assessment of consumers' ability to afford the mortgage' and gathering fees for remortgaging packages with little evidence that it was in consumers' best interest (Financial Services Association, 2007).

Studies also pointed to the unequal distribution of financial skills and money handling socialization. Although prevailing financial norms suggest that the promises of consumer culture visit those who are self-disciplined, prudent, rational, and able to balance their consumptive output with their income input, Allison Pugh's research suggests that relative access to income entrains distinct financial beliefs and practices (Pugh, 2004). Britain's GINI Index – the broadest measure of inequality of income – progressed towards equality throughout the post-war period, reversed in the 1980s and has yet to recover. Significant wealth had been generated on paper, but economic inequalities did not subside. Pugh documented how lower income families tended to view money as a matter of luck, fortune, or God's benevolence. Constantly under pressure to find ways to raise funds, Pugh found low-income families talked more about money and focused on the present. Middle classes relieved of the burden of struggling to acquire everyday items had less need to discuss money and could turn their attention to projecting their financial plans into the future.

Lamont (1992) reached conclusions similar to Pugh. Interviewing professionals and working-class people in the US and France about how they handled money, Lamont found that class background influenced the potential success with money-handling ventures. Lamont concluded professionals held forward-thinking attitudes and constantly looked out for investment opportunities. They were more likely to ensure that their debts could be written off against their business, to diversify their investments across various investment opportunities, and to save a percentage of their income for the purpose of investing. They also expressed considerable confidence in their understanding of investments and money management skills, which Lamont argued made them more secure about taking risks (Lamont, 1992). They gathered financial experience by playing the market in a safe way. Even young professionals were eager to start by buying a few stocks to gain knowledge of the stock market and to learn to play the odds. On the other hand, Lamont found working-class individuals in both countries had a less flexible approach to managing personal finance. Most lived from pay cheque to pay cheque – keeping debt to a minimum because they had less faith in their ability to control or understand of how they could benefit from credit instruments. Moreover, they showed little interest in trying to learn about investment beyond savings because they did not feel such knowledge would improve their situation. Clearly, with the retreat of post-war state supports, owning a home became the most palpable symbol of economic and social security.

British data suggests the dynamics of financial socialization are at play in property markets. The British middle class appeared to view property as an investment, using their superior lines of credit to leverage capital from their first home to speculate in rental property. When the crash hit, middle-class people experienced a devaluation in their property portfolio, but the working classes, in the context of rising unemployment rates, could only default on their mortgages. The Financial Services Authority reported in 2008 that there were 377,000 mortgage accounts in arrears, with repossessions rising by 68% (Haurant, 17 March 2009).

Thus, evidence suggests that the potential for wealth accumulation depends on class position and attitudes. While the middle class celebrated the home as an investment, low-income people reported they found maintaining a household a depressing and anxiety-ridden activity (Williams and Collins, 1995). Financial anxieties accompanied financial freedoms and opportunities. During the 1990s recession, Lunt and Livingstone reported the acute and paradoxical money anxieties experienced by British consumers. Other writers, subsequently, confirmed a strong correlation between economic inequalities, health, and psychological problems. Recent studies suggest half of all heavy debtors suffer from depression (Hickman, 2006).

The poor consistently report higher rates of 'psychological distress as well as other health problems' than the rest of the public and, in extreme cases, debt-related suicide. Those with few resources are twice as likely to 'report low subjective well-being as those who locate themselves in a more privileged position' (Smith & Easterlow, 2005). Those with high levels of unsecured debt reported higher levels of psychological torment and lower self-esteem (Bridges and Disney, 2003). Former banker Anthony Elliott's research documented a wide variety of mental and physical illnesses that visited indebted consumers. Even after they had paid their debt, debtors complained of long-term debilitating health problems. The indebted also frequently suffered from excessive food, alcohol, and drug abuse. Elliot estimated that up to 4 million people suffered ill-health because of over indebtedness (Treanor, 2005). As the economic crisis accentuated, the lower classes were not only financially but also psychologically at risk. Recognizing this fact, the banking community responded with therapeutic advertising, while governments funded debt counselling services completing the long march from debtors' prison to the psychiatrist's couch.

Irrationality, thy name is woman

Within popular discourses, women's consumption and financial management has long been deemed more crazy than men's. Patriarchy deemed women incapable of entering into credit contracts and defined them as vulnerable to the ways of the tallyman. Madame Bovary had to die for her debts. Nothing constrained women's lives more than their economic dependence on men, until women gained the legal right to enter into credit contracts, own property, and declare bankruptcy. Becky Bloomwood, a late modern female figure, represents an extremely conflicted version of women's place in the consumer culture. Freed from patriarchal control by virtue of her work and access to credit, Becky moved out of her humble origins. Yet, her financial independence was precarious. She continues to rely on a rich husband, wealthy friends, and tolerant bankers to manage her excessive debts. Mental energy once directed towards domesticity, placating husband, and family needs, were refocused on following the shifting markers of fashion and lacing commodities into daydreams. The numerous, exhausting denial strategies Becky must engage to manage her credit bills, however, curtail her marketplace pleasures and freedoms. She is called upon to exaggerate her earning potential, focus on instant gratification to repress creeping awareness of debt, rationalize her situation, and struggle to make her decisions appear respectable. This is the type of identity work required to maintain a place in consumer culture. Thus, Becky reminds us that women invested more than their incomes into the domestic economy: they invested their identities and psychic energies.

Further evidence of the disparaging insults against gender that circulate in contemporary discourses is found in Emma Casey's (2003) research. Casey explored the long-standing cultural tendency to construct working-class women's financial practices as deviant and irrational. Casey talked to low-income women about their playing the lottery, which was widespread and subject to popular cultural scorn. The women Casey interviewed expended effort to counteract the popular definitions of their financial performances. The women understood well the 'popular critiques of gambling behaviour' and their discord with 'norms of budgeting and money management'. To make National Lottery Play 'respectable', women stressed the prudent, family-oriented and utility-minded ways they employed their small winnings. Winnings, said women, helped to buy or replace household items, provide items for the children, or payoff debts. Casey concludes that working-class women's lottery play should be understood as people 'making the best' out of their subordinate economic situations.

British culture has not completely abandoned its thrift ethos. I found thrift lingered in press, psychological and popular literature that invoked champagne lifestyles, Madame Bovary Syndrome, shopaholics, and rate tarts. Just as Victorian women carried a disproportionate share of the weight of thrift, so too do some contemporary discourses construct women as foolish and pathological. When their consumption was deemed less than prudent, or appeared selfish, popular discourses deemed women's purchases irrational. This is not to deny that some women refuse to assume responsibility for their consumption and finances, but rather to highlight that women hold less debt and are more likely to pay back than men. Why do financial discourses subject women's financial practices to more ridicule? I assert that the construction of feminine financial folk devils is a cultural reflex utilized to deflect and ease anxieties about troubling economic relations.

The cultural projection of blame on women is as old as humanity, but why do these troubling and tired gender politics experienced by women continue when evidence has proven men equally irrational and irresponsible in handling the weight of the contemporary domestic economy? We have seen how the irrationality of bankers in their marketing of credit made them the targets of hatred during the current economic crisis. But bankers are a visible enemy. Much more distressing is the collective faith in the reason of the financial elite, a sentiment which is sadly misplaced in a deregulated market system. Aeron Davis (2005) interviewed fund mangers, the financial elites who controlled '80–90 percent of all shares and other financial products traded in the LSE' (p. 607). These men (women rarely held these positions) relied on the financial press, newswires and shared research material to make their decisions. The 34 fund managers Davis interviewed did not slavishly follow media messages, but he could not characterize their decisions as wholly rational.

Financiers, according to Davis, constantly, carefully, and rationally processed information. Fund managers qualify among the brightest minds in the country: highly educated, focused, calculating, and in possession of superior computer literacy, highly numerate with exceptional communication skills (Davis, 2005, p. 609). They even showed awareness 'of their own potential irrationalities and failings', admitting, 'No-one can claim to be totally objective' (Davis, 2005, p. 610). They

saw the tendency to rationalize contradictions as an unhelpful occu-
pational hazard. They tried to limit their irrationality through active
self-reflection and continual correction.

Despite their intelligence, reason, and noble efforts to filter out faulty
logic, fund managers made decisions that deviated from best interest.
The reason for this, notes Davis, is partly explained by the promotional
tone of the information upon which they must base their decisions.
Subjective assumptions enter into decision-making processes because
fund managers have to forecast the future based on constantly changing
valuation tools formulated on companies' promotional rhetoric (Davis,
2005, p. 611). The quality of the company's management emerged as
one of the most important measures of value, but the cult of the CEO
contributed to allegiances based on faith and charisma not reason.

Although the cultural framework fund managers worked in encouraged
them to act independently, their adherence to general market indicators
led to 'herd like behavior'. Davis noted how, 'When everyone follows
"index-tracking", a logical choice for individuals, "returns become worse
for everyone"'. All the fund managers said they felt pressure to follow
the herd. 'If it all goes wrong, it does so for the majority and no-one
gets blamed' (Davis, 2005, p. 617). The expansion of financial news
and Internet information added a new layer to the speculative booms.
Fund managers, aware that stocks are overvalued, feel pressured to buy
because media made it appear a considerable 'risk not to join the boom'
(Davis, 2005, p. 619). Davis concludes 'rational, self-interested individuals can, collectively, behave in mass, irrational ways, and in response to
common sources of media communications (Davis, 2005, p. 622).

The implications of Davis's study were chilling because they suggested
that bankers were not simply greedy or morally suspect, but that their
powers of rationality were as limited as Becky Bloomwood's. In chapters
5, 6, and 7, I outlined the expansion of financial media and promotion.
Regulators drew limits on the promotional messages directed to consumers, but no one considered the implication of promotional messages
on bankers' decisions. The culture is vulnerable to promotional hype
because it locks into deeper cultural hopes seeded in the idea of ever-
increasing wealth, the goodness of private property, and the ability of
consumerism to deliver happiness. This cultural history reminds us that
Becky's consumer dreams were caught in larger social discourses that an
unregulated financial system would deliver infinite economic expansion with no pains, no environmental disasters, no global discord, no
inequality, and no recessions. This was a dream as irrational as Becky's
belief that a pair of shoes would make her Cinderella.

Bibliography

'20 Years after "Big Bang" in the City of London; Forget Shares, Property Has Been the Big Winner Says Frank Knight', *Finfacts Ireland* (24 October 2006). Accessed on 13 January 2009.

Abelson, E. S. *When Ladies Go A-Thieving: Middle-Class Shoplifters in the Victorian Department Store* (NY: Oxford University Press, 1989).

Aboujaoude, E.; Faber, R.; Koran, L. M.; Large, M. D.; and Serpe, R. T. 'Estimated Prevalence of Compulsive Buying Behaviour in the United States', *American Journal of Psychiatry*, 163: 10 (2006), 1806–12.

Ackrill, M. 'Marketing in British Banking, 1945–1980'. In R. Tedlow & G. Jones (eds), *The Rise and Fall of Mass Marketing*. (London: Routledge, 1993).

Ackrill, M. and L. Hannah, *Barclays: The Business of Banking, 1690–1996.* (Cambridge: Cambridge University Press, 2001).

Allen, A. and Hollander, E. 'Is Compulsive Buying a Real Disorder, and Is It Really Compulsive?', *American Journal of Psychiatry*, 163: 10 (2006), 1670–2.

Anderson, A. R.; Drakopoulou-Dodd, S. L; and Scott, M. G. 'Religion as an Environmental Influence on Enterprise Culture – The Case of Britain in the 1980s, *International Journal of Entrepreneurial Behaviour and Research*, 6: 11 (2000), 5–20.

Andrew, J. and A. Oswald, The Housing Market and Europe's Unemployment: A Non-Technical Paper, Unpublished paper, Warwick: University of Warwick, May 1999). Available from http://www.warwick.ac.uk/fac/soc/economics/staff/faculty/oswald/homesnt.pdf. Accessed: October 19, 2009.

APACS, 'Plastic Cards in the UK and How We Used Them in 2007' (London: APACS, The UK Payments Association, 2007). Available from: www.apacs.org.uk/resources. Accessed on 3 July 2007.

Archer, B. Laughing All the Way to the Bank, London: *Guardian*, 15 September 1997, p. 30.

Ashworth, A. 'A Dangerous Message for the Financially Feckless', *Times* (14 May 2005), 3.

Atkinson, R., 'Lifelong Parenting: The Changing Shape of British Family Life', *Mortgage Strategy* (4 April 2007) 24.

Attwood, M., *Payback: Debt and the Shadow Side of Wealth* (Toronto: House of Anansi Press, 2008).

—— 'Let the Borrower Beware', *Times* (28 January 2006), 3.

Bailey, P. 'Will the Real Bill Blanks Please Stand Up?: Towards a Role Analysis of Mid-Victorian Working-class Respectability', *Journal of Social History*, 12: 3 (1979), 336–53.

Bain, A. D. 'The Cost of Motor Vehicle Hire Purchase', *The Journal of Industrial Economics*, 14: 2 (April 1966), 124–42.

Bali, G. and F. Capie, 'Concentration in British Banking 1870–1920', *Business History*, 24 (3) (1982) 280–92.

Bank of England, 'Table A5.2 Monthly Total Lending to Individuals: Net Lending Bank of England,' Monetary & Financial Statistics (October 2008).

Bardon, N. *Discourse Upon Trade*, (London: Tho. Milbourn, 1690). Archive for the History of Economic Thought, McMaster University. Available from: http://socserv.mcmaster.ca/econ/ugcm/3ll3/. Accessed on 6 February 2009.

Barr, N. The Economics of the Welfare State, 2nd ed. (Palo Alto, CA: Stanford University Press, 1993).

Barrow, B. 'Most Bankrupts Are in Their Twenties', *Daily Telegraph* (15 February 2005), 4.

Barty-King, H. *The Worst Poverty: A History of Debt and Debtors*, (Wolfeboro Falls, NH: Alan Sutton, 1991).

BBC News online. 'Number of Insolvencies "Falling"' (23 February 2007). Available from: http://news.bbc.co.uk/go/pr/fr/-/1/hi/business/6390383.stm. Accessed on 9 January 2009.

—— 'Barclaycard Tackles Over-spenders' (16 February 2007). Available from: http://news.bbc.co.uk/go/pr/fr/-/1/hi/business/6368339.stmo. Accessed on 9 January 2009.

—— 'Divorce "Can Boost Debt Levels"' (16 October 2006). Available from: http://news.bbc.co.uk/2/hi/business/6054532.stm. Accessed on 9 January 2009.

—— 'Older Men Have the Worst Debt Problems, According to Research from a Leading Debt Charity' (16 February 2007). Available from: http://news.bbc.co.uk/2/hi/business/6361295.stm. Accessed on 14 March 2008.

—— 'Store Cards "Need Rate Warning"' (21 December 2005). Available from: http://news.bbc.co.uk/go/pr/fr/-/1/hi/business/4549514.stm. Accessed on 9 January 2009.

—— 'The UK's Debt Footprint', (16 February 2007). Available from: http://news.bbc.co.uk/2/hi/in_depth/629/629/6365321.stm. Accessed on 9 January 2009

BBC One, 'Spend It Like Beckham', Panorama (30 November 2003). Reporter: Justin Rowlatt, Producer: Andy Bell, Assistant Producers: Shabnam Grewal, David Baxter, Deputy Editors: Andrew Bell, Sam Collyns, Editor: Mike Robinson.

BBC, 'Warning as City Toasts Big Bang', London, 26 October 2006. Available from http://news.bbc.co.uk/2/hi/business/6087748.stm. Accessed on 18 October 2009.

Beattie, J.; Dittmar, H.; and Friese, S. 'Objects, Decision Consideration and Self-Image in Men's and Women's Impulse Purchases', *Journal of Economic Psychology*, 16: 3 (1995), 491–511.

Benson, A. (ed.). 'I Shop Therefore I Am: Compulsive Buying and the Search For Self' (NY: Aronson, 2000).

Benson, J. 'Working Class Consumption, Saving and Investment in England and Wales, 1851–1911', *Journal of Design History*, 9: 2 (1996), 87–99.

Bentham, J. Defence of Usury, (London: Payne and Foss, 1818). Available from: http://www.econlib.org/library/Bentham/bnthUs.html. Accessed on 3 March 2009.

—— Defence of Usury, (London: Payne and Foss, 1787). Available from: http://socserv2.socsci.mcmaster.ca/~econ/ugcm/3ll3/bentham/usury. Accessed on 3 March 2009.

Bernthal, M. J.; Crockett, D.; and Rose R. L. 'Credit Cards as Lifestyle Facilitators', *Journal of Consumer Research*, 32: 1 (2005), 130–45.

Berwick, I. 'National Consumer Debt Approaches 1,000bn', *Independent* (5 June 2004), 28.

Bevon, T., 'The Battle for Personal Deposits Hots Up'. *Banking World* (1984) 1(4).

Bicker, M., *Factoring in the UK 2nd edn* (London: Department for Trade and Industry, HMSO, 1994).

Black, D. 'A Review of Compulsive Buying Disorder', *World Psychiatry*, 6(1) February 2007, 14–18.

Black, D. W. 'Compulsive Buying Disorder: A Review of the Evidence', *International Journal of Neuropsychiatric Medicine*, 12: 2 (2007), 124–32.

Black, D. and T. Moyer, 'Clinical Features and Psychiatric Comorbidity of Subjects with Pathological Gambling Behavior', *Psychiatric Services*, 49, November 1998, 1434–1439.

Blackwell, D. 'Dividend in Sight at Debt Free Direct', *Financial Times* (29 June 2005), 23.

Blackwell, T. and J. Seabrook, *A World still to Win: Reconstruction of the Postwar Working Class* (London: Faber and Faber, 1985).

Blumer, H. 'The Rejuvenation of Community Studies? Neighbours, Networks and Policy', *Sociological Review*, 33: 3 (1985), 439.

Booker, C., *The seventies* (Harmondsworth: Penguin Books Ltd, 1980).

Bosanquet, H. 'The Burden of Small Debts', *Economic Journal*, 6: 22 (1896), 212–25.

Bourdieu, P. Distinction: A Social Critique of the Judgement of Taste (Cambridge: Harvard University Press, 1984).

Bourdieu, P. *Acts of Resistance: Against the Tyranny of the Market*. Richard Nice (trans.) (New York: The New Press, 1998).

Bowden, S. and Collins, M. 'The Bank of England, Industrial Regeneration, and Hire Purchase between the Wars', *Economic History Review*, New series, 45: 1 (1992), 120–36.

Bowden, S. and Turner, P. 'The Demand for Consumer Durables in the United Kingdom in the Interwar Period', *Journal of Economic History*, 53: 2 (1993), 244–58.

Bowden, S. 'Credit Facilities and the Growth of Consumer Demand for Electric Appliances in England in the 1930s', *Business History*, 32: 1 (1990), 52–75.

Bowlby, R. (1985) *Just Looking: Consumer Culture in Dreiser, Gissing and Zola* (New York: Methuen Inc.).

Boyd Jr, H. W. and Piercy, I. 'Retailing in Great Britain', *Journal of Marketing*, 27: 1 (1963), 29–35.

Brantlinger, P. *Fictions of the State: Culture and Credit in Britain, 1694–1994.* (Ithaca, NY: Cornell University Press 1996).

Bridges, S. and R. Disney, Use of Credit and Arrears on Debt among Low Income Families in the United Kingdom (School of Economics, University of Nottingham, UK 2003).

Briggs, A. *Victorian Things* (Chicago: Chicago University Press, 1988), 214.

Bromley, C. and Humphrey, A. 'Home Sweet Home', *British Social Attitudes: 22nd Report* (London: Sage 2005), 63–86.

Brown, K. 'Debt Laws to Change: Result in Misery', *Financial Times* (27 March 2004), 27.

Brundson, C. 'Lifestyling Britain: The 8–9 Slot on British Television', *International Journal of Cultural Studies*, 6: 1 (2003), 5–23.

Budden, R. 'Bankruptcy Can Leave You Quids in Robert Budden Serious Money', *Financial Times* (12 February 2005), 27.

Burnett, J. *The Annals of Labour: Autobiographies of British Working Class People, 1820–1920* (Bloomington, IN: Indiana University Press, 1974).

Burroughs, R. J. 'Should Urban Land Be Publicly Owned?', *Land Economics*, 42: 1 (1966), 11–20.

Burton, D. 'Gender Relations in the British Banking Industry: Continuity or Change?', *The Services Industries Journal*, 16 (4) (1996) 527–544.

Bush, J. 'Christmas Spending Fails to Lift Economy', *Times* (24 December 1992), 3.

Cain, P. J. and A. G. Hopkins, 'Gentlemanly Capitalism and British Expansion Overseas II: New Imperialism 1850–1945'. *South African Journal of Economic History*, 2 (40) (1992) 1–26.

Calder, L. *Financing the American Dream: A Cultural History of Consumer Credit* (Princeton: Princeton University Press, 2001).

Callon, M. *The Laws of the Markets* (London: Blackwell Publishers, 1998).

Carey, J. *The Intellectuals and the Mass: Pride and Prejudice among the Literary Intelligentsia, 1800–1939*. (London: Faber & Faber, 1992).

Carter, P. 'Polite "Persons": Character, Biography and the Gentleman', *Transactions of the Royal Historical Society*, 12 (2002), 333–54.

Casey, E. 'Gambling and Consumption: Working-class Women and UK National Lottery Play', *Journal of Consumer Culture*, 3: 2 (2003), 245–63.

Cave, T. F. 'Overseas Investment Income Helps to Prop Up Current Account Deficit', *Financial Times* (30 March 2005), 10.

Cave T. F. 'Bankruptcies Increase to Record High in First Quarter', *Financial Times* (7 May 2005), 14.

—— 'Overseas Investment Income Helps to Prop up Current Account Deficit', *Financial Times* (30 March 2005), 3.

Chadwick, E. 'Post Office Savings' Banks'. *Journal of the Statistical Society of London*, Vol. 24(4), (1861), pp. 519–522.

Chaney, D. *Lifestyles* (London: Routledge, 2002).

Chapman, M., 'Sub-Prime Borrowers Face Repossession', BBC One, Panorama, 14 March 2007. Available from: http://news.bbc.co.uk/2/hi/business/7030723.stm. Accessed: 3 April 2009.

Chisholm, J. 'Credit Card Spending Fall Adds to Pressure For Rate Cut Personal Debt', *Financial Times* (5 January 2006), 3.

—— 'Shoppers Enthusiastic in Spite of Debts Retailing', *Financial Times* (21 January 2006), 4.

Church, R. 'Advertising Consumer Goods in Nineteenth-Century Britain: Reinterpretations', *Economic History Review*, New series, 53: 4 (2000), 621–45.

Cohen, D. *Household Gods: The British and their Possessions*. (London: Yale University Press, 2006).

Clapson, M. 'Working-class Women's Experiences of Moving to New Housing Estates in England since 1919', *Twentieth Century Brit History*, 10 (1999), 345–65.

Clark, G. L.; Thrift, N.; and Tickell, A. 'Performing Finance: The Industry, the Media and Its Image', *Review of International Political Economy*, 11: 2 (May 2004), 289–310.

Clark, R. 'A Nation Afloat on Debt', *Times* (30 May 2005), 20.

Coffin, J. 'Credit, Consumption, and Images of Women's Desires: Selling and Sewing Machines in Late Nineteenth – Century France', *French Historical Studies*, 18: 3 (1994), 749–83.

Coggan, P. 'You Will Have to Be Nimble to Ride Rally', *Financial Times* (6 December 2003), 30.

Coleman, D. C. 'London Scriveners and the Estate Market in the Later Seventeenth Century', *The Economic History Review*, Vol. 4(2) (1951), pp. 221–230.

Collins, M., *Money and banking in the UK: A history* (London: Croom Helm, 1988).

Cook, D. *The Commodification of Childhood* (Durham: Duke University Press, 2004).

Cooper, N. 'Rank, Manners and Display: The Gentlemanly House, 1500–1750', *Transactions of the Royal Historical Society*, 12 (2002), 291–310.

Cordery, S. 'Friendly Societies and the Discourse of Respectability in Britain, 1825–1875', *Journal of British Studies*, 34: 1 (1995), 35–58.

Croft, J. 'Aggressive Tactics Blamed For Borrowing Explosion', *Financial Times* (2 June 2004), 4.

Cruickshank, D. Competition in UK Banking: A Report to the Chancellor of the Exchequer (London: HM Treasury, 2000).

—— 'Barclays Tightens Its Lending Criteria Consumer Credit', *Financial Times* (30 November 2005), 3.

—— 'Credit Card Chief Condemns Bankruptcy Change Enterprise Act', *Financial Times* (12 February 2004), 5.

—— 'Maze of Debt Snares Hapless Borrowers Lending Policies Look Set To Be Toughened', *Financial Times* (30 December 2005), 3.

—— 'More Complain about Debt Collection Agencies', *Financial Times* (21 January 2006), 4.

—— 'Mortgage Repressions Expected to Soar Housing Market', *Financial Times* (22 February 2005), 5.

—— 'UK: Profits in the Billions Underline the Vital Role of Banking in the Economy', *Financial Times* (18 February 2006), 19.

Crompton, G. W. 'Self-Help: Voluntary Associations in Nineteenth-Century Britain by P. H. J. H. Gosden', *Economic History Review*, New series, 28: 1 (1975), 130–2.

Cumbo, J. Bankruptcy, 21 October 2005, p. 17.

Cunningham, J. and Roberts, P. *Inside Her Pretty Little Head: A New Theory of Female Motivation and What It Means for Marketing* (London: Cyan Communications, 2007).

Curran J. (foreword) and Burrows, R. (ed.). *Deciphering the Enterprise Culture: Entrepreneurship, Petty Capitalism and the Restructuring of Britain* (London: Thomson Learning, 1991).

Daley, J. 'Teenagers Are the Next Target for Expensive Plastic Providers', *Independent* (11 February 2006), 3.

Daily Telegraph, 'Bankruptcy's Soft Landing Highlighted', 12 January 2006, 2.

—— 'Banks Failing to Check Card Applicants' Income', 23 January 2006, 1.

—— 'Christmas on the Credit Card', 12 December 2005, 12.

—— 'Credit Crunch Awaits Brown', 14 February 2006, 2.

Daneshkhu, S. 'Unexpected Drop in Consumer Confidence Blamed Partly on Disasters', *Financial Times* (30 December 2005), 3.

D'Astrous, A. 'An Inquiry into the Compulsive Side of "Normal" Consumers', *Journal of Consumer Policy*, 13: 1 (1990), 15–31.

Davidoff, L. and Hall, C. *Family Fourtunes: Men and Women of the English Middle Class, 1780–1850*, (London: Routledge, 1987).

Davies, C. 'The Protestant Ethic and the Comic Spirit of Capitalism', *British Journal of Sociology*, 43: 3 (1992), 441–2.

Davies, P. J. 'Credit card companies invest their energies in attracting cautious consumers', *Financial Times* (15 April 2005), 4.

Davies, G, *A History of Money: From Ancient Times to the Present Day.* (Cardiff: University of Wales Press, 2002).

Davis, A. 'Media Effects and the Active Elite Audience: A Study of Media in Financial Markets', European Journal of Communications, 20 (3) (2005), pp. 303–26.

Davis, A. 'Media Effects and the Question of the Rational Audience: Lessons from the Financial Markets', *Media, Culture and Society,* 28 (4) (2006), 603–25.

Davis Burns, L. and Park, H. 'Fashion Orientation, Credit Card Use, and Compulsive Buying', *Journal of Consumer Marketing,* 22: 3 (2005), 135.

DeCloet, D. 'Selling the Back of GM is Probably a Sign of Desperation', *Globe and Mail* (20 October 2005), 6.

Derbyshire, D. 'Cash Going Out of Fashion as Plastic Debt Soars to New Record', *Daily Telegraph* (17 August 2005), 5.

Dimrock, M. 'British and American Utilities: A Comparison', *University of Chicago Law Review,* 1: 2 (1933), 265–82.

Dittmar, H. and Drury, J. 'Self-image – Is It In the Bag? A Qualitative Comparison between "Ordinary" and "Excessive" Consumers', *Journal of Economic Psychology,* 21: 2 (2000), 109–42.

Dittmar, H. 'Compulsive Buying – a Growing Concern? An Examination of Gender, Age, and Endorsement of Materialistic Values as Predictors', *British Journal of Psychology,* 96 (4) (2005), 467–91.

Dodd, N. *The Sociology of Money* (Cambridge: Polity Press, 1994).

Dow, S. and Hillard, J. Keynes, Uncertainty and the Global Economy. (Cheltenham, UK: Deward Elgar, 2002).

Downes, S. and Levene, T. 'Loan Consolidation or Individual Voluntary Arrangements?', *Guardian* (7 January 2006), 5.

Downham, J. S. and Treasure, J. A. P. 'Market Research and Consumer Durables', *Incorporated Statistician,* 7: 3 (1956), 108–17.

Dunn, D. 'Nip 'n' Tuck: Your Wallet Won't Look as Lovely as You', *Independent on Sunday* (22 January 2006), 32.

Dunn, S., 'Nip 'n' Tuck: Your Wallet Won't Look as Lovely as You', *The Independent,* 22 January 2006.

——— 'Lenders Play Hard to Get in the Loan Lottery', *Independent on Sunday* (4 December 2005), 27.

——— 'We Can't Afford to Lose This Gladiators' Contest', *Independent on Sunday* (24 October 2004), 31.

Easingwood, C. J. and C. Storey, 'Success Factors for New Consumer Financial Services', *International Journal of Bank Marketing* 9 (1) 1991, 3–10.

Eccles, S.; Elliott, R.; and Gournay, K. 'Revenge, Existential Choice, and Addictive Consumption', *Psychology and Marketing,* 13: 8 (1996), 753.

——— 'Plastic Money', 29 December 1979, 52.

Ehrlich, C. *The Piano: A History* (Oxford: Clarendon Press, 1990).

Einsig, P., 'The Dynamics of Hire-Purchase Credit', *The Economic Journal,* 66 (261) (1956), 17–24.

Elliot, L. '60 per cent per cent of UK Wealth is Tied Up in Homes', *Guardian* (24 July 2006), 20.

Elliot, L., 'Borrowers are Warned against Banking on Big Pay Rises'. *Guardian* 12 December 2003, p. 22.

Elliott, R., 'Addictive Consumption: Function and Fragmentation in Postmodernity', *Journal of Consumer Policy,* 17 (1994), 159–79.

—— 'Borrowers Are Warned against Banking on Big Pay Rises', *Guardian* (12 December 2003), 22.

—— 'Victims of London's Property Boom', *Guardian* (24 November 2006), 23.

Esty, J. 'National Objects: Keynesian Economics and Modernist Culture in England', *Modernism/modernity*, 7: 1 (2000), 1–24.

Evans, I. and Morgan, J. 'Cash Loses Its Currency as Plastic Flexes Its Muscle', *Times* (8 July 2004), 1.

Faber, R. and O'Guinn, T. 'Compulsive Buying: A Phenomenological Exploration', *The Journal of Consumer Research*, 16 (2) (1989), 147–57.

Farrell, P. 'Mortgage Choice is Good for Everyone', *Sunday Times* (22 January 2006), 4.

Farrow, P. 'Don't Give Your Kids This Pernicious Piece of Plastic', *Daily Telegraph* (29 January 2006), 2.

—— 'We'll Outlive Our Money, Fear Brits', *Sunday Telegraph* (4 September 2005), 1.

Faust, W. and M. Mooney, Brand Management in Financial Services. The Bankers Magazine, 178(1) (1995).

Feber, R. J. 'Money Changes Everything: Compulsive Buying from a Biopsychosocial Perspective', *America Behavioral Scientist*, 35: 6 (1992), 809–19.

Feeley, M. M. and Little, D. L. 'The Vanishing Female: The Decline of Women in the Criminal Process, 1687–1912', *Law & Society Review*, 25: 4 (1991), 719–57.

Financial Services Association, 2007. FSA Finds Poor Practice by Intermediaries and Lenders within Subprime Market. FSA Press Release, issued 4 July 2007.

Finn, M. *The Character of Credit: Personal Debt in English Culture, 1740–1914* (New York: Cambridge University Press, 2003).

Flugge, E. 'Possibilities and Problems of Integration in the Automobile Industry', *Journal of Political Economy*, 37: 2 (1929), 150–74.

Ford of Britain. (2008) Ford of Britain Homepage. Available from: http://www.ford.co.uk. Accessed on 14 February 2009.

Ford, D. and S. King, 'Banking on the Unbanked', *International Journal of Bank Marketing*, 1 (2) (1983), 27–40.

Fousek, P. G. 'Prerequisites for the Growth of Consumer Instalment Credit', *Journal of Finance*, 13: 2 (May, 1958), 163–75.

Francis, C. 'Credit Crackdown as Debt Levels Soar', *Sunday Times* (14 December 2003), 6.

Fraser, H. *The Coming of the Mass Market 1850–1914* (Hamden, CT: Archon Books, 1981).

Fraser, P. and D. Vittas, *The Retail Banking Revolution* (London: Michael Lafferty Publications, 1982).

Fray, K. 'Retail Figures Knock Hopes of UK Rate Cut', *Financial Times* (21 October 2005), 17.

Furlough E. and Strikwerda, C. (eds). *Consumers Against Capitalism? Consumer Cooperation in Europe, North America, and Japan, 1840–1990* (Lanham: Rowman & Littlefield, 1999).

Furnham, A.; Lewis, A.; and Webley, P. *The New Economic Mind* (Hemel Hempstead: Harvester Wheatsheaf, 1995).

Garcia, I. 'Compulsive Buying: An Irresistible Impulse or a Reflection of Personal Values?', *Social*, 22: 22 (2007), 125–36.

Gardner, E. P. M., P. Molyneux, J. Williams, and S. Carbo, 'European Savings Banks: Facing up to the New Environment', *International Journal of Bank Marketing*, 1997 Vol. 15 Issue 7 (1997), 243–254.

Gardener, E., B. Howcroft, J. Williams, (1999), 'The new retail banking revolution', *Service Industries Journal*, Vol. 19 No. 2, pp. 83–100.

Garrahan, P. 'Housing, the Class Milieu and Middle-Class Conservatism', *British Journal of Political Science*, 7: 1 (1977), 126–7.

Gibson, A. and O'Connor, R. 'Hidden Cost of a Spending Spree', *Times* (28 January 2006), 6.

Giles, J. '"Playing Hard to Get": Working-class Women, Sexuality and Respectability in Britain, 1918–1940', *Women's History Review*, 1: 2 (1992).

P. Giuliano, 'Living Arrangements in Western Europe: Does Cultural Origin Matter?', *Journal of the European Economic Association*, **5** (5) (2007) pp. 927–52.

Glatt, M. and Cook, C. 'Pathological Spending as a Form of Psychological Dependence', *British Journal of Consumer Research*, 82 (1987), 1257–8.

Glendinning, V. *Leonard Woolf: A Life* (London: Simon & Schuster, 2006).

Goodall, F. 'Appliance Trading Activities of British Gas Utilities, 1875–1935', *Economic History Review*, New series, 46: 3 (1993), 543–57.

Grady, J. and M. Weale, *British Banking, 1960–85*. (New York: St. Martins Press, 1986).

Graham, G. 'London Insiders Remember Big Bang', *Financial Times* (25 October 1996), 3.

Griffin, N. J. 'Scientific Management in the Direction of Britain's Military Labour Establishment During World War I', *Military Affairs*, 42: 4 (December, 1978), 197–201.

Griffiths, K. 'MPs Accuse Credit Card Users of Deceitful Practices', *Independent* (18 December 2003), 23.

Guest, K. 'Plastic is a Girl's Best Friend: The Motto of a Generation in Debt', *Independent* (23 July 2006), 6.

Gwen, J. E. and E. Nevin, 'The British National Debt', *Economica*, New series, 24: 96 (1957), 307–14.

Hall, J. and Watts, R. 'Personal Bankruptcies Hit Record', *Sunday Telegraph* (30 October 2005), 1.

—— 'Market Insight Mortgages', *Daily Telegraph* (8 January 2006), 9.

Hall, R. 'British Cooperative in Politics', *Public Opinion Quarterly*, 3: 1 (1939), 124–35.

Hall, S. 'Thatcherism – A New Stage?', *Marxism Today* (February 1980), 26–8.

—— *The Hard Road To Renewal: Thatcherism and the Crisis of the Left* (London: Verso, 1988).

—— 'When was "The Post-Colonial"? Thinking at the Limit', in I. Chambers and L. Curti (eds) *The Post-Colonial Question* (London: Routledge, 1996).

Hall, W. 'Mounting Personal Debts Help Lift DFD', *Financial Times* (12 January 2005), 23.

—— 'Small Talk', *Financial Times* (3 June 2005), 26.

Hallsworth, A. G. 'Short-Termism and Economic Restructuring in Britain', *Economic Geography*, 72: 1 (1996), 23–37.

Hampden-Turner, C. *Gentlemen and Tradesmen* (London: Routledge & Kegan Paul Books Ltd, 1984).

Hanley, A. and M. Wilhelm, 'Compulsive Buying: An Exploration into Self-Esteem and Money Attitudes', *Journal of Economic Psychology*, 13 (1) (1992), 5–18.

Hansard Orders of the Day Advertisements (Hire-Purchase) Bill February 1957, vol. 563, cc1323–4131. Available from: http://hansard.millbanksystems. com/commons/1957/feb/01/advertisements-hire-purchase-bill. Accessed on 2 January 2009.

Hardy, A. Debt Problems and Looming Personal Bankruptcy. *The Guardian* 10 January 2004, p. 2.

Hardy, A., 'Suffering a Festive Financial Hangover'. *Guardian*, 10 January p. 2.

Harris, J. 'Review: *An Edwardian Mixed Doubles: The Bosanquets versus the Webbs: A Study of British Social Policy, 1890–1929* by A. M. McBriar', *Economic History Review*, New series, 43: 3 (1990), 499–501.

Harris, R. and Hammet, C. 'The Myth of Promised Land: The Social Diffusion of Home Ownership in Britain and North America', *Annals of Association of American Geographers*, 77: 2, (1987), 173–90.

Hart, W. O. 'British New Towns Today', *Economics*, 32: 1 (1956), 57–68.

Harvey, D. *A Brief History of Neoliberalism* (Oxford: Oxford University Press, 2005).

—— *The Condition of Postmodernity* (Oxford: Basil Blackwell, 1990).

Hassay, D. and Smith, M. 'Compulsive Buying: An Examination of the Commotion Motive', *Psychology and Marketing*, 13: 8 (1998), 741–52.

Hattersley, G. 'Ipod Therefore I Whinge: The Truth about the Indulged Generation', *Sunday Times* (28 August 2005), 5.

Haurant, S., Repossessions up 68% in 2008. New Financial Service Authority Report. *Guardian* 17 March 2009. Available from http://www.guardian.co.uk/money/2009/mar/17/fsa-respossessions-arrears-rise, Accessed 3 April 2009.

Healy, G., 'Business and Discrimination', in R. Stacey, ed., *Strategic Thinking and the Management of Change: International Perspectives of Organizational Dynamics.* (London: Kogan Page, 1993), pp. 169–89.

Heelas, P. and Morris, P. (eds). *The Values of the Enterprise Culture: The Moral Debate* (London: Routledge, 1992).

Herbert, C. 'Filthy Lucre: Victorian Ideas of Money', *Victorian Studies*, 44: 2 (2002), 185–213.

Hewitt, M. 'Why the Notion of Victorian Britain Does Make Sense', *Victorian Studies*, 48: 3 (2006), 395–438.

Hickman, M. 'Britons in Debt to the Tune of £1.13 Trillion', *Independent* (3 January 2006), 1.

Hira, T. K. 'Financial Attitudes, Beliefs and Behaviours: Differences by Age', *Journal of Consumer Studies and Home Economics*, 21: 3 (1997), 271.

Hirschman, E. C. 'The Consciousness of Addiction: Toward a General Theory of Compulsive Consumption', *Journal of Consumer Research*, 19: 2 (1992), 155–79.

Holdsworth, W. S. *An Historical Introduction to the Land Law* (London: Oxford University Press, 1927).

Horrell, S. and Oxley, D. 'Crust or Crumb?: Intrahousehold Resource Allocation and Male Breadwinning in Late Victorian Britain', *Economic History Review*, 52: 3 (1999), 494–522.

—— 'Work and Prudence: Household Responses to Income Variation in Nineteenth-century Britain', *European Review of Economic History*, 4: 1 (2000), 27–57.

Hosgood, C. 'The "Pigmies of Commerce" and the Working-Class Community: Small Shopkeepers in England, 1870–1914, *Journal of Social History*, 22: 3 (1989), 439–60.

234   *Bibliography*

House of Commons Advertisements (Hire-Purchase) Bill, Hansard, 1803–2005, Vol. 563 (1957) cc1323–413.

Howard, E. *Garden Cities of To-Morrow* (London: S. Sonnenschein & Co. Ltd., 1902).

Howcroft, J. B. and J. Lavis, 'Image in Retail Banking', *International Journal of Bank Marketing*, 4 (4) (1986), 3–13.

Howe, D. W. 'American Victorianism as a Culture', *American Quarterly*, 27: 5 (1975), 507–32.

Hoyt, H. 1966. According to Hoyt. Washington, D.C.: Homer Hoyt.

Huggins, M. 'More Sinful Pleasures? Leisure, Respectability and the Male Middle Classes in Victorian England.' *Journal of Social History*, Vol. 33(3), (2000) pp. 585–600.

Hunter, T. 'Homeowners Say House Prices Will Carry on Rising', *Sunday Telegraph* (13 June 2004), 1.

Hurlston, M. 'Debt: France and Ireland are Worried. Why Isn't Britain?', *Independent* (3 January 2006), 2.

Hurren E. and King, S. '"Begging for Burial": Form, Function and Conflict in Nineteenth-Century Pauper Burial', *Social History*, 30: 3 (2005), 321–41.

Independent, 'Borrowing Can Be Liberating; Personal Debt', 3 January 2006, 28.

Independent, 'British Households Pass Debt Milestone', 3 July 2004, 16.

Independent, 'Britons in Debt to the Tune of £1.13 trillion', 3 January 2006, 1.

Ingham, G. 'Capitalism, Money and Banking: A Critique of Recent Historical Sociology', *British Journal of Sociology*, Vol. 50 Issue 1 (1996) 76–96.

Inman, P. 'Strategy Targets £1 Trillion Debt Pile', *Guardian* (20 July 2004), 14.

International Monetary Fund. World Economic Outlook: Housing and the Business Cycle. *World Economic Financial Surveys*. 2008 [online]. [April 2008]. Available from the World Wide Web: www.imf.org.

Jackson, P. 'How Much Does Your Household Debt Amount To?', *Independent* (11 January 2006), 2.

Jamieson, B. 'Beware Those "Consumer Spending Plunge" Blues', *Business* (13 November 2005), 10.

Johnes, M. 'Archery, Romance and Elite Culture in England and Wales, c. 1780–1840', *History*, 89: 294 (2004), 193–208.

Johnson, K. K. P. and Yurchisin, J. 'Compulsive Buying Behaviour and Its Relationship to Perceived Social Status Associated with Buying Materialism, Self-Esteem, and Apparel-Product Involvement', *Family and Consumer Sciences Research Journal*, 32: 3 (2004), 291–314.

Johnston, J. *Trades Unionism and Co-operation*. (London: LSE Selected Pamphlets, 1897).

Johnson, P. 'Conspicuous Consumption and Working-Class Culture in Late-Victorian and Edwardian Britain', *Transactions of the Royal Historical Society*, 5th series, 38 (1988), 27–42.

—— *Saving and Spending: The Working-Class Economy in Britain, 1870–1939* (Oxford: Oxford University Press, 1984).

Johnson, S. 'Women Account for 42% of Bankruptcies', *Financial Times* (16 May 2005), 4.

Jones, R., 'Banks Write Off £ 100,000 after Irresponsible Lending Claims'. *Guardian*, 28 January 2006, p. 11.

Jones, R. 'Mortgage Lending Hits April Record', *Guardian* (19 May 2006), 11.

Jones, N. *God and the Moneylenders: Usury and the Law in Early Modern England* (Oxford: Blackwell, 1989).

Jopson, B. 'Begbies Looks to Personal Bankruptcies', *Financial Times* (5 July 2005), 23.

Juster, F. T. *Household Capital Formation and Financing 1897–1962* (NY: Columbia University Press, 1966).

Kaletsky, A. 'The Public Knows Better than the Money Men', *Times* (6 May 2004), 20.

Kalliney, P. Cities of Affluence: Masculinity, Class and the Angry Young Men. MFS Modern Fiction Studies. Vol. 47(1) (2001) pp. 92–117.

Kassam, L. 'Don't Get Trapped in a Home Loan Hell', *Sun* (13 April 2005), 20.

—— 'IVA Way Puts 4,000 Back in Control of Their Lives', *Independent on Sunday* (13 November 2005), 20.

Kasser, T. *The High Price of Materialism* (Cambridge: MIT Press, 2002).

Kelly, V. 'The Equitable Consumer: Shopping at the Co-Op in Manchester', *Journal of Design History*, 11: 4 (1998), 295–310.

Kempson, E.; Mckay, S.; and Willitts, M. 'Characteristics of Families in Debt and the Nature of Indebtedness', *DWP Research Report No. 211* (Leeds: Corporate Document Services, 2004).

Kerridge, E. *Usury, Interest and the Reformation* (Aldershot, UK: Ashgate, 2002).

Keynes, J. M. 'Alfred Marshall, 1842–1924', *Economic Journal*, 34: 135 (September 1924), 311–72.

King, S. 'How Non-Customers See Banks', *Journal of the Institute of Bankers*, Vol. 1, 2 (1981), 27–40.

Kinmonth, E. 'Nakamura Keiu and Samuel Smiles: A Victorian Confucian and a Confucian Victorian', *American Historical Review*, 85: 3 (1980), 535–56.

Kinsella, S. *Confessions of a Shopaholic* (NY: Delta, 2001).

—— *Shopaholic Takes Manhattan* (NY: Delta, 2002).

—— *Shopaholic Ties the Knot* (NY: Delta, 2003).

Knight, R. 'Found at Last: Loads of Full Wallets', *Financial Times* (10 September 2005), 25.

Kollewe, J. 'Debt Market Rumours Damage Barclays', *Guardian Unlimited* (28 August 2007), 26.

Kopytoff, I. 'The Cultural Biography Of Things: Commoditization As Process', in. A. Appadurai (ed.) *The Social Life of Things, Commodities in Cultural Perspectives* (Cambridge: Cambridge University Press, 1988).

Koran, L., R. Faber, M. Aboujaoude, M. Large, R. Serpe, 'Estimated Prevalence of Compulsive Buying Behaviour in the United States', *American Journal of Psychiatry*, 163 October (2006) 1806–12.

Kowaleski-Wallace, E. 'The Needs of Strangers: Friendly Societies and Insurance Societies in Late Eighteenth-Century England', *Eighteenth-Century Life*, 24: 3 (2000), 53–72.

Kraepelin, E. *Psychiatrie*. 8th ed. (Leipzig: Verlag von Johann Ambrosius Barth, 1915).

Labastille, F. M. 'Methods of Extending Credit Facilities for the Export of Automobiles', *American Economic Review*, 22: 2 (1932), 208–33.

Lamont, M. *Money, Morals, and Manners: The Culture of the French and the American Upper-Middle Class* (Chicago, IL: University of Chicago Press, 1992).

Langford, P. A. *Polite and Commercial People: England 1727–1783* (Oxford: Oxford University Press, 1989).

Langland, E. 'Nobody's Angels: Domestic Ideology and Middle-Class Women in the Victorian Novel', *PMLA*, 107 (2), (1992), 290–304.

Larsen, P. T. 'Big Bang Still Brings Much to London Finance', *Financial Times* (25 October 2006).

Lash, S and J. Urry, *Economies of Signs and Space*, (London: Sage, 1994).

Laux, J. M. 'Some Notes on Entrepreneurship in the Early French Automobile Industry', *French Historical Studies*, 3: 1 (1963), 129–34.

Lee, M. *Consumer Culture Reborn: The Cultural Politics of Consumption* (NY: Routledge, 1993).

Lee, S. and Mysyk, A. 'The Medicalization of Compulsive Buying', *Social Science & Medicine*, 58: 9 (2004), 1709–18.

Leisure, Respectability and the Male Middle Classes in Victorian England. Journal of Social History, Vol. 33(3), pp. 585–600.

Lejoyeux, M.; Bailey, F.; Moula, H.; Loi, S.; and Ades, J. 'Study of Compulsive Buying in Patients Presenting Bbsessive-Compulsive Disorder', *Comprehensive Psychiatry*, 46: 2 (2005), 105–10.

Lemire, B. 'Savers in Training: Education, Savings Banks and the Nineteenth-Century English Working Class', *EBHA Conference* (Barcelona: 16–18 September 2004).

—— *The Business of Everyday Life: Gender, Practice and Social Politics in England, C.1600–1900* (Manchester: Manchester University Press, 2005).

Leppert, R. 'Sexual Identity, Death, and the Family Piano: 19th-Century Music', *Music in Its Social Contexts*, 16: 2 (1992), 105–28.

Leyshon, A. and N. J. Thrift, *Money/space: Geographies of Monetary Transformation.* (London: Routledge, 1996).

Leyshon, A. and Thrift, N. *Money/Space: Geographies of Monetary Transformation.* (London: Routledge, 1997).

Lindgren, K. E. 'The Consumer Credit Act 1974: Its Scope', *Modern Law Review*, 40: 2 (March 1977), 159–73.

Lin, P. Y. 'National Identity and Social Mobility: Class, Empire and the British Government Overseas Evacuation of Children During the Second World War', *Twentieth Century Brit History*, 7 (1996), 310–44.

Loeb, L. *Consumering Angels: Advertising and Victorian Women* (USA: Oxford University Press, 1994).

Lynch, D. C. and L. Lundquist, *Digital money: The New Era of Internet Commerce*, (New York: John Wiley & Sons, Inc., 1996).

Lunt, P. K. and Livingstone, S. M. *Mass Consumption and Personal Identity* (Buckingham: Open University Press, 1992).

Lury, C., *Consumer Culture.* (New Brunswick, NJ: Rutgers University Press, 1996).

Lutyens, D. 'Nightclubs and Luxury Spas Are By Definition in the Business of Indulgence', *Observer* (12 February 2006), 6.

Lysack, K. *Come Buy, Come Buy: Shopping and the Culture of Consumption in Victorian Women's Writing* (Athens: Ohio University Press, 2008).

MacKinnon, M. H. 'Calvinism and the Infallible Assurance of Grace: The Weber Thesis Reconsidered', *British Journal of Sociology*, 39: 2 (1988), 143–77.

Marchand, R. 'Customer Research as Public Relations: General Motors in the 1930s', in. S. Strasser, C. McGovern, M. Judt, and D. Mattern (eds), *Getting and Spending: American and European Consumer Society in the Twentieth Century* (Cambridge: Cambridge University Press, 1986), 85–110.

Market Assessment Publications. *Financial Service Retailing Chesham: Market Assessment Publications Ltd.,* 1995.

Marsh, P. UK Credit Market, Research Report (London: DataMonitor, 2006).

Martin, J. L. 'The Myth of the Consumption-Orientation Economy and the Rise of the Desiring Subject', *Theory and Society,* 28: 3 (1991), 425–53.

Mathiason, N. 'From Big Bang to Whimper: Welcome to the New City', *Observer* (11 January 2009), 7.

Masculinity, Class and the Angry Young Men. MFS Modern Fiction Studies. vol. 47(1) pp 92–117.

Mawson, J. 'Household Debts are Soaring and Bankruptcy Has Been Made Less Painful', *Financial Times* (3 January 2005), 24.

May, O.; Tudela, M.; and Young, G. 'British Household Indebtedness and Financial Stress: A Household-Level Picture', *Bank of England Quarterly Bulletin* (Winter, 2004), 422.

McClymont, G. 'Socialism, Puritanism, Hedonism: The Parliamentary Labour Party's Attitude to Gambling 1923–31', *Twentieth Century British History,* 19: 3 (2008), 288–313.

McCombs, M. E. and Shaw, D. L. 'The Agenda-Setting Function of Mass Media', *Public Opinion Quarterly,* 36 (1972), 176–87.

McElroy, S. L.; Keck, P. E.; Garrison, G.; Pope, M. D.' Smith, M. R.; and Strakowski, S. M. 'Compulsive Buying: A Report of 20 Cases', *Journal of Clinical Psychiatry,* 55: 6 (1994), 242–8.

McKendrick, N.; Brewer, J.; and Plumb, J. H. *The Birth of a Consumer Society: The Commercialization of Eighteenth Century England* (Bloomington: Indiana University Press, 1982).

McKibbin, R. I. 'Social Class and Social Observation in Edwardian England', *Transactions of the Royal Historical Society,* 5th series, 28 (1978), 175–99.

McManus, J. J. 'The Consumer Credit Act 1974', *British Journal of Law and Society,* 2: 1 (1975), 66–75.

Millard, R. 'Debt Juggling, the New Middle-Class Addiction', *Sunday Times* (3 April 2005), 5.

Miller, R. 'FSA Fears Consumers Can't Afford Debts', *Daily Telegraph,* (26 January 2006), 3.

Mingione, E. *Social Conflict and the City* (Oxford: Basil Blackwell, 1981).

Mini, P. V. 'Keynes on Markets: A Survey of Heretical Views', *American Journal of Economics and Sociology,* 55: 1 (1996), 99–111.

Minkes, A. L. 'The Decline of Pawnbroking', *Economica,* New series, 20: 77 (1953), 10–23.

Moore, M. and Watts, R. 'Debt Helpline Swamped by Anxious Callers', *Daily Telegraph* (15 January 2006), 1.

Mobiot, G. 'Three Million Homes?', *Guardian* (27 November 2007), 7.

Monks, H. 'Ways of Getting On the Ladder', *Observer* (15 May 2005), 17.

Morgan, J. 'Credit Card Firm Targets Teen', *Times* (26 January 2006), 3.

—— 'Credit Card "Health Warnings"', *Times* (17 May 2005), 42.

—— 'Friday MPs Seek Action over Credit Card Lending as Debt Soars', *Times* (16 April 2004), 31.

Mooney, J. L. and M. S. Blodgett, 'Letter of Credit in the Global Economy: Implication for International Trade', *Journal of International Accounting, Auditing and Taxation*, 4 (2) (1995), pp. 175–83.

Morrell, J. G. 'Furniture for the Masses', *Journal of Industrial Economics*, 5: 1 (1956), 24–9.

Morris, R. J. 'Samuel Smiles and the Genesis of Self-Help: The Retreat of a Petit Bourgeois Utopia', *Historical Journal*, 24: 1 (1981), 89–109.

Moules, J. 'Bankruptcy Hits More under-30s', *Financial Times* (10 June 2005), 22.

Moynihan, C. J. *Introduction to the Law of Real Property* (St Paul, MN: West Publishing Co., 1982).

Muldrew, C. The Economy of Obligation: The Culture of Credit and Social Relations in Early Modern England (Basingstoke: Palgrave Macmillan, 1998).

Mullineux, A. W. *UK Banking after Deregulation*. (London: Croom Helm, 1987).

Muller, A. and De Zwaan, M. 'Current Status of Psychotherapy Research on Pathological Buying', Verhaltenstherapie. 14: 2 (2004), 112. Available from: www.content.karger.com. Accessed on 22 March 2008.

Muller, C. 'British War Finance and the Banks', *Journal of Business of the University of Chicago*, 16: 2 (1943), 77–99.

Mullins, D.; Murie, A.; Leather, P.; and Lee, P. *Housing Policy in the UK* (London: Palgrave Macmillan, 2006).

Murray-West, R. 'Credit Card and Heating Bills Add to the Burden for Indebted Pensioners', *Daily Telegraph* (10 January 2006), 4.

National Centre for Social Research, Living in Britain: A Summary of Changes over Time Housing Tenure: Great Britain, 1971 to 2002 (2004). Available from: www.natcen.ac.uk. Accessed on 3 January 2009.

National Consumer Council, *A Better Class of Consumers*. (London: National Consumer Council, 1980).

National Statistics, National Accounts/Economic Activity, UK Gross Domestic Product, 2003, http://www.statistics.gov.uk, accessed, January 20, 2008.

Nava, M. 'Modernitiy's Disavowal: Women, the City and the Department Store.' In Mica Nava and Alan O'Shea (eds) *Modern Times: Reflections on a Century of English Modernity* (London: Routledge, 1996).

Nava, M., Blake, A., MacRury, I., Richards, B. (eds). *Buy This Book: Studies in Advertising and Consumption*. (New York, London: Routledge, 1997).

Needham, C., *The Reform of Public Services under New Labour* (Basingstoke: Palgrave Macmillan, 2007).

Neuner, M., G. Raab, L. Reisch, 'Compulsive Buying in Maturing Consumer Societies: An Empirical Re-Inquiry', *Journal of Economic Psychology*, 26 (4) (2005) 509–22.

Nicolson, P. 'Unfair Lending to the Desperate Poor', *Independent* (18 January 2006), 28.

Nisse, J. 'Bankruptcy Overhaul Mooted as Too Many Walk Away from Debts', *Independent on Sunday* (19 September 2004), 3.

Nugent, L. 'Bankrupt Women Paying for Credit Cards', *Times* (16 May 2005), 25.

Observer, 'Older and Wiser – With Deep Pockets', 18 December 1994, 18.

O'Connell, S. 'Credit, Debt and Guilt: Cultural and Moral Obstacles to the Development of Consumer Society', in Niall Ó'Ciosáin (ed.), *Explaining Change in Cultural History* (Chester Springs, PA: Dulfour Editions, 2004).

O'Connor, R. 'Primed for Top Deals', *Times* (23 January 2006), 4.

Office for National Statistics, 'Wealthier and Healthier, But Are We Happier?', *Social Trends*, 38th ed. (London: Office of National Statistics, 8 April 2008).

OFSTED. Developing Financially Capable Young People (Unpublished report, March 2008).

O'Hara, M. 'Consumer Debt is $ 109bn and Rising', *Guardian* (20 January 2004), 16.

Olney, M. *Buy Now, Pay Later: Advertising Credit, and Consumer Durables in the 1920s* (Chapel Hill: University of North Carolina Press, 1991).

Ornstien, E. J. *The Marketing of Money*. (Epping: Gower Press, 1972).

Owens, W. and Furbank, P. 'efoe and Imprisonment for Debt: Some Attributions Reviewed', *Review of English Studies* (1986), xxxvii, 495–502.

Palmer, G., P. Kenway, S. Wilcox, *Monitoring Housing and Neighbourhoods Trends* (York: Joseph Rountree Foundation, 2006).

Parakilas, J. *Piano Toles: Three Hundred Years of Life with the Piano* (New Haven, CT: Yale University Press, 1999).

Parker, G. *Getting and Spending Credit and Debt in Britain* (London: Gower Publishing Group, 1990).

Paterson, L. 'Big-Spending Britons Rack Up Debts of £1 Trillion', *Times* (22 May 2004), 1.

Persky, J. 'Retrospectives: From Usury to Interest', *Journal of Economic Perspectives*, 21: 1 (2007), 227–36.

Pilston, T. 'Customers Shut Out as Newcastle Goes Back to Its Roots', *Independent on Sunday* (14 August 2005), 19.

Polany, K. *The Great Transformation*, 2nd ed. (Boston: Beacon Press, 2001).

Pollock, F. *The Land Laws*, 3rd ed. (London and NY: Macmillan and Co., 1986).

Pratt, J. T. *The History of Savings Banks in England, Wales, and Ireland*. (London: C.J.G. & R. Rivington, St. Paul's Church-Yard, 1830).

Preston, R. 'Dismal Debts', *Sunday Telegraph* (24 April, 2005), 3.

Prosser, D. 'Record Level of Bankruptcies Prompts Debt Warning', *Independent* (6 August 2005), 44.

Psychology Today, 'The Call of the Mall', 12 December 2007. Available from: www.psychologytoday.com. Accessed on 28 March 2008.

Pugh, A. 'Windfall Child Rearing: Low-Income Care and Consumption', *Journal of Consumer Culture*, 4: 2 (2004), 229–49.

Qureshi, H. 'Is Shopping Your Drug of Choice?' *Observer* (18 February 2007), 7.

Rae, G., *The Country Banker: His Clients, Cares, and Work, From an Experience of Forty Years*. (New York: Charles Scribner's Sons, 1886).

Ramachadran, N., 'The Parent Trap: Boomerang Kids', *U. S. News & World Report*, 139 (22) (2005) pp. 64–4.

Rappaport, E. *Shopping for Pleasure: Women in the Making of London's West End, 1860–1914* (Princeton: Princeton University Press, 2000).

Redmond, A. 'Household Debt has Broken New Barrier'. *Financial Times*, 19 June 2004, p. 27.

Reed, C. *Bloomsbury Rooms: Modernism, Subculture, and Domesticity* (New Haven, CT: Yale University Press, 2004).

Reich, L. 'Buy Now, Pay for the Rest of Your Life', *Daily Telegraph* (2 July 2004), 23.

Reith, G. 'Consumption and its Discontents: Addiction, Identity and the Problems of Freedom', *British Journal of Sociology*, 55: 2 (2004), 283–300.

Richards, J. 'Spreading the Gospel of Self-Help: G. A. Henty and Samuel Smiles', *Journal of Popular Culture*, 16: 2 (1982), 52–65.

Riddell, M. 'It is not just Farepak that is sick at heart', *Observer* (12 November 2006), 4.

Riley, C. 'No crash yet but who knows what is round the corner?', *Times* (27 January 2006), 2.

Ritzer, G. *Explorations in Sociology of Consumption: Fast Food, Credit Cards and Casinos* (London: Sage, 2001).

—— *Expressing American: A Critique of the Global Credit-Card Society* (Thousand Oaks: Pine Forge Press, 1995).

Roberts, D. 'Bankruptcy Laws Could be Stifling Start-Ups', *Financial Times* (16 June 2005), 27.

Roberts, J. A. and Jones, E. 'Money Attitudes, Credit Card Use, and Compulsive Buying among American College Students', *Journal of Consumer Affairs*, 35: 2 (2001), 213–40.

Roe, A. 'Bankers and Thrift in the Age of Affluence', *American Quarterly*, 17: 4 (Winter, 1965), 619–33.

Rogers, P. 'Defoe in the Fleet Prison', *Review of English Studies*, New series, 22: 88 (1971), 451–5.

Ronson, J. 'Who Killed Richard Cullen?', *Guardian* (16 July 2005), 19.

Rothwell, M. and P. Jowett, *Rivalry in Retail Financial Services*. (Basingstoke: Macmillan, 1988).

Rowland, T. 'Human Touch Still Counts for a Lot', *Times* (24 January 2006), 57.

Rozenberg, G. 'Shoppers Rein in Their Borrowing', *Times* (5 January 2006), 48.

Rozmovits, L. *Shakespeare and the Politics of Culture in Late Victorian England* (Baltimore, MD: The John Hopkins University Press, 1998).

Rubin, G. 'From Packmen, Tallymen and "Perambulating Scotchmen" to Credit Drapers Association, 1849–1914', *Business History*, 28: 2 (1986), 206–25.

Ryle, S. 'Store card chief who wants to take all of the credit', *Observer* (15 May 2005), 5.

Sacks, P., *New Product, New Risks: How Bankers are Adapting to the New International Marketplace* (New York: HarperBusiness).

Samuel, R. 'Mrs Thatcher's Return to Victorian Values', *Proceeds of the British Academy*, 78 (1992), 9–29.

Scanlon, J. 'Making Shopping Safe for the Rest of Us: Sophie Kinsella's Shopaholic Series and Its Readers', *Americana: The Journal of American Popular Culture*, 4: 2 (2005). Available from: http://www.americanpopularculture.com/journal/index.htm. Accessed on 12 January 2009.

Scherhorn, G., L. A. Reisch, and G. Raab, 'Addictive Buying in West Germany: An Empirical Study,' *Journal of Consumer Policy*, 13, (1990) 355–87.

Schneiders, B. 'Will Those High-Rise Bank Profits Come Tumbling Down?', *Independent on Sunday* (24 July 2005), 6.

Schwartz, G. L. 'Instalment Finance: The Nature of Consumer Credit', *Economica*, New series, 3: 10 (1936), 182–95.

Scott, M. 'Why Enjoying the High Life Can Come Back to Haunt You?', *Observer* (22 January 2006), 14.

Scott, P. 'The Twilight World of Interwar British Hire Purchase', *Past and Present*, 177 (2002), 195–225.

—— *Triumph of the South: A Regional Economic History of Early Twentieth Century Britain* (Burlington, VT: Ashgate, 2006).

Seabrook, J. 'An Easy Stroll from Thrift Street to Credit Crescent', *Guardian* (2 February 2004).

Seager, A. 'City Bonuses Hit Record High with £14bn Payout', *Guardian* (28 August 2007), 27.

—— 'Growth at Risk as Shopping Boom Runs Out of Steam', *Guardian* (17 February 2006), 27.

—— 'Survey Eases Fears of "Debt Meltdown"', *Guardian* (16 March 2006), 29.

Searjeant, G. Britain Has Bloomed by Striking Out its Winters of Industrial Discontent. 2006, *The Times*, 17 February, p. 63.

Seaver, P. *Wallington's World: A Puritan Artisan in Seventeenth-Century London.* (Stanford University Press, 1985).

Senior, A. 'Bankruptcy among the Young does Them No Credit', *Times* (19 February 2005), 3.

Shaw, E. 'Borrowers Go Full Steam Ahead for a Debt Iceberg', *Independent on Sunday* (22 May 2005), 23.

Shaw, E. 'Two Houses, Two Salaries, But Each Month is a Struggle', *Independent on Sunday* (29 January 2006), 18.

—— 'You Didn't Ask For It, So Do You Need This Credit Gift?', *Independent on Sunday* (11 December 2005), 20.

Simmel, G. *The Philosophy of Money*, 2nd ed. (London: Routledge, 1990).

Simonds, J. 'The Finance of Hire-Purchase Agreements', *Modern Law Review*, 3: 3 (1940), 239–40.

Slater, D. and Tonkiss, F. *Market Society: Markets and Modern Social Theory* (Cambridge: Polity Press, 2001).

Slater, D. *Consumer Culture and Modernity* (Cambridge: Polity, 1999).

Smart, E. 'The Banks and Personal Consumers'. *Banking World*, 1 (5) 1984.

Smith, D. 'Trends: Consumers Living in a House of Plastic Cards', *Times* (25 February 1987), 5.

Smith, G. 'Karl Marx and St George', *Journal of the History of Ideas*, 2: 4 (1941), 401–19.

Smith, I. & Boyns, T. 'Scientific Management and the Pursuit of Control in Britain to c. 1960', *Accounting Business & Financial History*, 15: 2 (July 2005), 187–216.

Smith, N. 'Of Yuppies and Housing: Gentrification, Social Restructuring and the Urban Dream', *Society and Space*, 25 (February 1987), 151–72.

Smith, S. J. and D., Easterlow, 'The Strange Geography of Health Inequalities', *Transactions of the Institute of British Geographers, New Series* 30 (2005), 173–90.

Smithers, R. 'Spend, Spend, Spend: Britons Lap Up the High Life', *Guardian* (4 March 2006), 3.

Stafford, D. and King, S. 'Banking on the unbanked', *International Journal of Bank Marketing*, 1 (2) (1983), 27–40.

Stallybrass, P. 'Marx's Coat', in. P. Spyer (ed.) *Border Fetishism: Material Objects in Unstable Spaces*, (NY: Routledge, 1998).

Stamp, J. C. 'The Report of the Macmillan Committee', *Economic Journal*, 41: 163 (1931), 424–35.

Stanley, V. 'Mummy, Can We Go to Conran?', *Sunday Times* (29 January 2006), 54.

Stein, E. 'The Consumers' Cooperative Movement', *Journal of Educational Sociology*, 6: 7 (1933), 427–36.

Stenberg, K. Y. 'Working-Class Women in London Local Politics, 1894–1914', *Twentieth Century British History*, 9 (1998), 323–49.

Stevenson, R. 'Personal Bankruptcies Hit All-Time High as Debt Levels Rise', *Independent* (5 February 2005), 48.

Straus, S. W. 'Promotion and Practice of Thrift in Foreign Countries', *Annals of the American Academy of Political and Social Science*, 87: 1 (1920), 190–6.

Sutton-Ramspeck, S. *Raising the Dust: The Literary Housekeeping of Mary Ward, Sarah Grand, and Charlotte Perkins Gilman* (Athens: Ohio University Press, 2004).

Swann, C. 'Risks to a Heroic Spending Spree the US', *Financial Times* (20 January 2006), 17.

Szmigin, I. 'The Aestheticization of Consumption: An Exploration of "Brand New" and "Shopping"', *Marketing Theory*, 6 (2006), 107.

Taylor, A. *Working Class Credit and Community since 1918* (London: Palgrave Macmillan, 2002).

Taylor, L. 'Gardening Lifestyle Television From Ways of Life to Lifestyle: The "Ordinari-ization" of British', *European Journal of Communication*, 17 (2002), 479.

Taylor, B. and Rogaly, B. '"Mrs Fairly is a Dirty, Lazy Type": Unsatisfactory Households and the Problem of Problem Families in Norwich 1942–1963', *Twentieth Century British History*, 18: 4 (2007), 429–52.

Thatcher, M. 'Speech to Conservative Party Conference' (Brighton, Speech, 13 Oct 1978) Available from http://www.margaretthatcher.org/speeches/displaydocument.asp?docid=103764. Accessed on 3 February 2009.

Thatcher, M. 'Speech on Women in a Changing World. 1st Dame Margery Corbett-Ashby Memorial Lecture' (Institute of Electrical Engineers, London, Speech, 13 Oct 1978) Available from http://www.margaretthatcher.org/speeches/displaydocument.asp?docid=105007. Accessed on 3 February 2009.

Thatcher, M. Conservative Women's Conference, Speech (Westminster: Central Hall, 21 May 1975).

——— 'Interview for Sunday Times', *Sunday Times* (1 August 1980) 945–1100. Available from: http://www.margaretthatcher.org/speeches/displaydocument.asp?docid=104214. Accessed on 3 February 2009.

——— 'Interview for The Sun', *Sun* (8 July 1985), 1055–155. Available from: http://www.margaretthatcher.org/speeches/displaydocument.asp?docid=105828. Accessed on 3 February 2009.

——— 'Radio Interview for IRN' (Conservative Leadership Election) (House of Commons, 31 January 1975). Available from: http://www.margaretthatcher.org/speeches/displaydocument.asp?docid=102602. Accessed on 3 February 2009.

——— Speech at Lord Mayor's Banquet' (London: Guildhall, 10 November 1986). Available from: http://www.margaretthatcher.org/speeches/displaydocument.asp?docid=106512. Accessed on 3 February 2009.

——— 'Speech at St Lawrence Jewry' (London: St Lawrence Jewry, 4 March 1981). Available from: http://www.margaretthatcher.org/speeches/displaydocument.asp?docid=104587. Accessed on 3 February 2009.

——— 'Speech in Aberdeen' (Aberdeen: 8 September 1975). Available from: http://www.margaretthatcher.org/speeches/displaydocument.asp?docid=102768. Accessed on 3 February 2009.

—— 'Speech to Christchurch Conservatives', *Christchurch Times*, 14 December 1974. Available from: http://www.margaretthatcher.org/speeches/displaydocument.asp?docid=102442. Accessed on 3 February 2009.

—— 'Speech to Conservative Party Conference' (Blackpool: Winter Gardens, 9 October 1987).

—— 'Speech to Conservative Rally in Edinburgh' (Edinburgh: Leith Town Hall, 25 April 1979).

—— 'Speech to Conservative Women's Conference' (London: Barbican Centre, 25 May 1988). Available from: http://www.margaretthatcher.org/speeches/displaydocument.asp?docid=. Accessed on 3 February 2009.

—— 'Speech to General Assembly of the Church of Scotland' (The Mound, Edinburgh: Assembly Hall, 21 May 1988). Available from: http://www.margaretthatcher.org/Speeches/displaydocument.asp?docid=107246. Accessed on 3 February 2009.

—— 'Speech to Overseas Bankers' (London: Plaisterers' Hall, 7 February 1978).

—— 'Speech to Parliamentary and Scientific Committee' (London: Savoy Hotel, 25 February 1981).

—— 'Speech to Press Association' (London: Savoy Hotel, 8 June 1988). Available from: http://www.margaretthatcher.org/speeches/displaydocument.asp?docid=107258. Accessed on 3 February 2009.

—— 'Speech to Small Business Bureau Conference' (Frimley, Surrey: Lakeside Country Club, 8 February 1984). Available from: http://www.margaretthatcher.org/speeches/displaydocument.asp?docid=105617. Accessed on 3 February 2009.

—— 'Speech to the Annual Dinner of the Scottish CBI' (Glasgow: 8 September 1988).

—— 'This is Your Choice', *Signpost* (1 September 1959).

—— 'We Cannot Prosper With Dud Cheques', *Daily Express* (1 May 1979).

Tedlow, R. S. and G. Jones, *The Rise and Fall of Mass Marketing*. (London: Routledge, 1993).

Thomas, J. 'Bounded in by History: The Winter of Discontent in British Politics, 1979–2004', *Media, Culture and Society*, 29: 2 (2007), 263–83.

Thompson, E. P. *The Making of the English Working Class* (London: Victor Gollancz, 1963).

Thompson, E. P. (1967) Time, Work-Discipline and Industrial Captialism Past & Present, 381: 56–97.

Thompson, F. M. L. 'Social Control in Victorian Britain', *Economic History Review*, New series, 34: 2 (1981), 189–208.

Thompson, K. C. 'Varieties of Victorianism: The Uses of a Past', *Victorian Studies*, 42: 4 (1999/2000), 661–4.

Thomson, H. 'More Britons are Going for Broke', *Sunday Telegraph*, (19 December 2004), 12.

Thornton, P. and Brown, J. 'At £1 Trillion and Rising: British Households Pass Debt Milestone', *Independent* (3 July 2004), 16.

Thornton, P. 'Rising Bad Debts Fuel Slowdown Fears', *Independent* (9 January 2006), 56.

—— 'Spending by Plastic Hits 11-year Low', *Independent* (5 January 2006), 52.

Times, 'Bank Charge', 27 October 2004, 19.

Times, 'Debt Helplines', 21 January 2006, 2.

Tosh, J. 'Gentlemanly Politeness and Manly Simplicity in Victorian England', *Transactions of the Royal Historial Society*, 6th series, 12 (2002), 455–72.

Tratner, M. *Deficits and Desires: Economics and Sexuality in Twentieth Century Literature* (Stanford: Stanford University Press, 2001).

Treanor, J. '4m Affected by Debts that Cannot Be Paid', *Guardian* (4 March 2005), 11.

—— 'Clear Debts with Barclaycard Loan', *Guardian* (2 January 2004), 20.

—— 'Lenders Fighting to Save Revenue Worth up to £1bn', *Guardian* (20 February 2006), 27.

Trentmann, F. *Free Trade Nation: Consumption, Commerce, and Civil Society in Modern Britain* (Oxford: Oxford University Press, 2008).

Trexler, A. 'Economic Ideas and British Literature, 1900–1930: The Fabian Society, Bloomsbury, and The New Age', *Literature Compass*, 4: 3 (2007), 862–87.

US Census Bureau, 'Section 25 Banking, Finance, and Insurance', *Statistical Abstract of the United States* (2008), 73.

Valence, G., A. d'Astous, and L. Fortier, ('Compulsive Buying: Concept and Measurement', *Journal of Consumer Policy*, 11, (1988) 419–33.

Vaughan, A. 'How I Found Myself Bankrupt', *Times* (17 January 2006), 16.

Vickery, A. 'Golden Age to Separate Spheres? A Review of the Categories and Chronology of English Women's History', *Historical Journal*, 36: 2 (1993), 383–414.

Vohs, K. and R. Faber, 'Spent Resources: Self-Regulatory Resource Availability Affects Impulse Buying', *Journal of Consumer Research*, 33, March (2007) 537–47.

Walker, G. A. *International Banking Regulation: Law, Policy and Practice*, (London: Kluwer Law International, 2001).

Walkowitz, J. 'Going Public: Shopping, Street Harassment, and Streetwalking in Late Victorian London', *Representations*, 62 (1998), 1–30.

Warwick-Ching, L. 'Banks Accused of Fuelling Personal Debt "Crisis"', *Financial Times* (10 May 2005), 4.

—— 'Debt Loses Stigma as a Four-Letter Word', *Financial Times* (13 May 2005), 28.

—— 'Political Parties Scramble for the Grey Vote', *Financial Times* (30 April 2005), 22.

Watts, R. 'Bankruptcies Soar to a 10-year High', *Sunday Telegraph* (1 May 2005), 1.

Weber, M. *The Protestant Ethic and the Spirit of Capitalism* (NY: Scribner, 1958).

Weiler, P. 'The Conservatives', *Search for a Middle Way in Housing, 1951–64'*, *Twentieth Century British History*, 14: 4 (2003), 360–90.

Weiner, N. and T. A. Mahoney, 'A Model of Corporate Performance as a Function of Environmental, Organizational, and Leadership', *Academy of Management Journal*, 24 (3) (1981), 453–70.

Wheatcroft, P. 'Brown Can't Sleep through This Nightmare', *Times* (6 May 2005), 49.

—— 'Opposition Must Act to Protect UK PLC', *Times* (7 May 2005), 93.

Wicke, J. 'Mrs Dalloway Goes to Market: Woolf, Keynes and Modern Markets', *Novel: A Forum of Fiction*, 28: 1 (1994), 5–23.

Wicks, J. and Asato, J. *The Family Report 2002: Lifelong parenting and the changing face of British family life*. Lever Faberge and Social Market foundation report 2002.

Wilk, E. *Economies and Cultures: Foundations of Economic Anthropology* (Boulder, CO: Westview Press, 1996).

Williams, D. R. and C. Collins, 'US Socioeconomic and Racial Differences in Health: Patterns and Explanations', *Annual Review of Sociology* 21 (1995), 349–86.

Williams, P. 'Building Societies and the Inner City', *Transactions of the Institute of British Geographers*, New series, 3: 1 (1978), 23–34.

Williams, R. *Culture and Society, 1780–1950*, 2nd ed. (NY: Columbia University Press, 1983).

Williams, R. *Culture and Materialism: Selected Essays*. (London: Verso, 2005).

Wilson, D. S. 'A New Look at the Affluent Worker: The Good Working Mother in Post-War Britain', *Twentieth Century British History*, 17 (2005/6), 206–29.

Winton, J. R. *Lloyds Bank, 1918–1969* (Oxford: Oxford University Press, 1982).

Zelizer, V. *The Social Meaning of Money* (Princeton: Princeton University Press, 1997).

Index